D0368678

BREAKUP

BREAKUP

The Coming End of Canada
and the Stakes for America

LANSING LAMONT

W · W · NORTON & COMPANY
New York   London

The text of this book is composed in Times Roman,
with the display set in Times Semi Bold.
Composition and manufacturing by The Maple-Vail Book Manufacturing Group.
Book design by Jacques Chazaud.
Poetry on page 226 from *Return to Canada* by Patrick Anderson.
Used by permission of the Canadian publishers, McClelland and Stewart, Toronto.

Library of Congress Cataloging-in-Publication Data

Lamont, Lansing.
Breakup : the coming end of Canada and the stakes for America / by
Lansing Lamont.
p.   cm.
Includes bibliographical references (p.   ) and index.
1. United States—Relations—Canada.   2. Canada—Relations—United
States.   3. Nationalism—Québec (Province)   4. Regionalism—Canada.
5. Canada—History—Autonomy and independence movements.   I. Title.
E183.8.C2L27   1994
303.48′273071—dc20   93-43809

ISBN 0-393-03634-0

W. W. Norton & Company, Inc., 500 Fifth Avenue, New York, N.Y. 10110
W. W. Norton & Company Ltd., 10 Coptic Street, London WC1A 1PU

2 3 4 5 6 7 8 9 0

For Gilles at the bar in Chicoutimi,
for Celia and Tung Chan in Vancouver,
Theresa in Bird Cove, Newfoundland,
Chief Crowe in Regina,
Catherine and Gus in Calgary,
and for Nancy and
the boys of summer in Williamstown, Ontario,
where the Loyalists came to rest.
For Canada.

Contents

———◆———

Glossary

allophone—Canadian whose mother tongue is neither French nor English

anglophone—English-speaking Canadian

bilingual—Fluent in both English and French

francophone—French-speaking Canadian

Quebecers—Combined anglo-, franco-, and allophone populace of Quebec

Québécois—Francophone, largely nationalist citizenry of Quebec

"We are a great country and shall become one of the greatest in the world if we preserve it. We shall sink into insignificance and adversity if we suffer it to be broken."

SIR JOHN A. MACDONALD,
Canada's first Prime Minister

"Most Canadians understand that the rupture of their country would be an aberrant departure from the norms they themselves have set, a crime against the history of mankind."

PRIME MINISTER PIERRE ELLIOTT TRUDEAU
addressing U.S. Congress,
February 1977

"The very existence of our country is at stake. . . . And the truth is that the end of Canada would be one of mankind's greatest failures."

PRIME MINISTER BRIAN MULRONEY,
Calgary, Alberta
April 1991

Author's Note

In writing this book, I readily acknowledge having broken three rules.

The first is never to waste ink on a subject allegedly as boring as Canada. Over the years Canadians have shrewdly ceded the headlines to Israel, Somalia, and Bosnia-Herzegovina in favor of peace, order, and the good life. Still, the notion that Canada is boring reflects more truthfully our short attention span and ignorance about the place, as well as faint contempt for a too familiar neighbor. Canada is dull only to the unseeing eye.

The second rule is that in discussing Canadian politics, to paraphrase an oft-quoted observation, one should either write sparingly about the comprehensible or unsparingly about the incomprehensible, but never mix the two. Sorry, couldn't get around that one.

The third rule, in assessing Canada's English-French cultural dilemma, is never to forget where you're coming from. While I have tried faithfully to record both sides of the issue from works by and interviews with both francophones and anglophones, I have also viewed much of the Quebec scene through the prism of an English-speaking media. And I am guilty of having done so as a unilingual, Scots-descended American.

Politics aside, I am an unabashed Canadaphile and have been since the age of ten when I strapped on my first skis in St. Jovite, Quebec, in the heart of the Laurentians. I have seen a bit more of the country since: sailed the Cabot Strait from Nova Scotia to the fogbound southern coast of Newfoundland, canoed the rushing streams of the Western Selkirk range, searched for golden eagles in British Columbia, and fished for Arctic char beneath the year-round ice of Ellesmere Island.

Along the way, small epiphanies: Kingsmere under a pale moon, Mackenzie King's abandoned statuary cast in ghostly shades, testament to the Ozymandian bent of Canada's most eccentric Prime Minister; the hotel bar, one night in Vancouver, where I found the unsung brother of Erroll Garner weaving lacy jazz patterns on the piano for an audience of one. I remember, too, a long-ago morning, standing by frozen Lake Hazen near the top of the world, not far from where Peary had shoved off for the Pole, experiencing a moment of transcendency. I had closed my eyes, held my breath, and heard . . . nothing. No human voice, no animal sound, no bird or wind song, no sigh of air or crack of ice, only total, otherworldly silence.

One spring day in the early 1970s, on a small uninhabited island above the Arctic Circle off the Yukon coast, I found a kinsman. He lay beneath a rolling field of tundra in a solitary plot enclosed by a white picket fence. The simple inscription on the grave marker noted one Robert Lamont, who had died in the very early 1900s in the service of the Royal North-West Mounted Police.

After that, I never felt alone again in Canada.

L.L.
New York City
April 1994

BREAKUP

(continuation of main map, same scale)

Baffin Bay

A R C T I C

O C E A N

Lake Hazen

Ellesmere

GREENLAND

Island

Baffin Island

Baffin Bay

Devon I.

O R I E S

Hudson Strait

Labrador Sea

Hudson

Bay

UNGAVA

N E W F O U N D L A N D

TERRITORY

LABRADOR

ST. JOHN'S

La Grande R.

Chisasibi

Q U E B E C

James Bay

St. Lawrence R.

Cabot Strait

S H I E L D

Laurentian Mountains

Gaspé Peninsula

CHARLOTTETOWN

Saguenay R.

P.E.I.

Louisbourg

N T A R I O

Chicoutimi

NEW BRUNSWICK

FREDERICTON

Lake Superior

QUEBEC

MAINE

HALIFAX

NOVA SCOTIA

Lake Nipissing

North Bay

Montreal

Oka

A T L A N T I C

Cornwall

Plattsburgh

M I C H I G A N

OTTAWA

St. Lawrence Seaway

Akwesasne

N.H.

Massena

Kingston

Thousand Islands

VT.

WISC.

Lake Huron

TORONTO

Lake Ontario

N.Y.

O C E A N

Lake Michigan

Niagara R.

Buffalo

Detroit

Lake Erie

Detroit R.

PENN.

OHIO

CHAZAUD

Introduction

Nations, like stars, burn out. Amid the world's constellation of 180 or so countries, some, like Austria or Greece, supernovas in their day, have seen their once brilliant empires and cultures dim or go dark, leaving their mother nations lusterless bit players on the international stage. Others, brief comets of glory or conquest, have flamed out, becoming forgotten epochs or black holes of social and political chaos, civilizations in abaddon.

Half a world away the Soviet Union has torn itself apart, leaving its core of Russia in turmoil. Americans were transfixed by the drama, although we shared little with the Russians this past half century other than nuclear masterdom and the dread of mutual annihilation. Yet across our northern border, Canada—most of whose 28 million people share with us the same language, democratic ideals, and a galaxy of commercial enterprises—also faces the prospect of dissolution. North America's once dismissable attic of the inconsequential—now our primary trading partner and strategic shield against still formidable nuclear forces—could splinter into two or more states before the century's end. And Americans seem largely indifferent to, or unaware of, the consequences.

Canadians have been questioning the survivability of their country since its birth about ninety years after the Declaration of Independence. In the 1990s the question has become painfully acute: Will Canada still exist as a country at the end of the decade, or will it have disintegrated, a victim of the tensions of its troubled past and present? Nearly half of Canada's populace, when polled a while back, answered yes to the second part of the question.

Largely, it is the gaping wound of Quebec's disaffection. Its French-speaking majority has for more than two centuries agitated for English Canada to recognize the province and its status for what most Québécois in their souls fervently believe: Quebec, in all but the formalities, is already a separate nation. Now, finally, spurred by the sulfurous defiance of Quebec's separatists and the sense of betrayal among English Canadians, Canada's two founding peoples, hunkered in their separate quarters under the same roof, seem bent on dissolving their marriage.

English and French Canadians, outwardly civil to one another, have managed until now to submerge their differences in the interests of serving each other's needs: English Canada's for retaining a vibrant franco-phone culture within the nation to lend it greater distinctiveness; Quebec's for staying allied to a strong and supportive national economy. But as that economy, hobbled by debts and systemic failings, has in the early 1990s faltered through recession and a shaky recovery, Quebecers have turned further away from the rest of Canada. Forever sure of their cultural superiority, they now feel confident enough to oversee their economic destiny as well.

Quebec's independentist trend has rekindled other frictions that are abrading the thin fabric of national unity: the stubborn resentments nurtured by the country's besetting regionalism; the vying demands of Canada's other powerful provinces; the insistent claims and sometimes ugly protests of its aboriginal peoples; the know-it-all arrogance of its nannying federal bureaucracy in distant Ottawa, coupled with collapsing public confidence in political institutions; and, always, the specter of an embracing United States threatening Canada with further loss of identity through its invasive culture and the inexorable pull of trade currents toward some unwanted, homogenizing continentalism. All feed the sense of disarray that hangs like a pall over Canadians. Not even successive rounds of negotiations to restore national unity through constitutional reform have been able to reverse the seemingly relentless slide.

Other countries face one, possibly two, kinds of crises simultaneously. Canada today is struggling with three: economic, political, constitutional. And Canadians, alarmed by the portents of economic decline, weary of the constitutional bickering and despairing of their political leadership, are beginning to sense the nightmare of their country one day fracturing along the faultlines of race and regionalism. The old Canada is dying, victim of those divisive forces, a western political leader recently proclaimed. The old Canada is dying a psychologically painful death, a noted pollster in Toronto agreed. Canada is simply dying, the chief editorialist of Quebec's largest newspaper has stated unequivocally.

Exhausted by the failure of the last constitutional roundelay in 1992, Canadians welcomed the pause as a cancer patient welcomes remission. The fires of dissension were banked for the time being, perhaps for a generation. Yet Canada's history denies such hopes. The cancer might lie dormant for a spell, but Canadians know it will never disappear. It will fester indefinitely, our own version of hell or purgatory, a senior legislator in British Columbia confided. No one should suppose that within five years or less the Quebec nationalists won't be back again, the premier of Newfoundland told me. Canada is headed for another constitutional crisis within the next four years, predicted the former chief of staff to Prime Minister Brian Mulroney. That was in the waning months of 1992. Canadians are adept at muddling through, but in the fire next time, he concluded, those prospects are no better than 15 percent.

At its birth as a British dominion in 1867, Canada's existence was predicated on its fear of annexation by the United States, its pride and security in belonging to the mightiest empire since Rome's, and the need for a protected economy to ward off its omnipotent southern neighbor. As none of those reasons apply any longer, and having no new ideological underpinnings to help validate its national purpose, Canada is becoming increasingly vulnerable to fissure. One of two outcomes seems inevitable: reconfederation that meets Quebec's and the other provinces' demands without seriously enfeebling the federal government; or dissolution.

Apocalyptists, who have seldom found Canada fertile ground for research, outline a five-stage progression toward breakup: growing resentment between anglophones and francophones; open hostility; separation by Quebec; imposition of a police state; civil war. The scenario seems absurd, even if one contemplates the depth of the antagonisms involved, the history of violence, and recent incidents of racial strife in Canada, not to mention the paranoid excesses of French-language enforcers in Quebec. More serious scenarists take note of the impact of the last federal elections in October 1993 that elevated Quebec's separatist-leaning Bloc Québécois in the Canadian Parliament even as they established a new Liberal government in Ottawa; the critical provincial election in Quebec in 1994; and, depending on the outcome there between the ruling Liberals and the Parti Québécois, a crucial referendum on independence in the province before 1995 is out. Should the referendum pass, Quebec could then unilaterally declare its sovereignty. The final unraveling of Canada will have begun.

Most Americans comfortably assume that Canadians are too decent, too passive a people to propel themselves into breakup. The world has been suckered by such assumptions for much of the century. A more realistic view is that Canadians, surfeited by their antagonisms and stymied in resolving them, might let their nation sunder by default. If that happens, they, we, and the world will share painful costs. Gone for Canadians would be much of the economic reward of their union, their hard-won international stature, and their enviable tradition of civility. For the United States and the rest of the world, the stakes encompass the fate of Canada as our biggest partner by far in trade and finance, our closest NATO ally, and a reliable force for good in international councils around the globe.

This book was written as a wake-up call, an alert to the implications of Canada's crisis. *Breakup* is not a prediction of what will happen. It is an informed surmise of what could happen in the worst circumstances. It is a fable for our time, based on history as well as the concerns of scores of Canadians and Americans whom the author interviewed. It is a fable that could become at least part truth. The scenarios that appear throughout the book are of course fictitious, but derived from published references and interviews with scholars, government officials, and other experts.

Maybe Canada is not meant to survive. Maybe it isn't destined to live out its span as a nation. Perhaps it was fated from the start to be a bifurcated land of insecure naggers, at once the most civilized, tolerant, and backbiting of societies. In 1992 Canadians warred among themselves constitutionally almost to the brink of self-destruction. They did not slip over the brink then, although some thought it a very close call. The next time, the betting is they will. A nation, even one as survivalist as Canada, can suffer only so many near breakdowns before the system rends apart for good.

Consider, then, one vision of Canada in the year 2002, the 135th anniversary of its birth as a nation:

Quebec, a fledgling nation-state of 6 million francophones, saddled with still anemic birth rates and a paucity of new immigrants, struggles for cultural headroom on a continent of 350 million English and Spanish peoples. The former province's half-million or more anglophones have mostly dispersed, finding the climate set by Quebec's authoritarian new government too constrictive. Quebec's departure has upset the balance of power between central Canada and the rest of the country, leaving Ontario, with almost half the population, top-heavy in political and economic clout. The western Prairie Provinces—Alberta, Manitoba, Saskatchewan—have patched together a regional alliance to counterbalance Ontario. On the extremities, British Columbia, cocooned by geography from the rest of Canada, tilts economically toward the Pacific Rim, while its political needle fluctuates between choosing sovereignty for itself or accepting American statehood. The orphan Atlantic Provinces—New Brunswick, Nova Scotia, Prince Edward Island, and Newfoundland—find themselves marooned, cut off from Canada by the interposal of sovereign Quebec. Grudgingly, they form an economic union and jockey for closer ties to New England, and perhaps later, political absorption by the United States. In scattered pockets across the country, Canada's sullen natives—Indians, Inuits, Métis—compound the chaos by staging acts of civil disobedience in the cause of reclaiming long-lost territories. Canada's population has crested and already begun its predicted decline. The economy, like the body politic, has fragmented. Its resource-driven robustness has given out, its once proud safety net of social welfare programs become shredded due to massive indebtedness and the public's insatiable appetite for cradle-to-grave security. As federal coffers have emptied, with Quebec expropriating a quarter of the former nation's tax base, Ottawa has surrendered to the provinces ever more financial levers. The shift in power has taken its toll of Canada's generous redistribution ethic: richer provinces, which once succored the less fortunate ones, have exchanged the obligations of federalism for Darwinian competitiveness. Old ways and traditions have marched into memory with the nation's dismantlement: even the Royal Canadian Mounted Police guarding Ottawa's Gothic Parliament buildings seem less spit-and-polish, a trifle tackier, to visiting tourists. The shine has gone from the Mounties' brass buttons. Everywhere the shine has gone.

PART I

CANADA AT THE CROSSROADS

"Our day is tomorrow."

STEPHEN LEACOCK,
October 1941

"There is a fury in the land. Canada looks to Canadians like
a pessimist's nightmare of hell."

KEITH SPICER, Chairman
Report of The Citizens' Forum
on Canada's Future
June 1991

1

Anger Beneath
the Smiling Land

In the summer of 1992, on its 125th anniversary, Canada had just been awarded the good housekeeping seal of approval by the United Nations. This ranked the nation number one in the world, replacing Japan, in terms of economic prosperity, life expectancy, and education commitment. Canada's economy was the world's seventh largest, despite its low population ranking, and its citizens, per capita, enjoyed unparalleled purchasing power. Its Social Security, income support, and health programs were exceeded by none. No Canadian was denied medical care or was likely to suffer the misery of slum life and runaway crime. Canadian cities worked, potholes were few and homicides fewer, proportionately about one fifth the U.S. rate. As a fillip, the Toronto Blue Jays were on their way to becoming the first Canadian team to win the World Series. In other words, the best place on earth to live was this Canada. Surely, God's chosen people.

The country, "that hemless, hardly peopled continuum of water and land and sky," as Edmund Wilson described it, seemed to glow under the summer sun that year. The verdant fields and farms of Ontario sparkled along its Great Lake, the corn stalks almost as high as the passenger cars of the train rolling lazily north along the shore route from Toronto to Montreal. Beyond Kingston, along the St. Lawrence Seaway, the river, which Charles Dickens had once christened "this noble stream," still wound its way among the wooded Thousand Islands, some so small they appeared "mere dimples on its broad bosom."

The affluence of Toronto late that summer was mirrored in the vast, glass-enclosed shopping mall, Eaton Centre, where shoppers strolled along tiers of marbled walks under electrified snowflakes and miniature trees dripping tinsel composed of scores of tiny lightbulbs, all in early anticipation of a fat Christmas. At the other end of the rail line, in Montreal, the cafés in francophone Outremont and anglo Westmount brimmed with gabbling young people; on Sherbrooke Street, the city's fashionable main artery that lies below the graceful sweep of streets rising toward Mount Royal, the hotels seemed awash in elegant consumption, guests sipping Perrier in the Ritz Carlton bar or gorging on fresh salmon at Les Quatres Saisons. The simpler pursuits of an older Quebec, family and church, flourished, too, beyond the city's clangor, in the rural towns and villages beneath the silver steeples and the tin roofs of steep wooden homes.

Eastward, in the cool mists of the Maritimes, the countryside seemed equally at peace with itself. The neatly tilled farms of Prince Edward Island, strewn with their wheels of fresh-cut hay and surrounded by houses painted in blue and red pastels, bespoke the serenity of an English landscape, far removed from worldly tensions. In the harbor of Halifax, under a lowering sun, the schooner *Blue Nose II,* restored testament to the glory days of Nova Scotia's fishing hegemony, tacked across placid waters with its complement of tourists.

To the west, the panorama of optimism seemed boundless as the towering skies and vast spaces. At sunset in Regina the wheat fields stretched to the horizon from the hub of Saskatchewan's capital, bottomless breadbaskets for an apparently contented people. In the 200 miles between Regina and its idyllic sister city, Saskatoon, the only mournful note to be heard was the distant fugue of a train whistle, like some lost prairie lamb. In Edmonton, children frolicked in an enormous reflecting pool just a whoop and holler from the nearby Legislative Building where Alberta's lawmakers pondered the future of their province's oil bounty, in between verbal assaults on irksome Quebec and Ottawa's federal grabbers.

Astride the fork in Manitoba where the Assiniboine meets the Red

River, even barren Winnipeg, home of the subfreezing winter gust, seemed happily at ease amid its bustling refineries, bulging grain elevators, outsized streets and avenues, and more surreptitious delights: pocket-size Japanese gardens squeezed among some of the most ghastly corporate architecture in North America.

Beyond the Prairies and the barrier Rockies, British Columbia, its back turned to the rest of Canada as it gazed toward the Pacific, reveled in newfound prosperity. The province was riding a wave of small business and real estate wealth impelled by Asian immigrants, mostly ambitious Hong Kong Chinese. In Vancouver, now the preeminent port of the continent's West Coast, the handsome skyline sprouted a forest of building cranes as ubiquitous as the soaring new office structures they helped advance. Across the city's heavily trafficked bay new residential manses dotted the hills. Sleek yachts crammed the marinas. Two hours north, skiers still raced down the season's last snowfields atop Blackcomb Mountain at Whistler.

This was no Potemkin Village scene. Yet neither, arguably, was it ever really summer that year in Canada. Beneath the surface, behind the glow, the nation believed itself teetering on the edge of breakdown.

More and more Canadians were grappling with the reality of economic stagnation and potential upheaval of their system. The recession of the past two years would end, of course, but many felt the future would be one of diminished expectations. To visitors, Canadians prattled on a bit too defensively about their compassionate society, seeking to represent themselves as a truly kinder, more humane folk than those frenetic money grubbers south of the border. The feel-good talk seemed to cloak a gathering darkness in the national soul.

Soothsayers predicted that the 1990s for Canada would be a decade of declining living standards and limited growth. Editorialists opined that Canadians were experiencing doubts about their future unparalleled in history. An aging former leader of the Conservative Party wondered whether Canadians deserved to survive as a country. He concluded they would somehow, if only from habit. Others wondered if Canadians had outlived the habit.

To outsiders, Canada's angst seemed mystifing. Such a blessed people: peace, order, good government, with Uncle Sam and Florida to guarantee their national security and a haven from the relentless Canadian winter. How could they blow such a deal? The notion was surreal. "This country sometimes likes to bite its own tail," marveled a former U.S. Ambassador to Ottawa, "whereas most of the rest of the world would like a one-way ticket to Canada." The logic of the place viewed from outside, one of its own, the Montreal-born journalist Robert MacNeil, agreed, always seemed to make ten times more sense than it did inside.

Canada, thanks to the Precambrian Shield, is more than half rock, and a lot of outsiders that year understandably thought much of it was located in Canadians' heads.

One could trace the malaise to sea-changes in the quite recent past. Canada's never robust psyche had been buffeted over the last four decades by the nation's final severance of its umbilical ties to Britain and Empire; the rise of its new trade and economic dependency under the American Colossus; the emergence of a militant Quebec in the 1960s; and successive waves of immigrants to its shores who had changed the ethnic mix of large urban centers like Toronto and Vancouver, threatening to marginalize Canada's once-ruling Wasps.

Since the 1970s, when the growth in public demand for social entitlements and regional economic aid took off, Canadians had witnessed the gradual contracting of the federal largesse they had for so long taken for granted. By the 1980s it had become clear their government no longer had the wherewithal to maintain the old level of public services or to create the kind of megaprojects—a continental railroad, bilingual broadcasting network, universal health insurance—which had once helped sustain the national bond. The first signs of disillusionment appeared, then a mounting aggravation with the system and its managers.

Uneasily, Canadians also sensed the abandonment of some of their long-held catechisms and perceived virtues, a subtle bending to the inevitability of the American way. To the Constitution they had repatriated from Britain in 1982, they added an American-style Charter of Rights. Later in the 1980s they curbed their timeworn bias against economic continentalism by supporting with two cheers a free trade accord with the United States. And at the end of the decade a number of Canadians were agitating for an elected U.S.-style Senate instead of the amiable body of political appointees that comprised their own. Raised to believe that the

Canadian mosaic of non-assimilating ethnic minorities was a superior model to America's melting pot, Canadians nevertheless were preparing to shuck that, too, in favor of henceforth integrating newcomers into the national mainstream, whatever that was.

By the 1990s, external developments, too, had forced Canadians to reassess themselves and alter their comfortable ways of doing business. Rapid globalization of the world economy and the rush to meld North America's three economies were transforming business cultures, allowing trade and investment flows to transcend national borders like America's and Canada's 49th parallel. For all that, internal pressures continued to consume Canadians. English Canadians nationwide and separatists and federalists within Quebec argued bitterly among themselves over the kind of governing system Canada needed for the new century. When the penultimate constitutional proposal, the so-called "Meech Lake Accord," collapsed in acrimony in mid-1990, the yawning chasm between English Canada's and Quebec's visions of Canada could no longer be ignored. The two peoples could agree only that the process of constitutional change had been badly tarnished. The idea of Canada, its very nature, seemed to be dying on both sides of the linguistic divide.

As the pain of Meech Lake finally receded in that summer of 1992, Canadians girded warily for the next constitutional hurdle, the much-touted Charlottetown proposal, which was to be voted on that fall, already suspecting that they lacked the national cohesion to clear it.

In this broad-shouldered giant of a country, the world's second largest, where Jonathan Swift chose to site his mythical Brobdingnag, there were no giants that summer of '92 to lead Canadians out of their morass—only a despised Prime Minister whose popularity rating had sunk below the prime interest rate, and a passel of opposition party leaders whose mediocrity confirmed the country's sense of hopelessness. One veteran poll taker asserted that in thirteen years of surveying, he had never seen a Canadian public so cynical and rudderless.

The irony was that while the elites believed the disunity issue to be the country's most critical, ordinary Canadians chose the economic slump as the less abstract focus of their concern. Millions of them raged against lost jobs, eroding incomes, and tax burdens that had seemed tolerable in flusher times. Canada might share roughly the same population as California, but seldom if ever had it shared the same populist revulsion against high taxes. The almost universal condemnation of Ottawa's new Goods and Services Tax, however, for once allied Canadians and Californians in their anger at government. Government in Canada was assailed by the rich provinces as increasingly irrelevant to their welfare and by the poorer ones for reneging on its commitment to unlimited federal aid forever. Canada, one of its philosophers observed, would be defined in the 1990s by populism and perestroika.

The business community, meanwhile, bemoaned the uninviting investment climate brought on by the divisiveness. Forgotten were the not so long ago years from 1984 to 1989 when Canada's rate of economic growth had been second only to Japan's among the world's richest economies. The mood was reflected in the warnings of one Toronto executive who assessed the possible convulsive impact of separation by Quebec: "The market will go to hell. The Canadian dollar will go into freefall. Interest rates will soar. It'll be an unholy mess." In fact, politically, it was already that.

The divisiveness pitted "haves" against "have nots"; federalists against provincialists; westerners against easterners; hard-fisted Calgarian risk takers against the cautious traditionalists of Toronto; dispossessed Natives against the governing establishment; older ethnics against the bumptious new immigrants; insular nationalists against free traders; and a host of newly empowered special-interest groups against almost everyone. All this formed a dissonant Greek chorus to the focal division between English and French Canadians: their failure to resolve the differences they had fought over 230 years earlier on Quebec's Plains of Abraham. "I think we could lose the country this year," its Constitutional Affairs Minister, Joe Clark, told a television audience in early 1992.

The multiplicity of divisions only confirmed the feeling in Quebec that over recent years a political agenda had been developing in Canada that included Quebec less and less as the most justifiably aggrieved dissident of all. In the new Canada, the very foundation of Quebec nationalist belief—that two founding races, the French and English, had forged the nation—was under assault. Canada was no longer promoted as a bicultural society officially conversing in two languages, but as a sprawling multicultural one. And that, according to a top separatist official, was not only a strategic misuse of history but had led to an ocean of misunderstanding between the two races. "If this is not to be a two-nation adventure," the official told me, "it's no longer an adventure for Quebec."

If Quebec was losing the debate over its historical legitimacy as cofounder, English Canada's attitude toward it had also changed. The anglophones' slow burn over Quebec's incessant demands had escalated to angry exasperation over the perception that the province received favored treatment from Ottawa, over Quebec's enforcement of a unilingual French-language policy at the same time the rest of the country had bowed to a bilingualism mandate from Ottawa, and over Quebec's fervid support of free trade with the United States, which in some quarters like Ontario was viewed as turncoat. Time was when Canadians turned somersaults to keep Quebec happy and in the family. But by the early nineties the phrase *tant pis* (enough) was heard across the land, and a Gallup Poll showed that 75 percent of English Canadians were willing to risk Quebec's separation rather than submit to its demands for more powers.

It was this unsettling lull, the sense of resignation and finality on both sides, that stirred the armageddonists. "If Quebec separates, it is the end of Canada, the complete end," warned Bruce Hutchison, Canada's venerated social chronicler, a short while before his death. Once there had been boisterous marches and terrorist acts to mar the separatist cause and sober the hotheads on both sides before the breach became irreparable. Now, Quebecers seemed to have already crossed the emotional divide of separation, and English Canada had wearily accepted the fact.

The mood that summer of discontent was a mix of the volatile, the destabilizing, and the eerily calm. A generation of Canadians had grown up under the shadow of constitutional wrangling, believing it somehow the norm. That anniversary year, a cause for celebration, turned out to be more a reminder of how impossibly difficult Canada had become to govern. For historians it recalled the year 1787 and America's own trial by constitutional fire, when the fragile union was in danger of splitting into thirteen parts. "We are acting out a tragedy," one of Canada's elder statesmen of the arts, Mavor Moore, wrote an American friend, "and one of the definitions of tragedy is that everyone can see it coming but no one knows how to stop it." That meant, in this case, neither Canada's citizenry, caught in a crash of expectations, nor its leadership and the mandarinate in its national capital.

The two men, patrician, wise, and experienced, were among the best that
Canada's public service offers, both former ambassadors to Washington.
They sipped drinks with a guest in the hush of Ottawa's Rideau Club,
exclusive ganglion for the capital's movers and shakers, where the gold-
draped windows framed a view of the solidly massive Parliament buildings a few blocks away. Their view, however, was not of national solidity
but of a Canada mired in parochialism and provincial self-interest, a prescription for a disintegrative future. Eastward down the Ottawa Valley,
in Montreal, in his sunlit twenty-fifth-floor law office high above René
Levesque Boulevard, Pierre Elliott Trudeau assessed the coming storm.
Canada's onetime philosopher-prince, his nation's last world-class Prime
Minister, was a spent political force but still an influential rhetorician
capable of stirring passions. His latest polemic, condemning Quebec's
nationalists for "blackmailing" the rest of Canada, had created a furor. In
shirtsleeves and loosened tie, he was the picture of a man at ease with the
row he'd caused, oblivious to the idea that his spite against his fellow
francophones might not in any way change Quebec's course. "For the
separatists," he told a visitor, "enough is never enough. There's no way
out that is happy."

In this context, it was agreed, Canada needed unity more than anything
else as the summer of 1992 wound down. The unity crisis stemmed from
the 1982 repatriation and updating of Canada's Constitution. Quebec had
refused to sign the new document because it failed explicitly to recognize
Quebec's distinctiveness. In fact, this problem of unity was rooted deeply
in the original Constitution of 1867, in the reluctant union of economic
interests and U.S.-induced fears that produced it.

From the start, Canada's unity never embraced an instinctive cohesion.
Instead, it was cosseted, protected, and artificially maintained by trade
barriers and by a range of government-backed institutions and programs,
from the Canadian Pacific Railway and the Canadian Broadcasting Corporation (CBC) to old-age security and regional assistance, which over
time became icons of unity to Canadians. It wasn't the abstract concept
of nationhood that held them together; it was the compact with their government to provide a universal safety net of social and economic aid programs. Add hockey and a shared love of the land, and the circle was
about complete.

These icons were cracking from economic and other pressures, and it was this that made Canadians begin to suspect they were living in a centrifuge. The Canadian Pacific sought to shut down its line between Quebec and New Brunswick, thus severing at one end the nation's Atlantic-to-Pacific rail link. The CBC moved to cut back some of its more costly programming. Ottawa tightened up its giveaways and transfer payments to the provinces. Near the end of 1992, a poll taken by Toronto's Environics Research Group Ltd. revealed that Canadians had become more enamored of provincial autonomy and less wedded to the importance of many of their national symbols. Ominously, more of them identified with their provinces than with their country.

Overshadowing all were the irreconcilable differences between English and French Canada. The two peoples disagreed on history, on language, and on the nation's governing system. By early 1993, another nationwide poll showed that virtually seven out of ten Canadians rejected the view that Canada was a contract between its two founding races, as Quebec believed history had originally intended. Politically, Canadians outside Quebec sought a strong central government, while most Quebecers argued for a weak federal government role within their province. Language above all defined the incompatibility of the two groups. Three fourths of Canadians had grown up speaking English, and the rednecks among them enjoyed booing when the national anthem was sung in French at sports events outside Quebec. That province, meanwhile, continued to prohibit English from appearing on commercial signs. It was no comfort to anyone that the failure to assimilate minorities had broken up such federations as Yugoslavia and the Soviet Union.

In January 1993, *Maclean's* magazine, Canada's national weekly, reported that 56 percent of the country believed that the generation being born then would turn out to be worse off than their parents. A resident deep thinker observed that good fortune over the years had dulled his countrymen's ears to the deeper rhythms of history, so that Canadians seldom heard any more "the footsteps of God in events." They could hear them now.

* * *

In some ways Canadians have been hearing God's footsteps, in fact, for much of their troubled history. Raw nature, awesome and forbidding in its vastness, has along with the Church influenced the shaping of their character as a people. And that character, bred by climate and historical transiency, is part of Canada's woes in the late twentieth century.

Canada, one of the world's younger nations, may also be the oldest of lands. Its great shield of Precambrian granite, surrounding Hudson's Bay and comprising the central geological ring of inner Canada, is some 600 million years old. The ice sheet which once covered it shaped the stark beauty of the hills and inland seas, even as it defined the desolate northernness that in time has become Canada's most nearly distinctive quality.

To this day that northernness permeates the psychic landscape, a line, according to the Canadian historian W. L. Morton, "that delineates frontier from farmstead, the wilderness from the baseland, the hinterland from the metropolis." The consciousness of northernness and space, at times almost theological, is the link between Canadians and a handful of other peoples—Scandinavians, Russians, Icelanders. Canadians, the novelist Robertson Davies has noted, have a stronger attachment to the lands of Ibsen and Strindberg than to anything to the south. Yet to Canada's earliest settlers the encounter with that hostile environment—an implacable emptiness of bog, rock, water, mountain, and sky—seemed devoid of romance or a caring God. For them it was less a harsh appreciation of the Almighty's work than a venture into a "frozen hell of utter moral nihilism," in the words of the late critic Northrop Frye. The explorer Jacques Cartier, in 1634, thought it "the land God gave to Cain." The name "Canada" itself, so one doubtful theory goes, came from sixteenth-century Spanish fishermen off Newfoundland, who remarked that there was *aca nada,* nothing there. The experience forced Canadians, as a matter of survival, to adopt collectivist means of coping with the elements—there were few if any of the kind of individual heroics so admired by Americans—while it imparted a certain skeptical stoicism in the Canadian character. It was surely not an experience to inspire a desperately foraging people with the vision to lay great plans for a new nation.

As if the cruel environment were not enough to sap their spirit, the very origins of early Canadians hardly built confidence. The place would become not so much a country as a "holding tank filled with the disgruntled progeny of defeated peoples," to quote a character in Mordecai Richler's novel, *Solomon Gursky Was Here.* Chief among those founding peoples were French *colons,* abandoned by mother France to the mercies of the British after their conquest of Quebec; Jacobite Scots, who had fled religious persecution by the English back home; and loyalists to the Crown, who had fled north from the American revolutionaries. Later, adding to this dubious porridge, came famine-stricken Irish, Ukrainians, Poles, and other political refugees from nineteenth-century Europe. These in turn helped overwhelm Canada's native peoples, relegating them to the bottom of the social and economic ladder.

Even after these early settlers had coalesced into nationhood, Canada was a transient entity, bouncing from colonial status under Great Britain to satellite status under the United States. It became Canada's fate to endure scorn from the Brits ("a great white waste of time") and indifference from the Yanks ("Nebraska north"). Lester B. Pearson, Canada's most influential statesman of the post–World War II decades, recalled that as a young man he and his compatriots were Canadians, yes, but in a British sense. "Our foreign policy was made on Downing Street." And just at the time when Canada emerged chesty from the war, "when we could have built up something specially our own, we fell under American economic imperialism." Having seen so much of their infrastructure created through the intervention of outsiders, it is small wonder that Canadians have accrued a more tenuous faith than most in the legitimacy of their institutions, further undermining their self-esteem.

Theirs became a society of borrowed traits whose character seemed grounded on respect or distaste for other societies. From the British, they inherited their deference to authority; their aversion to disorder; their preference for understatement, the raised eyebrow instead of the raised fist; their practice of paternalism in government; their slowness to salute success and encourage upward mobility; their sense of loyalty, their modesty, their ability to turn self-deprecation into an art form. "Mike" Pearson's quiet bow tie and self-effacing wit were attractive badges of the Canadian style; Brian Mulroney's yen for braggadocio, by contrast, was a turnoff. From the Scots, who peopled the Maritimes and later drove the business-success ethic in the big cities, Canadians inherited their financial conservatism and a suspicion, abetted by the church, that artistic and literary life are somehow subversive.

From their determination *not* to emulate Americans, at least the pushy side of our makeup, Canadians came to downplay exuberance; to abhor swagger; to mistrust excellence, preferring to reach for the bronze, not the gold; to resist the urge to attack every task with unremitting professionalism; to cultivate, in short, a more laid-back style. This has led to criticism of Canadians' complacency and low-octane economic performance. When Lee Kuan Yew of Singapore visited British Columbia a while back, he told the locals that if the Asian economy was like a high-compression engine, Canada's is closer to its low-compression counterpart.

For every generalization, of course, exceptions abound in the Land of the Big Eh. Despite their vaunted reticence, Canadians are born lecturers, especially when it comes to advising the rest of the world, America in particular, on its shortcomings. They can beat their breasts in fine moral fervor over the inequities of poverty and hunger abroad, even as they husband in their Scots-English bones the knowledge of what a cornucopia they have accumulated for themselves, by world standards a relatively small populace. And not all of that populace are shy Victorian prigs by a long shot. Canadians, according to Seymour Martin Lipset, in his estimable study *Continental Divide,* have since the 1960s held more permissive attitudes than Americans toward premarital and extramarital sex. The women of Canada had a high old time in 1992, baring their breasts en masse at public rallies to protest the unequal treatment of their anatomy (provocative) compared to the male chest (harmless). Perhaps the French observer who described the Canadian settlers of the early 1700s as "light-minded and inclined to debauchery" was onto something.

Some countries become emergency cases so fast that their people have virtually no time to search for the roots of, let alone answers to, their predicament. Not so Canadians, inveterate navel-gazers. They are the only people, it is said, who regularly pull themselves up by their roots to see if they are still alive. Introspection is built into their genes, and much of it is directed at trying to discover who they are and what if anything distinguishes them—the old identity hangup.

Québécois have little trouble with this, having spent most of their history trying to deny the Conquest of 1759 (France left them in the lurch even as it was shorn of its North American holdings) while at the same time charging a litany of humiliations at the hands of the English victors and their descendants. This is not only good for fueling nationalist passions in Quebec. The Québécois know exactly who they are: historical losers reborn as shrewd custodians and promoters of a distinctive culture.

For the English Canadian majority, there is no such unequivocal role they can easily play. Theirs has been, instead, an oddly negative attempt to define themselves—anything but American, thank you—and to grasp onto a muscular national credo. If climate and Crown helped forge their character, geography explains their tortured search for a true identity.

Within Canada's nearly 4 million square miles, stretching through seven time zones from Newfoundland to the Yukon-Alaska border—*a mari usque ad mare,* as the Dominion motto proclaimed—a handful of people inhabit barely a fraction of the land, most of them wedged in a Chile-like strip within 100 miles of the U.S. border. Only about 7 percent of the country is fully settled, and there are still only about seven inhabitants per square mile. Physically, the place could absorb Britain forty times over, France eighteen. Laid over a map of Europe, Canada would reach all the way from deepest Asia, east of the Urals, across the continent to the west coast of Ireland. Brendan Behan remarked, "T'will be a grand country when they get it finished." Except that its sheer size and intimidating distances make that unlikely.

Canadians are so formidably separated from each other by the Rockies, the Laurentians, the Prairies, plus the 1,000-mile swath of the uninhabitable Shield, that it is a wonder any sort of national unity has managed to flourish. Such obstacles precluded in the past large movements of population from east to west to fill up the country. The barrens of northern Ontario still cut off central Canada from its Prairies; wilderness Maine does much the same to the Maritimes. Unlike the United States, where the megalopolises sometimes seem almost to flow into one another, blurring regional distinctions, Canada's cities resemble medieval fortress towns, discrete and remote from one another. There are no interlocking urban galaxies, no network of Clevelands, Detroits, and Chicagos stretching across the land, a natural transmission belt which, in the United States, ensures that Americans, even without radio or television, can always in effect hear the tribal drums from one community to the next.

The disconnectedness imposed by geography has muddied Canadians' sense of obligation to a national family that lives and plays together. The great disparities in distances and travel costs alone persuade many, for example, to spend their weekends or holidays in foreign climes. Quebecers find it less expensive to fly to Paris than to Vancouver. Newfoundlanders can go cheaper to London than to Toronto. And Vancouverites can trip to San Francisco or Los Angeles more easily than to eastern Canada. The result is that the country, as its novelist Margaret Atwood lamented, remains "an unknown territory" for its people, many of whom show their ignorance of it variously. An editor in Winnipeg ruefully cites the visiting reporters from Ottawa who have no idea of the size of his city's population. The journalist Peter Newman jokes that most Canadians think the Precambrian Shield is a birth control device. And there is the classic story of the federal bureaucrats in Ottawa who insisted on pressing thousands of dollars worth of fireworks on the Yukon territorial government to help them celebrate the 115th anniversary of confederation in July 1982, only to be advised that at that time of year it was never night in the far north.

These are minor if symbolic lapses. A deeper ignorance is Canadians' fuzziness about their intermittent progress from colony to dominion to fully independent nation, a journey so pocked with little milestones of reluctant British accommodation that Canadians have ended up settling for an evolutionary definition of their identity. As a historian observed, it is not important to know when Canada became independent; it is important to understand that no one really knows. That, unlike America's conclusive revolution, has delayed and obscured Canadians' attainment of a staunch identity, an integrating vision of nationhood.

It does not help Canada's search that at the hour of its birth in 1867, and for some time afterwards, the new nation had no culture or distinctive living style to speak of, while its independence was more chimera than reality. Britain still held much of Canada's land as Crown domain, as well as certain taxing powers; Britain's wars were Canada's wars. Until the 1930s, while the Québécois called themselves "Canadiens," English Canadians considered themselves British subjects and, until 1947, carried the designation on their passports. Too many of Canada's new towns bore names imported from British history: Regina, Kitchener, Windsor, Waterloo. The national symbol was the beaver, a fur-bearing creature whose Protestant work ethic, someone pointed out, was largely dedicated to the destruction of trees. Understandably, Northrop Frye concluded, a society valued mainly for its beaver pelts, its softwood forests, and the troops it could supply for other countries' wars was unlikely to develop any cultural phenomena *beyond* a problem of identity.

Lacking a guiding ideology or popular mythology like America's, Canadians come by their symbols of patriotism haltingly; in fact, the whole idea of tear-in-the-eye patriotism is an embarrassment to them.

There were, after all, no Napoleons or Wellingtons or Washingtons in their past, no decapitated kings or Daniel Boones, no inspiriting Gettysburgs, no Bataans. In their original Constitution, the British North America Act, they eschewed poetry and uplift, as they did again in the preamble to their Constitution Act of 1982. No Canadian schoolchildren recite the prose of either or pledge allegiance to their concept. Canadians dithered eight years before making their national anthem, "O Canada," legal in 1980, then let it become the target of feminists, pacifists, and atheists for the political incorrectness of its lyrics. Finally, it took them ninety-eight years to get a flag, the Maple Leaf, which didn't start fluttering until 1965. Canadians loved Mort Sahl's reply in the 1950s to the Toronto reporter who spluttered to him that the country lacked a flag. "That's a start," Sahl said.

Canadians are, agreed the historian George Woodcock, unafflicted by "the fevers of aggressive patriotism." But Quebec's noted parliamentarian and journalist Henri Bourassa thought otherwise. "So long as we have no Canadian patriotism," he said, "there will be no Canadian nation." It is instructive, then, that American draft dodgers who fled to Canada in the Vietnam years could happily discover that patriotism was not a prerequisite of Canadian citizenship, that in Canada people were free to denounce their Canadianism without fear of McCarthyite hassling, that an entire people like the Québécois could threaten secession, giving the finger to Confederation while still reaping its benefits. Still, none of this moved the search for identity further along its path, other than to underscore the internal conflicts over what it meant to be Canadian.

Despite the fact that they fought and died bravely by the tens of thousands in two world wars—losing 60,000 dead alone in World War I from a population of only 7.5 million—Canadians remain basically untested and unscarred in their own land, innocent of revolution, civil war, assassinations, and other traumas that have tempered Americans. Bereft of heroes, epic victories or tragic defeats, the legendary links in a unifying history, Canadians still pine to define their national soul. This need has become much more pronounced since 1982, when one failure after another to resolve broader constitutional differences has called into question Canada's governing system itself, perhaps paramount to the nation's sense of identity. Today's crisis, thus, is as much as anything about the potential upheaval of Canadian society's whole organizing premise.

provincial influence, moved Canada down the unintended track of a more decentralized country, while America took the opposite road. Americans, absent the race issue, had sorted out most of their states' rights problems by the end of the last century; Canadians are still hotly arguing theirs in the 1990s.

For one thing, Canada's provinces lack balance in their size, while most of America's states are roughly equal in their proportions. The disproportion, in a nation of only ten provinces, between a vast Quebec or Ontario and a tiny Prince Edward Island or Newfoundland is not only staggering but in its way destabilizing. Too many large dominant parts of a federation can breed resistance to compromise, a desire to go one's own way. It is hard to imagine any American state, even one with a Spanish-speaking majority, that could have caused the continuous commotion that Quebec has over the years. Even beyond Quebec, in the Maritimes, the Prairies, and British Columbia, secession movements have flickered over the years, so disposed toward challenging the federal government have the provinces become.

Their assertiveness has grown relative to the nation's own confidence chart. For the first seventy years of Confederation Britain's Privy Council, not Ottawa, shaped the limits of federal power in Canada. Only after World War II, when Canada fully emerged from dominion status and was throwing its federal weight around in certain provincial jurisdictions, did the provinces seriously begin to flex their own muscles. As their natural resources were developed and taxing powers increasingly relegated to them, they came to assume in their eyes an equality of status with the federal government that would have been unthinkable in the United States. No President, one of Ottawa's wiser mandarins pointed out, would dream of sitting down with fifty governors to hammer out some agreement on domestic policy; but Canadian prime ministers regularly climbed into the pit with the provinces' ten premiers, or, as they are pleased to call themselves, "first ministers" of the land. If political success in the United States ultimately means going to Washington, in Canada it doesn't necessarily mean moving to Ottawa.

Not only did Canada's founders misjudge the growth of the provinces' power, its early leaders concocted an economic development.scheme that so favored central Canada at the expense of the rest of the country that westerners and Maritimers down through the years have convinced themselves that, while federalism has served Ontario and Quebec well, it has

:ois. They may still lay shaky claim to provincial governments in
itario, British Columbia, and Saskatchewan, but in terms of real power
nada's former third party has been consigned to the margins.

The parlous state of Canada's federal system, the fact that its political
nter has been further diffused to the point where it now embraces *five*
rties, only one of them nationwide in scope, reflects the obvious: a
arth of credible national leadership at one of the most dangerous cross-
ids in the nation's history.

With the secessionist Bloc Québécois ascending and the Parti Qué-
cois marshaling its separatist forces in Quebec, the political climate has
;couraged any effective voice for federalism in that province. More
·ious, the country itself has become starved for any rousing pan-Cana-
in fervor, a voice from on high summoning the spirit of unity and
tional purpose. The last Prime Minister, a Quebecer whose support
rived from that province, has become too discredited over the years to
)unt a credible defense of federalism. The new Liberal Prime Minister,
o a Quebecer, has been a committed but *sotto* federalist, an accommo-
ting politician rather than a call-to-arms national leader. Once, there
d been leaders like Trudeau who nourished a vision of Canada and
sited attainable goals. The visions may have gone sour, but Canadians
uld at least recognize clarity and principle in those who led them. Paul
nnedy, author of *The Rise and Fall of the Great Powers,* wrote in
92 that at least some visionary leaders in the United States were setting
irkers for the future. "Is there anyone in a responsible position in Can-
a who is doing the same?" he asked.

Part of the problem has been systemic. Canada has no effective farm
igue like the U.S. governorships to groom potential leaders of the
tion; it must rely on its House of Commons. Provincial premiers,
mersed in their local affairs, become too regionally identified, hence
gets of electoral hostility in competing regions. So, no Bill Clintons or
•nald Reagans are likely to reach the top rung; in Canada's modern
itory no premiers have ever made it to the office of Prime Minister. But
this time of doubt and shrunken dreams the absence of any Churchillian
? to light the nation's spirit is especially missed. The hollow prose, the
:k of music or poetry in the language of its leadership is a void shared
America, too. As Wolfe was rowed toward the shores of Quebec City
it fateful night in 1759, his officers overheard him reciting Gray's
?gy in a Country Churchyard, including the premonitory passage, "The

disadvantaged them. The response of these aggrieved provin
fashion their own economic policies without Ottawa's involve
moting their own welfare regardless of the nation's interest.
consequences has been to divide Canadians' political allegian
their provinces and the national agenda.

Federal and provincial political parties of the same stripe h
strangers to each other, frequently taking opposite sides on pc
Over the last decade, as public confidence has waned in the
and performance of the three national parties—Progressive C
Liberal, and New Democratic—the federal-provincial split ha
Alberta's Conservatives and Quebec's Liberals, for exampl
themselves from their federal namesakes in Ottawa. The di
even led to the rise of two powerful new regional parties, th
bécois and the West's populist Reform Party. The former ha
effect the federal arm of Quebec's separatist Parti Québéco
conservative in cast, has been hostile to the Quebec caus
anglophone togetherness, reform of the Canadian Senate
decentralization. Both parties have by now become contenc
reckon with on the national scene as a result of the most r
elections in late 1993.

Those elections devastatingly altered the political face of (
savaged two of the three mainstream parties, nearly ob
incumbent Conservatives. They dramatically empowe
regional protest parties, which expanded their representatior
one hundred seats between them in the federal Parliament a
way for the Bloc Québécois to become, of all things, Car
Opposition Party. And they reestablished the Liberals unc
tien, the new Prime Minister, as the country's dominant go
The Liberals, who have bestrode federal politics for most o
century, now enjoy a clear parliamentary majority althou
tional support from Quebec has withered under the onslau;
Québécois. The once proud Conservatives, who under Mi
power in 1984 with a coalition of western Tories and Queb
are now an enfeebled political force, their coalition crumb
ern support evaporated; the Tories command barely a tok
Parliament. As for the socialist New Democrats, they were
in the elections and now join the Tories at the bottom of th
political ladder, well below the Liberals, Reform, and

paths of glory lead but to the grave." As he ended his recitation, the British general was reported to have said, "Gentlemen, I would rather have written those lines than take Quebec."

No leader in Canada today would even contemplate making that kind of swap in the interests of stirring the nation to put aside its sectional grievances and unite.

If any elegy was appropriate in Canada's 125th anniversary year, it would have been one to the nation's history itself, a history that far from providing Canadians with a common identity and vision, has tended in the end to divide them. It bequeathed them a neurosis, reflecting the fact that Canada's has been not one but three histories: its mainstream saga; Quebec's story; and America's role.

"We have come to a period in the history of this young country when premature dissolution seems to be at hand."

—SIR WILFRID LAURIER,
Prime Minister, 1890

2

A Brave
and Troubled Past

The earliest probes of Canada, by Icelandic warrior-farmers who penetrated the fogs off Newfoundland around A.D. 1000, hardly presaged what were to become the two great themes of Canadian history: the French-English conflict and Canada's struggle for independence. Not till five hundred years after the Vikings, when John Cabot had reached Newfoundland and claimed it for England and Jacques Cartier had planted the fleur-de-lis on the Gaspé Peninsula in France's name, did the first stirrings of English-French rivalry in the New World begin.

Cabot, operating from Venice under Henry VII's aegis, was the forerunner of all those God-fearing, cod-fishing, land-tilling British colonists who came eventually to settle along the northern Atlantic seaboard. The Breton Cartier, commissioned by Francis I to find a passage to China, sailed up the St. Lawrence, stumbled on what the locals called *Québec* (for "the place where the river narrows"), and became the precursor to Champlain, Frontenac, and a succession of Jesuit Black Robes, fur traders, and hardscrabble farmers. By 1750, they numbered some fifty thousand in New France. A French visitor observed that the new habitants were "extremely sensitive to slights" and "by nature hard to govern." They built their society on the pillars of language, Catholicism, and mistrust of outsiders. Church and State did their part to nurture the new community—the papal ensign got equal billing with the fleur-de-lis—but of the two the Church was far the more committed. While France supplied shiploads of *filles de roi* as brides for the settlers, the conversionary Jesuits joined the fur traders in exploring the interior, contacting and gaining the alliance of the Indian tribes; they effectively pushed the Quebec frontier south into the Ohio Valley territory of the colonial English traders. The subsequent rivalry over territory and trade led to a protracted series of skirmishes between the French and English settlers, and their Indian allies, that climaxed in 1759 on the heights of Quebec City, the first of two events on which Canadian history has centered.

During the bloody walkup to Quebec City, American settlers had played a contributing role in the humbling of New France. Massachusetts regulars in 1755 had assisted the British in expelling the hapless Acadians from their century-old French settlement in Nova Scotia, scattering the peasant tribe by the thousands to New Brunswick and faraway Louisiana. A decade earlier, two thousand armed New Englanders had helped force the surrender of Louisbourg, the French fortress on Cape Breton, which was finally destroyed by the British in 1758. Two years after that, following the conquest of Quebec City, hundreds of American Rangers joined British forces in repelling French counterattacks until reinforcements arrived. The New Englanders' roles there and at the siege of Louisbourg emboldened the colonists a short while later to press their revolution against the British, the second of the events so crucial to Canadian history.

The fall of Quebec City and the resulting Treaty of Paris in 1763 ended French territorial ambitions in North America: Louis XV formally ceded to Britain virtually all of New France east of the Mississippi. In one half-hour battle, in which both opposing generals perished, the British won most of the Franco-American empire, freed their thirteen colonies from the need for protection from the French, and inadvertently set the stage for American independence. The Conquest gave to English Canada a welcome shot of confidence, a sense of superiority that, in the historian Ramsay Cook's view, later became a valuable component of their nationalism. But for French Canada, the event proved a disaster: its middle class was decimated by the abandonment of most of the administrative, military, and merchant upper crust. The leavings were a small professional class, an illiterate peasantry, and a priesthood that soon moved into the leadership vacuum.

After a failed attempt to assimilate its new Quebec subjects into an English-speaking colony with English laws and customs, Britain reversed course and, in what seemed a remarkable stroke of generosity, granted the Québécois full retention of their French-speaking culture and legal system, in effect recognizing the colony's distinctiveness. The habitants got to keep their rural ways and the priests were elevated into the politically powerful reaches of the new English regime. To placate the English-speaking merchants of Montreal, who had begun taking up residence shortly after the Conquest, Britain returned the rich fur-trading lands of the Ohio Valley to Canada. By thus appeasing all factions, Britain secured the peace and loyalty it needed from Quebec, no small trade-off, for there were already rebellious rumblings from within its American colonies. The Quebec Act of 1774 turned out to be an incendiary red flag to the Americans: it sanctioned next door to them an alien culture and an unrepresentative form of government that ran counter to the limited liberties they enjoyed. Worse yet, the return of the Ohio territories, coveted by the Americans, to French Canadian jurisdiction effectively shut off the Americans' route to western settlement, hemming them in along the Atlantic seaboard. No one was more angered than a Virginian squire named George Washington.

Already aggravated by high British taxes and the likelihood of more repressive British laws, the American colonists in 1775 organized the First Continental Congress. Following the Minutemen's baptism of fire at Lexington and Concord, they laid plans for military resistance and set about trying to persuade the Quebecers to join their cause. "Have not the Canadians sense enough to attend to any public affairs," scolded the Congress in a manifesto to the Quebecers, "(other) than gathering stones from one place and piling them in another? Unhappy people!" It was not a politic approach. As outposts of a maritime empire, the Americans had the advantage of considerable autonomy and latitude with their town meetings and assembly form of government; by contrast, the Quebec colonists, perceived by France as outriders of a land empire who needed a short tether in matters of government and military defense, had little familiarity with responsible government. Furthermore, Quebecers had grown accustomed to the general tolerance of their new masters. The Americans' entreaties fell on unreceptive ears.

Even Benjamin Franklin, the Americans' nonpareil diplomat who'd been dispatched to Montreal to plead the revolutionary cause, got a cool welcome. (One of his traveling companions from Philadelphia, a French-emigrant printer named Mesplet, stayed behind after Franklin had returned, and three years later published Montreal's first newspaper.) Diplomacy exhausted, the Americans moved to prevent the British governor from using Quebec as a military base; they marched two hastily organized armies north to capture Montreal and Quebec City, briefly occupied the former, failed to subdue the latter, and abandoned the whole enterprise by early 1776. The rest of the war went better. The imperatives of European great power rivalry eventually brought France in on the side of the revolutionaries. By 1781, when Cornwallis found himself cornered at Yorktown, half or more of his attackers were French. The French-speaking colonists of Quebec, however, never did join the Revolution. They remained neutral or actively supportive of Britain during America's long ordeal to attain its nationhood. At the same time, the Continental Army's incursions settled in the Canadian soul the beginning qualm over America's expansionist bent and its designs on Canada.

In addition to dividing the continent between the United States and British North America, the American Revolution generated the first important anglophone community in Canada. The 50,000 Loyalists who in the immediate postwar years turned their backs on the new American republic and trekked north to settle in Nova Scotia and Quebec, along the shores of the St. Lawrence and the lakes west of Montreal, began new lives they hoped would markedly differentiate them from their rebellious cousins to the south. Over time, their United Empire Loyalist ancestry would become as valuable to their social ambitions as *Mayflower* genealogy has been to those of many Americans. But their arrival in Canada also intensified the growing tensions between anglophones and francophones. Unwilling to join Quebec's Catholic, rurally wedded society, the new refugees successfully petitioned for the introduction of English political practices. Thus, in 1791 the British Parliament passed an act splitting the country into English-speaking Upper Canada (later to become Ontario), and Lower Canada (Quebec), which remained a French-speaking preserve. The Loyalist émigrés from America had, in effect, impelled the first act of separatism in Canada.

America would loom large in Canadians' consciousness for much of the next century, two wars in particular influencing their outlook and the course of British North America in the 1800s.

If the literature of that period conveyed the feeling that Britain's northern possession was a hermit kingdom, a kind of "non-criminal penal colony designed for remittance men and Irish housemaids," as Northrop Frye had it, Canadians were equally scathing about their southern neighbors. American republicanism was deemed irreligious and materialistic, its democracy close to anarchy. "The frequency of their elections," complained one observer, "keeps them in a continual broil." The bad feelings were linked to the border problems which continued to unsettle Anglo-American relations. These in turn were linked to many Americans' frustration that their War of Independence would never be completed unless they rid themselves for good of the Indian menace, halted the egregious British insults to their flag on the high seas, and liberated the British-oppressed people to their north. Accordingly, President Madison in 1812 declared a second war of independence against Britain and sent American troops to invade its colony.

The Americans, incompetently led, managed to gain control of the Great Lakes and pillage the Canadians' capital at York (later Toronto), but were unable to hold any territory. The British, in retaliation for York, burned much of Washington and sacked the White House. The war dragged on for two years with neither side emerging as a clear winner. Still, America exulted in having shown Britain that U.S. independence was not to be trifled with. Canada took the more parochial view that its integrity had been saved from defilement by the Americans. The Treaty of Ghent ended hostilities and brought some order to the border disputes; in 1818, the 49th parallel was accepted as the definitive boundary between Canada and the United States.

The War of 1812 may have been a postscript in British annals and relatively inconsequential to Americans, but to Canadians it reaffirmed their faith in the Empire, the security it afforded, even as it fueled their suspicion of U.S. intentions and a general animus toward the new republic. For the first time, Canadians had encountered a different kind of American, not the easygoing farmers who lived just across the Detroit and Niagara rivers, but, in the Canadian author Pierre Berton's words, "backwoodsmen, brawlers and eye-gougers." From then on, Canadians viewed their American neighbors ever more guardedly.

For the next twenty-five years, as waves of immigrants began washing over British North America, most of them settling in anglophone Upper Canada, the colony addressed its own growing political roil that would eventually precipitate rebellion in both Canadas. The overarching issue was the denial of democracy in the governing process. In Upper Canada, however, the reform movement led by William Lyon Mackenzie was pale beer compared to the racially spiced protest brew in Quebec. There, the friction between the francophone majority and the anglophone business class seeking to transform Quebec into a commercial society ignited when Britain bowed to the businessmen and enforced a policy of anglicization. Quebec's National Assembly was dissolved, francophone militia officers were cashiered, and the principal francophone newspaper was suppressed, its owners sent to jail. London, embarrassed by the turmoil, reconsidered its action. But by then French Canada had found its own *beau provocateur* in Louis-Joseph Papineau.

The fiery young lawyer challenged an unyielding Catholic clergy and Britain's proconsuls to permit some democracy in Church and State. When they continued to balk, Papineau, invoking the cause of the rebellious American patriots, led his own *patriotes* in 1837 in an armed uprising which was ruthlessly quelled. The government in London had heard, however. Lord Durham, the emissary it sent to investigate the troubles, found not so much a struggle of principle between his government and Canada as a conflict between races, francophones and anglophones, "two nations warring in the bosom of a single state." The Québécois, he reported, brooded in silence over the memory of their fallen countrymen, their burnt villages, "their humbled nationality." Durham anticipated from then on "an indiscriminating and eternal animosity." In fact, when the francophones later sought compensation for property damages suffered in the revolt, passions exploded again; mobs rioted in the streets of Montreal and the city was put to the torch.

In retrospect, one might argue that Britain right then should have cut its losses and the unruly French Canadians adrift, leaving them to nurse their grievances as a permanently separate tribe sinking into a long coma of retrogressive conservatism. That the French Canadians eventually came to this anyway is beside the point. Britain, instead, in 1840 imposed its Act of Union, under which the Québécois became reluctant members of a new legislative union with English Canada. The Act rejoined the two Canadas in a single province; but it was a unitary state in name only and did little to cool the ferment. By the 1860s the feuding had convinced Britain that a federal union of all its North American possessions might be the most promising solution.

America's Civil War, by then in full clang, served to hasten matters. Well before the war, Canada had been the terminal of the "underground railroad"; some forty thousand slaves, scarred by bullwhips and chains, had made their way from the Confederate South to Ontario. Along the way they'd sung, "Farewell, old master / don't come after me / I'm on my way to Canada / where colored men are free." The experience of one of them, the Reverend Josiah Henson, became the basis for Harriet Beecher Stowe's *Uncle Tom's Cabin*. None of that assuaged northern U.S. sentiment after the war, which was for pursuing America's "manifest destiny" to acquire or annex Canada and make the continent an American hegemony. Americans were angered that Canada's British keeper had tacitly supported the Confederacy; Canadians suspected the deeper rationale for U.S. truculence was territorial and the need, in America's postwar depression, for more favorable trade arrangements. In 1865, the United States abrogated its reciprocal trade treaty with Canada. The worried Canadians, meanwhile, had massed some two thousand militiamen along the U.S. border. Two years later, wary of the mounting discord, the border raids by fanatical Irish-American groups, and the prospect of its western lands being absorbed in the spillover of America's onrushing colonization of its own West, Canada prepared to defend its interests in perpetuity. It announced the establishment of a new federal union under the protection of Britain.

The British North America Act didn't pop out full-grown in 1867. It was the product of three years of squabbling negotiations begun in tiny Charlottetown, the capital of Prince Edward Island. There, fortified by some of the $13,000 worth of Champagne they had brought along, the future fathers of Confederation convened in a second-floor chamber of the handsome neoclassical Capitol, or Province House. Warmed by the bubbly and the blaze from two black marble fireplaces, they began what seemed to be in danger of becoming an interminable argument over how federal and provincial powers would be divided under the new Canadian Constitution. The bickering moved the nineteenth-century historian Goldwin Smith to observe later that "The father of Confederation was deadlock."

He was, in fact, a bulbous-nosed, shrewd manager of men named John

A. Macdonald. As the new dominion's first Prime Minister, he would
come to dominate Canada's post-Confederation scene for more than a
quarter of a century. The Scottish-born Macdonald was no florid orator,
but a clever enough speaker, graced with quick wit, a warm affability
(frequently livened by demon rum), and the persuasive skills to convince
his fellow delegates at Charlottetown that a central government with
strong powers was the key to an enduring federation. Macdonald didn't
get his way with naming the new nation the Kingdom of Canada, which
was a bit too elevated for Whitehall's taste; but he was instrumental in
seeing that the British North America Act reflected Quebec's status even
then as a distinct society by authorizing it as the only province where
French was to be officially used. The English Canadian "must make
friends with the French . . . must respect their nationality," he had written the editor of the *Montreal Gazette* eleven years earlier. "Treat them
as a nation and they will act as a free people generally do, generously."
Macdonald went on to found Canada's Conservative Party and to lead his
infant country through the first decades of its teething pains.

The covenant forged by Macdonald and his colleagues by no means
covered every base. It omitted a formula for amending the Constitution,
assuming Ottawa would petition the British Parliament for any needed
changes—an assumption that would return to haunt Canadians more than
a century later. And the new federation's debut was hardly a universal
smash. The *Prince Edward Island Herald* assured its readers that "a beg-
garly 'nationality,' with a large minority of its people discontented and
ripe for revolt at the very outset of its career, cannot be of long duration."
Americans greeted Canada's birth tepidly, slow to recognize that the new
country was, in the late Canadian diplomat John Holmes's definition, "an
indigenous resistance movement, not an imperial plantation" of Great
Britain. At least one New York journal, the Catholic Church's influential
Tablet, gave the event its due. "A star has risen in the northern sky," it
editorialized, "and who may calculate its future magnitude?"

As if in answer, Canada's business and political leadership began planning in earnest to tame and reap the rewards of the country's infinitely
bounteous West. If ranchers, robber barons, gunslingers, and other
rogues had boldly defined the early American West, Canada's western
frontier became a corporate and largely law-abiding one, the preserve of
the Hudson's Bay Company, the Canadian Pacific Railway, countless
bank branches, and, of course, the Mountie. Once this infrastructure was

in place, the territory began to fill up fast and expand. In 1867, the United States had acquired Alaska from Russia. British Columbia, next door and already overrun by American gold miners panning from the Cariboos to the Cascades, feared a U.S. takeover and struck a deal with Ottawa: it would join Confederation if the Macdonald government guaranteed the province a railroad east. Macdonald did, and British Columbia became a province four years later. By 1870 the Hudson's Bay Company's extensive northern landholdings and the Arctic had become Canada's Northwest Territories. The rush to settle the Plains was on.

One Catholic, French-speaking colony emplaced along the Red River at Fort Garry, the present site of Winnipeg, perceived the heavy westward migration of mostly Protestant settlers from Ontario as a threat. The Métis of the area, half-breed progeny of seventeenth- and eighteenth-century fur trappers and their Indian wives, were alarmed by the incursion of eastern farmers and land surveyors. When their leader, a self-styled messiah named Louis Riel, organized a resistance by seizing Fort Garry, taking a number of prisoners, and proclaiming a provisional government in defiance of Ottawa, the Red River Rebellion was on. Riel summarily executed one of his prisoners, an Ontarian, enraging Canada's anglophone populace. Ottawa, fearing any impotence on its part would encourage the United States to consider annexing the Red River territory, moved swiftly to snuff the rebellion and negotiate the creation of Manitoba as Canada's fifth province, with Winnipeg its capital. Riel, now wanted for murder, fled to Montana, only to be enticed back to Manitoba to lead another rebellion in 1884. This time, as he paced behind the rifle pits, waving his crucifix and praying for his outnumbered followers, his luck ran out for good. Riel was captured, convicted by an English-speaking jury, and hanged.

English Canadians applauded the verdict and punishment; French Canadians, viewing Riel as a martyr to their Church and culture, reacted otherwise. One of them had predicted that when Riel fell through the gallows' trap, "at that moment an abyss will be dug," forever separating Quebec from English-speaking Canada. The Red River Rebellion was as close as Canada had come to civil war, and the death of Riel widened the anglo-francophone divide another crack.

Despite Riel, Canada's western migration continued unabated: Hungarians, Icelanders, Poles, Ukrainians, Mennonites from Russia, Hutterites from Germany, all lured by the promise of cheap land. They settled on the fertile soils of Manitoba and Alberta, the wheatlands and potash beds of Saskatchewan, and some trekked across the Rockies to the virgin forests and Pacific shores of British Columbia. The transcontinental railroad that Prime Minister Macdonald had promised British Columbia got its final spike in 1885 and helped bear many of the immigrants westward. Yet the Canadian Pacific, as unifying a force as any in the nation's history, was also becoming a symbol to westerners of the unequal treatment they felt their region had become subjected to.

The scheme that Toronto's merchant princes and Ottawa's visionaries had concocted decades before to develop the nation's markets was grounded on expectations that the western wheatlands would become the granary of the British Empire and the whole region eventually the engine of the Canadian economy. To realize the dream required tight control by Ottawa, which wanted to avoid what it viewed as the six-shooter anarchy and private-interest grab-all that had characterized the development of America's West. The process resulted in a squeezing of western Canadian producers for the benefit of eastern businessmen, and the Canadian Pacific was seen as a facilitator of the squeeze. Western farmers resented the railroad for the soaring freight rates it charged to transport their goods; they resented even more the high prices charged for eastern-made goods, part of the tariff structure designed to protect manufacturers in central Canada. By the mid-1880s the West's dudgeon was at a crest.

The discontent surged into the 1890s. Riel's death had plunged anglo-francophone relations to new depths. In an eerie forecast of the 1990s, Quebec was already seeking more powers not just for itself but for all the provinces. The Maritimes had joined the West in outrage over federal policies favoring central Canada; Nova Scotia was actually threatening secession. In his mid-seventies, near the end of his life, Sir John Macdonald conceded he was "a good deal discouraged as to our future," even as he girded for his final election campaign in 1891. He won it on the rhetoric of anti-Americanism, but was dead within the year. Canadians wondered who could possibly replace Macdonald, who could reconcile the conflicting parties and make them act in ways contrary to their prejudices but vital to national unity. It was, concluded Goldwin Smith, "work which will have to be done if a general breakup is to be avoided. Things will not hold together on their own."

On Canada's twenty-fifth anniversary in 1892 the troubles looked to many to be insuperable. The new Prime Minister-in-waiting, Wilfrid

Laurier, warned: "We have come to a period in the history of this young country when premature dissolution seems at hand."

By the turn of the century it seemed that Laurier and the idea of dissolution had been happily premature. The new nation had not only survived its initial growing pains, it appeared to have sufficient steam to have persuaded Laurier, its first French Canadian Prime Minister, to do a *volte-face* and proclaim that the twentieth century belonged to Canada.

Immigrants were flooding in and further opening up Canada's West. The amplitude of the country's natural-resource wealth was becoming more apparent by the day. Rebellion in Quebec and on the Plains had subsided. Relations with the United States, though still edgy, were moving toward greater harmony. In 1910, both countries established a permanent International Joint Commission to deal with the Great Lakes and other use-of-water issues; both made ready to benefit from a proposed new accord on trade reciprocity. Laurier was moved to rhapsodize about "the spectacle of two peoples living side by side along a frontier nearly 4,000 miles long with not a cannon, not a gun, facing across it from either side. . . ." It was the beginning of what would become known, in rhetorical terms, as the longest undefended cliché in Canadian-American relations.

It was also the beginning of the end for Laurier and his Liberals. Much of Canada was still obdurately anti-American, suspicious of any trade accord that might hasten the advent of continentalism and vitiation of the Canadian national dream. Laurier's Conservative opponents rode the climate to victory in the brass-knuckled election campaign of 1911, warning: "No truck nor trade with the Yankees." In the same election, Quebec's Conservatives expressed disdain for Laurier as a tool of British imperialism, presaging the fissure between English and French Canada which burst open anew six years later during World War I.

Canadian governments had from the start hedged their loyalty to Empire whenever far-afield British police actions seemed irrelevant to Ottawa's interests: in 1885, Macdonald had refused to send troops to aid a British military expedition in the Sudan, and Laurier in 1899 had declined to order Canadians to serve in the Boer War. But when World War I brought distinction to Canada and to the thousands of its soldiers who fought, choked, and died in the mud of Passchendaele and Vimy

Ridge or amid the swirl of poison gas at Ypres, any thought of renouncing nationwide military conscription seemed traitorous. Quebec's bitter opposition to conscription, coming at a time when French-language rights were under assault in parts of Canada, enraged English Canada even as it underscored French Canadians' unwillingness to participate in the wars of an Empire whose anglophone constituents denied them equal rights at home. The conscription crisis shattered any semblance of national unity; in Quebec, the federal militia fired on labor unionists protesting the Ottawa government, killing three workers.

The century's two world wars would become as defining for Canada as the War of 1812 and America's Civil War had been. The Canadian Army's performance in World War I infused the nation with massive new confidence; it brought respect from London and the realization that Canadians deserved a larger dose of autonomy. Although the war served to further divide anglos and francophones, it restored, however briefly, the influence of the federal government. In the interim between the world wars, Canada effectively shed dominionhood, gained control of its own foreign policy, named its first envoy to Washington, and stirred uneasily as the provinces amassed more influence and expanded their spending powers while those of the federal government declined. Around this time, too, the first murmurings of constitutional change were heard, intimations of the drama that would engross the nation's leadership for much of the century's last quarter.

In the late 1920s Canada's leaders, tired of having to beg London's permission every time they wanted to amend their Constitution, started negotiations among themselves that would lead to more than six decades of rancorous bargaining and, in the end, failure. No one could agree on a simple and effective means of changing the nation's governing legal document as the times required. (Much later, the repatriated Constitution would contain at least four stupefyingly complex formulas for the record.) The simplest thing that could be said about the history of the amending formula, one scholar noted, was that it went from unwritten to unwieldy without ever passing through understandable. And for much of this period the Constitution, unwanted in Canada until some consensus emerged, continued to reside in Westminster.

The country, meanwhile, took the decades in stride, more or less. It suffered through the Depression, erected in 1930 the highest tariff wall in its history to guard its still adolescent manufacturing economy, and cemented closer relations with the United States, as war approached, by setting up a Permanent Joint Board on Defense. When World War II broke, Canada was again tragically generous in its sacrifice—nearly 42,000 dead or missing—and more wisely accommodating on the matter of conscription, which Quebec once more opposed. This time the issue provoked more a momentary burp of protest than widespread mutiny. A key reason was Canada's flawlessly unigniting Prime Minister, William Lyon Mackenzie King.

King had seemingly been around forever. He'd first assumed the prime ministership in 1921, and thereafter, with only a few periods out of office, had managed to bury successive challengers under the weight of his oratorical sludge and ponderousness. No one worshipped more successfully at the altar of dullness than Mackenzie King—a dumpy, unimposing little man with tidy straight hair, a leader possessed of such patience and capacity for compromise that he could blunt the most pointed debate or crisis in the making. He was an Everyman politician whose durability through war and domestic crises has been attributed to the fact that he divided Canadians the least. But King was also a canny accommodator, who foresaw early the coming exchange of Canada's wardship to Britain for its dependency on the United States. To the country's and his career's later advantage, King focused his postgraduate education in the United States, connected with the right American institutions (Harvard, the Rockefellers), and befriended the right President, Franklin D. Roosevelt. On his way to power, King also divined what some have called the dirty little secret of Canadian politics, namely, the leader who leads least governs longest. His would be the lengthiest on-and-off rule of twentieth-century Canada.

It was only after he died in 1948 that King's charismaless persona took on a bizarre dimension. Although tales of his consorting with prostitutes in Ottawa, the better (he said) to reform them, had become well known during his lifetime as a bachelor, his diaries posthumously revealed King as a genuine oddball who held nocturnal séances. Through a medium, he regularly consulted the departed spirits of his mother, his Liberal predecessor Laurier, and his pet terrier Pat. It was reported that he even reached Leonardo da Vinci for advice on the design of some statuary for his ruins at Kingsmere, the Prime Minister's country home. King admittedly contributed to a lot of the doubts about his reputation; but even in ridicule, he remained a towering figure in Canada's political life. Or, as the poet F. R. Scott observed, he will be remembered "Wherever men honor ingenuity / ambiguity, inactivity, and political longevity."

As it had in World War I, Canada's federal government assumed broad new powers in mobilizing for World War II: the provinces surrendered for the war's duration control of all fiscal policy. Emerging in 1945 with massive surpluses of industrial goods and the world's third largest navy, Canada entered the ranks of industrialized states with a renewed sense of national unity, at least in English Canada. Before the decade was over, a tenth province, Newfoundland, had been added to the federation and Canada had joined the new North Atlantic Treaty Organization (NATO) as one of its founding members. The Cold War threatened, but Canada, under the leadership of King's successor, Louis St. Laurent, was poised to enter the 1950s on a wave of economic prosperity.

Key to this was the development, fueled by foreign capital, of Canada's abundant natural resources: nickel by the mineload, wood pulp for newsprint production, vast ranges of iron ore in northern Quebec, rich timber preserves in British Columbia, Alberta's oil and natural gas fields, Saskatchewan's potash, and recently discovered uranium beds in Ontario. By the late fifties, export trade in these and other commodities had been markedly enhanced by the opening of the St. Lawrence Seaway, which offered access to the inland ports and trading centers of the Great Lakes. To help guard this cornucopia and the encompassing continent, Canada in 1957 joined the United States to form a joint command under the North American Air Defense (NORAD) Agreement. The prosperity continued into the sixties, although the era of sunnier Canadian-American relations hit squalls with the succession of John Diefenbaker to the prime ministership.

Diefenbaker's six-year tenure, during which he clashed with the Kennedy administration over the issue of arming nuclear weapons on Canadian soil, and refused to put Canada's NORAD forces on alert at the time of the Cuban missile crisis, undid much of the binational progress of the St. Laurent years. Diefenbaker's contentious governing style, which led eventually to his downfall, mirrored not only the man—insecure, dogmatic, suspicious—but the mood of many Canadians who'd grown uneasy at increasing U.S. influence over their economic development and their foreign policy. Diefenbaker's defensiveness, his anglophilia and hopeless attempts to speak French also incorporated much of English Canada's concern about the massive changes occurring in Quebec and

the newly assertive role of that province's 5 million or more francophones. The coming Pearson and Trudeau eras would address, with
mixed results, English Canadians' looming crisis of identity in both these
spheres, especially concerning Quebec.

The 1960s were Quebec's decade, a transforming time in which the province literally burst the bonds of its feudal past and pushed its way into the
modern age.

Quebec in its earlier incarnation had been a largely forgotten North
American tribe, a semi-literate village society, according to one observer,
that spoke a language unknown to Parisians and was dominated by priests
and doctors. The province had slumbered for almost 150 years since the
British-imposed division of Upper and Lower Canada, its citizenry lost
like Brigadoon's in a pastoral time warp as the rest of Canada marched
ahead. Quebec's francophones were kept aside from business life and
away from the cities, in Pierre Trudeau's words, "reduced to a minority
role and deprived of influence in a country which, after all, they had
discovered, explored and settled."

For two decades, from the late 1930s through the 1950s, Quebecers
had groped through *la grande noirceur,* the great darkness that enveloped
the era of Premier Maurice Duplessis, a reactionary strongman who exercised near-dictatorial power. Under Duplessis's rule, graft and philistin-
ism flourished, civil liberties lapsed, and the provincial police bashed
unions and strikers' heads at will. More than thirty years after Duplessis's
death in 1959, the true dimension of Quebec's primitiveness in those
times was revealed: thousands of illegitimate children had been stamped
as social outcasts and systematically shunted off to state-sponsored men-
tal institutions run by the Church, where they had been deprived of
schooling and many subjected to unspeakable abuse. History has not
absolved Duplessis for his excesses, simply reapportioned some of the
blame: according to revisionist theory, Duplessis was *le roi nègre,* a
French Canadian manipulated by the real rulers of Quebec, the English,
much as certain puppet rulers in Africa had been controlled by earlier
colonial powers. Not surprisingly, that kind of rationale went far in nur-
turing the shoots of francophone nationalism in Quebec.

When those flowered into the "quiet revolution" of the early sixties,
under the Liberal government of Premier Jean Lesage, Quebec turned

rapidly from a backwoods society of French Canadians into a bustling, urban one of Québécois. In the rush to assert their status as *maîtres chez nous,* the Québécois tore themselves from the Church's embalming grip and plunged into an orgy of secularizing change. Education was transferred from the priests to a network of junior colleges. The provincial government mobilized the economy for the new age, nationalizing the private electric utilities to form the blockbuster Hydro-Québec company and setting up other corporations with mandates for economic development. For the same purpose Quebecers' savings were organized and pooled under a co-operative of *caisses* or savings banks, while the province established its own pension fund to manage Quebecers' growing capital. As power drained from the Church into the hands of the state, there emerged a new francophone middle class of corporate businessmen, civil servants, and other professionals. The era of change, the common enterprise on which Quebecers had embarked, infused the province with a cohesiveness absent elsewhere in Canada, with the French language becoming ever more central to Quebec's progress. The first tremors of eruptive Quebec nationalism and francisization began finally to register on English Canada.

The fruits of the "quiet revolution" persuaded ever more Québécois that their future lay with Quebec alone, that Confederation had become too confining, the Constitution antiquated and in need of reform. But Canada's newest Prime Minister, less a Quebec expert than an accomplished internationalist, had other priorities. Lester Pearson, who took power in 1963, had already, as Canada's foreign minister, won renown and the Nobel Prize for his peacekeeping efforts during the 1956 Suez crisis. As Prime Minister he proved adept at restabilizing Canadian-American relations which had frayed under Diefenbaker, less so in dealing with the strains at home. Pearson's compromising instincts did little to assuage Quebec's restlessness; when he launched what he thought was a pacifying initiative, an official inquiry into the state of bilingualism and biculturalism in Canada, Quebecers nodded and western Canadians denounced it.

In Quebec, the first whiffs of terrorism charged the air. Between 1963 and 1969 a series of bombings, Molotov cocktail attacks, and raids on armories in the Montreal area were carried out by the Maoist Quebec Liberation Front (FLQ). The FLQ had pledged to sabotage anglophone establishments as well as those of "American colonialism." The U.S.

Consulate was targeted, along with the Montreal Stock Exchange, where an explosion injured twenty persons. The violence shocked Montrealers even as it provided a backdrop for the initial victory of a rising politician who would become the most remarkable Canadian of his generation.

When the rocks began flying that June day in 1968, as a mob of radical separatists tried to break up the annual St. Jean Baptiste parade in Montreal, Pierre Elliott Trudeau was one of the few dignitaries who did not flee the reviewing stand. Trudeau had chosen to end his baptismal campaign for Prime Minister by attending the parade in honor of Quebec's patron saint. Three days after he contemptuously faced down the mob, he scored an overwhelming triumph at the polls, sweeping Quebec in the bargain. By the time he relinquished power, sixteen years and three elections later, Trudeau had become the enduring enemy of Quebec separatism and Canada's most impassioned voice for national unity.

He was a well-born, rose-in-the-lapel aristocrat whose millionaire father indulged him trips to Europe and Asia at an early age and a cosmopolitan education that included, after his Jesuit schooling, stints at Harvard, the London School of Economics, and the Sorbonne. At home but antsy in the world of academe, Trudeau vaulted from his career beginnings as a University of Montreal law professor and contributing essayist at the scholarly *Cité Libre* journal into the larger limelight of Liberal Party politics. His sharply reasoned, anti-nationalist essays had already drawn an attentive audience beyond Quebec. As the scion of parents rooted in both French and English traditions, he saw his mission in politics as helping to ensure that neither would Quebec voluntarily leave Canada via separatism nor would English Canada force Quebec out through narrow-mindedness. In the Cartesian logic that shaped his views, Trudeau saw no merit in the separatist arguments and little more in those championing regional and provincial loyalties. He was a true-believing centralist, and in Ottawa that proved no hindrance to his swift rise as a Member of Parliament through the Cabinet ranks of the Pearson government, thence to his final ascension in 1968.

Canadians weren't sure what they had gotten in their new fluently bilingual, break-the-mold leader. Quebec's francophones saw Trudeau proudly as one of their own; Canada's anglophones, especially in the West, saw him as the Prime Minister who would "put Quebec in its place." Millions of ordinary voters, who whipped up the "Trudeaumania" that swept him to office, thought him a magnetic Kennedyesque figure.

Trudeau's avant-garde flair was just the flavor for the times. Intellectuals welcomed his philosophic breadth, a man who could quote Racine at will. Canadian youth, brought up to revere the stately paternalism of past prime ministers, reveled in Trudeau's slangy informality and exuberant athleticism, even his bohemian threads. He favored rakish hats, roll-neck shirts, capes, and sandals, as well as late-night discothèquing, sliding down bannisters, and doing the boogaloo. A bachelor at the time, he enjoyed being photographed with beautiful women. He seemed an intriguing cross between the aesthetic Zhou Enlai and Leslie Howard's fop in *The Scarlet Pimpernel*. Another nascent swinger, the young U.S. Senator Edward Kennedy, remembered he first met Trudeau at Eisenhower's funeral in Washington and found him spell binding.

A year later, some of the spell had begun to dissipate. Trudeau's ground-breaking Official Languages Act, which made English and French equal in the conduct of federal business throughout Canada, was a well-intentioned effort to broaden the opportunities for francophone citizens while blunting the nationalist thrust in Quebec. But Quebecers seemed indifferent to the Act, while millions of English Canadians resented it altogether. The Trudeau style of governing, viewed by many as too technocratic, too preoccupied with global charts, and too given to precision instead of compromise, had begun to grate. The Prime Minister's court, led by a man who'd never had to scramble to pay the rent, had "too much computer and not enough heart," as the saying went. The Trudeauites' guiding urge was to impose logic on the course of events without seeming to comprehend the country's bedrock incompatibilities.

Behind the crisp management style was the man himself, a growing enigma to many Canadians. Trudeau's persona—a mix of arrogance, charm, aloofness, and frequent petulance—was beginning to fray at the edges. He seemed wanting some touch of charity in his makeup, the ability to bleed with people a little. Even after a decade of politics, one writer observed, Trudeau remained "about as knowledgeable of the human condition as a Trappist monk." His response to the outrage of opponents was aptly embodied in the title of a book-length critique of his governance: *Shrug*. His glamorous dating habits (movie stars, television notables, etc.) were also wearing thin. Hustle wheat, not women, came the reported advice from unamused western farmers. Even Trudeau's elitist sporting life had an air of unnecessary bravado: during a post-election ski holiday in British Columbia's Bugaboo peaks, he had come tearing down one slope and rocketed past his waiting guide and fellow skiers, heading full-throttle for a hidden hundred-foot-deep crevasse before frantic cries from his party brought him to a halt.

In his essentially European temperament, Trudeau was the least Canadian of all the nation's prime ministers, according to his biographer, Richard Gwyn. Yet Canadians, because they understood the magnitude of his vision, allowed Trudeau to dominate their political life and their consciousness in a way that no other leader had ever done.

With the 1970s under way, Trudeau was centerstage in the struggle heating up between the forces of unity and divisiveness. The new decade would be an epochal period for Quebec as the independence movement gathered steam and respectability. It would also be an unsettling time for other parts of the country as Ottawa displayed ever more power to effect jarring social and economic change, and a decade of souring Canadian-American relations.

Straightaway, the Prime Minister became embroiled in Canada's worst terrorist crisis to date. He managed to quash an incipient rebellion by the separatist FLQ, which had kidnapped Quebec's labor minister and the British Trade Commissioner. In the October 1970 crisis, Trudeau suspended civil rights, invoking a repressive act used only in wartime. Eight thousand federal troops imposed martial law on Montreal; the FLQ murdered the labor minister; and the Canadian government alerted U.S. border guards that some of the terrorists might try to flee to the United States. The crisis burnished Trudeau's reputation as a decisive leader if not a great civil libertarian. It also undermined, though not for long, the legitimacy of the independence movement in Quebec.

The diminishment of the Church's role in Quebec had accelerated a serious decline in the province's birth rate. The threatening trend moved the province to push for even more powers to preserve its special identity. It continued to scuttle the nation's occasional attempts at constitutional change, attempts which in Quebec's view failed to address its needs. Meanwhile, other power-seeking provinces began to side with Quebec's cause, an alliance that challenged Trudeau's efforts to clarify and strengthen the federal government's authority. Canada, the Prime Minister snapped, was far more than his opponents' view of it as just a collection of shopping centers. But Quebec and its allies remained defiant.

Quebec even stepped up the pace of its francisizing. Over the protests of its anglophone minority, it officially installed French as the language of Quebec's workplace and government. Years ahead of the federals in Ottawa, it enacted in 1975 its own comprehensive Charter of Human Rights and Freedoms. And at a time when only 26 out of Quebec's top 165 corporations were owned by Québécois (although they comprised 80 percent of the population), the province took steps to ensure that French Canadians would never again be excluded from the levers of economic power. When René Levesque was elected as Quebec's new premier in 1976, the battle between Trudeau and the separatists for the soul of Quebec was finally joined.

Levesque, a committed *indépendantiste,* had been a driving force in the "quiet revolution," but had grown impatient with Lesage's moderate Liberal Party and deserted it in the late sixties to found the separatist Parti Québécois. A chain-smoking, raspy-voiced little man who peppered his conversation with profanities and was known affectionately as *Tit-Poil* ("Little Baldy") for his sparse, usually uncombed hair, he was everything Trudeau was not: born in a remote coastal village in the Gaspé, provincially educated, a war correspondent in Europe and Korea, later a television commentator, unabashedly emotional, a man who cultivated the image of a four-star hick. When he met the patrician banker David Rockefeller on Wall Street a year after his election, Levesque sported a brown leather overcoat and suede Wallabees. From the beginning, he was suspicious of the urbane Trudeau, hostile toward his intellectual manner, and convinced that Trudeau was little more than a francophone poseur spouting basically anglophone ideas. In Levesque, Trudeau saw personified all the outdated myths and wounded sensitivities that hung like millstones around Quebecers' necks. "We must break the chains that bind us to them," he and his government in Ottawa declared in an action paper. "Let us forget once and for all about the Plains of Abraham. . . . Let us 'decolonize' Quebec in our minds." But, of course, that was not part of the separatists' strategy.

The Levesque government, in fact, proved surprisingly effective in restoring some of the luster to the separatist cause. For two terms it ran a corrupt-free administration in Quebec that abolished political patronage and set up an efficient civil service. Anglophones by the thousands departed Montreal as Levesque's ruling Parti Québécois fixated on establishing the primacy of the French language at every level. The righteous fervor of the separatist cause, fanned by Levesque's *péquistes,* as his party members called themselves, continued to antagonize English Canadians; but among his own people, *Tit-Poil* was revered.

That was more than could be said for the Prime Minister. After almost a decade in office, Trudeau bestrode the country less like a Colossus than a St. Sebastian braving the next arrow. The leader of a parliamentary democracy, he was accused of appropriating ever more power from Parliament and grafting it on to what had become an exorbitantly inflated executive branch. His new policy of "multiculturalism," emphasizing the diversity of Canada's ethnic society, constituted in Quebec's eyes another effort to downgrade francophones' status. In the West, they loathed him: under pressure from Ontario nationalists, Trudeau was preparing to break the hold of U.S.-dominated multinationals on the oil and gas industry, Alberta's bread-and-butter ticket.

Abroad, Trudeau was perceived as a rather dashing if ineffectual figure, an eloquent advocate for Third World interests and greater north-south dialogue, a classy leader of a middle power with diminishing muscle. In his determination to advance more and costly domestic social programs, he had managed to starve Canada's military forces almost to the bone and reduce its contribution of manpower to NATO by half. In America, Trudeau was viewed as an unfriendly maverick bent on discouraging U.S. investment in Canada through the protracted screening procedures of his Foreign Investment Review Agency and on abandoning Canada's long affair with the U.S. trade establishment for other world markets via Ottawa's so-called "third option" strategy.

About the only happy note had been Trudeau's farewell to bachelorhood at the age of fifty-one to marry a lovely twenty-two-year-old flower child who bore him three sons and was so incorrigibly fey that it was said she almost convinced him his Cabinet should take up transcendental meditation.

Trudeau's continued drive to repel Quebec separatism while bolstering national unity got a prod at the beginning of the new decade. His National Energy Program in 1980 to "Canadianize" the oil and natural gas industry decreed that 50 percent of the nation's energy assets were to be owned or controlled by Canadian interests within the decade. At the same time, Ottawa levied production and export taxes on the industry while ordering its oil and gas to be priced at less than half the world market value. For good measure, Ottawa took billions of dollars in royalty revenue from the producing provinces and diverted the funds to the federal budget. The consequences—among them, the mass departure of oil-drilling rigs and delays in developing new oil fields—devastated the industry and permanently alienated westerners and much of the U.S. business community from Trudeau. The program, however, succeeded to a degree in increasing the level of Canadian control, and as a gesture of old-fashioned Yankee bashing it played well elsewhere in the country. In Quebec, where a suspenseful referendum on the issue of independence was defeated, Trudeau received an even more important lift.

Quebec's 1980 referendum had pitted Trudeau against René Levesque's ruling separatists, who sought with the voters' approval to open negotiations with Ottawa on the question of sovereignty-association for Quebec—in effect, economic alliance with Canada but full political autonomy. When Quebecers rejected the referendum by a 6–to–4 margin, English Canada breathed a sigh of relief. Except, Trudeau had promised Quebecers that if they sunk the referendum he would see that their problems were resolved soon within a "renewed federation." That was not to be. Nor did the referendum's defeat spell the end of Levesque and his Parti Québécois, much less the independence movement.

Flushed with his triumph over the separatists, at the same time frustrated by the stumbling pace of constitutional reform, Trudeau two years later powered ahead on his own and, in a historic though controversial act, repatriated Canada's Constitution from Britain. With all of the provinces except Quebec approving, his government incorporated into the 1982 Constitution Act two major innovations: a Charter of Rights and Freedoms, resembling America's due-process Bill of Rights, and a mechanism for amending the Constitution. The Charter moved Canadians closer to becoming a society that emphasized individual (as opposed to collective) rights and gave Canada's courts a more influential role; the amending formula, which had many loopholes and opting-out provisions, only opened the door to more trouble. If a province disagreed with the courts' interpretation of a clause in the Charter, it could simply make its own rules, notwithstanding the Constitution.

The revised Constitution went into effect over Quebec's staunch objection. Levesque's *péquiste* government had fought Trudeau's repatriation efforts from the start. Now it objected because the new package had been passed without its consent, offered none of the powers Quebec had sought, particularly in the sensitive education and immigration areas, and denied Quebec its traditional veto over key constitutional changes. The new Constitution signaled Canada's final and complete independence from Britain, but it also confirmed the continuing English-French divide. Flags on public buildings in Quebec flew at half-mast; provincial legislation was ordered to be excluded from the provisions of the Constitution. Popular disaffection flamed not only in Quebec but in other provinces where politicians objected to Trudeau's steamroller tactics or feared that the new Constitution's emphasis on the courts would further weaken Parliament's historic prerogatives.

In repatriation's contentious aftermath, many Canadians wondered whether there had been any compelling reason to bring the Constitution home in the first place other than to ensure a solid legacy for the Trudeau government. Many, like columnist Jeffrey Simpson of the *Globe and Mail,* worried that constitutional reform would become not Canada's holy grail to salvation, but instead the charcoal for the nation's "bonfire of grievances." The old Newfie joke never seemed apter, that the best way to keep milk from going sour was to keep it in the cow.

Even as he finally secured Canada's crowning symbol of independence, Trudeau sensed he had overstayed his welcome with the electorate. His achievements had been monumental—preserving the nation's integrity in the face of Quebec's insurgents, opening the country to its French-speaking citizens through official bilingualism, and giving Canadians a charter of fundamental freedoms. But he had also become the lightning rod for Canadians' discontent, the meddlesome steward of an imperial prime ministership. For all his panache, as the *New York Times* editorialized, Trudeau's reach had exceeded his grasp. His indifferent understanding of the economy and his attempts to exert greater federal control over it had led to inflation, stagnancy, and pervasive debt. He had lost affection and now credibility among his people. Canada's business sector had come to hold him in such low esteem that when Trudeau announced in 1983 that he was finally stepping down, the Toronto Stock Exchange jumped more than sixteen points.

A year later Trudeau's Liberal successor, John N. Turner, a handsome former Rhodes Scholar at Oxford, standout Cabinet minister in the early Trudeau administration, and a blue-chip Toronto lawyer whose political skills had rusted, became one of the shortest-lived prime ministers in

Canadian history, buried under an electoral landslide that brought Brian Mulroney and the Progressive Conservatives to power.

Mulroney roared in, determined to harmonize matters between Ottawa and the provinces and between Ottawa and Washington, both of which relationships had soured under Trudeau. Among other things, Mulroney planned to forge an enduring political bond between his party and two habitually alienated regions, the West and Quebec, his home base; he had already formed a politically expedient alliance with many of Quebec's ardent nationalists in order to win office. Mulroney would also change the direction of Canada's overlarded economy. He would govern by consensus rather than Trudeauesque fiat. Like Ronald Reagan, a convivial master of symbolic form, Mulroney would elevate the politics of bonhomie to high art. As a former labor negotiator, he had always been more a reconciler than a persuader, more peacemaker than visionary. As time went on, unfortunately, Mulroney would prove to be more a back-slapping dealmaker than a long-distance nation builder.

He was born into middle-class obscurity, the oldest son of an electrician whose Catholic forebears had fled the Irish potato famine and come to rest on the northern coast of the St. Lawrence in a papermaking town called Baie Comeau. Mulroney was still in short pants when he began earning tips warbling standards like "Danny Boy" to Colonel McCormick of the *Chicago Tribune* whenever the publisher visited one of his paper mills in the area. He was street-smart, possessed of an incandescent smile, and knew how to flatter the right people. After studies at a minor university in Nova Scotia, Mulroney graduated from law school and joined an anglophone firm in Montreal. The backwoods boyo came in for his share of snubs from the local Protestant establishment, but at the age of thirty-three he was made a partner of his law firm and four years later was contesting the leadership of the national Conservative Party. Mulroney lost that one, but regained his momentum as president of the Iron Ore Company of Canada for six years and, following his election at last as leader of the Conservatives in 1983, went on to become Canada's eighteenth Prime Minister.

The Mulroney years were pot-stirring ones that for a start shook Canadians from their welfare-dependency torpor. The Tories' drive to deregulate key economic sectors, reform the tax structure, and privatize some of the more sluggish, state-supported companies riled many of Canada's leftish opinion makers as well as much of the cozy business establishment. Right off, the new Prime Minister dismantled Trudeau's National Energy Program and removed the most egregious features of the Foreign Investment Review Agency (FIRA) which had antagonized American businesses. The screening agency had been established at the height of Canada's economic nationalist fervor in the mid-seventies and had assumed wide-ranging authority to apply stricter controls on foreign investment. In cases where such investment would result in little more than extending a company's foreign market power into Canada, with no substantial benefits to the local economy, FIRA could block it in the "national interest." Such cases were rarer than supposed, but the agency's potential for arbitrary judgments and harassment of foreign firms was a source of bilateral irritation.

Mulroney's administration also took measures to curb the government's deficit spending, not that much had been left in the coffers to spend, and began steering Canada's economy toward a rate of average growth that would become the fastest in the industrial world for a time. Early on, despite his previous opposition to the idea, Mulroney initiated talks with the United States that led in 1989 to the pioneering Canadian-American Free Trade accord. He undertook a good deal of this at about the same time his new administration was plagued with beginner's pratfalls: alleged scandals, nasty Cabinet resignations, and club-footed policy reversals. By 1988, however, Mulroney's record was sufficient for the voters to return him and his party to power in an election that, along with the one in 1984, resulted in the first back-to-back majorities for a Canadian leader in thirty-five years. And then within a paddy's twinkle it all started to come a mucker.

As Canada's first Conservative Prime Minister to be reelected since 1872, Mulroney had seen his Tories move commandingly to displace the once dominant Liberals as the nation's perennial party of government. But in winning his 1988 campaign, Mulroney, though he'd held Quebec comfortably, had failed to gain a majority of the country's English-speaking voters. Too soon, his approval ratings dropped like a stone. Many Canadians, the second time around, found Mulroney's policies and the man wanting. Not a few of his successes had come early and been perceived as more corrective than innovative. Some faulted his consensus style and impatiently accused him of giving consultation a bad name. Others resented his being an agent of drastic change. Mulroney's government had substantially reduced spending, but many Canadians still hankered for the extravagant giveaways of the Trudeau years. Mulroney's foreign policy proved adequate enough ("Oh, Brian, he may not be a heavyweight, but he rows well behind Reagan and me," Britain's Prime Minister Margaret Thatcher told a visiting Canadian executive at the time). But Mulroney's unapologetic pro-Americanism earned him more brickbats than huzzahs at home; Canadians saw him as a toady for U.S. business interests. The journalist Peter Newman wrote that it seemed Mulroney was blamed for every dead sparrow that fell from the sky.

No matter his successes. What really peeved Canadians was Mulroney's self-applauding air about them, especially those that existed largely in his hyperbole. He was marked as a name-dropping blarneyist with a craving for approval, a man of shallow intellectual depth with a vindictive streak when it came to dealing with associates who were not up to snuff. He courted the press unashamedly, and they repaid him with a lack of respect they never showed Trudeau. When the Prime Minister spoke, his mellifluous basso tones seemed to ooze insincerity, "like listening to chocolate melting," as one reporter said. Rightly or wrongly, Canadians may have sensed in Mulroney a man whose first-rate ambitions and achievements could never quite overcome the second rate in his character and personality. Instinctively, some may have suspected that in American politics Mulroney would have become at best a colorful Senate committee chairman, behind the scenes an artful log-roller and after-hours raconteur. Like his friend George Bush, he epitomized the triumph of perseverance over talent.

If the Prime Minister tended to identify Canada's fate with his political fortunes (Après moi, le déluge), the outcome of the decade's most ambitious attempt to achieve constitutional reform and return Quebec to the fold proved a truly damaging blow to Mulroney.

Despite reservations in many quarters about reopening the constitutional question after the turmoil over repatriation, Mulroney and the provincial premiers met in early 1987 at Quebec's Meech Lake, just north of Ottawa, to thrash out an agreement that would meet Quebec's minimal conditions for rejoining the federation in a legal sense. The accord they signed, named after the lake which had once been known for its nudist beach, recognized Quebec as a "distinct society"; that was one of several constitutional changes recommended with Quebec's enthusiastic approval. All ten provincial legislatures would have to ratify the Meech

Lake Accord within three years, or it would expire. Before the ink was dry, the sniping began. Some argued that the accord empowered the provinces with too many new rights that would render the federal government impotent and its leaders virtual eunuchs. There were complaints that the accord had been crafted too secretively behind closed doors. But most of the wrath was directed at the special status accorded Quebec, which ignored the agendas of Canada's aboriginals, its westerners, and prominent ethnic groups of more recent lineage. Mulroney was accused of having made a Faustian bargain with Quebec, while former Prime Minister Trudeau heaped scorn on the Québécois leaders as a "bunch of snivellers" and "spoiled adolescents."

Despite the growing criticism, the Meech Lake Accord was approved within months by provinces accounting for almost 94 percent of the population. In the interim, however, power had shifted in three smaller provinces to new governments whose premiers had second doubts. And in Quebec, the provincial government had not only stonewalled any suggestions for modifying the accord, it had flaunted the nation's Supreme Court by overriding the Court's decision that Quebec's ban on English-language outdoor signs was unconstitutional. That, effectively, blew it. In towns across Ontario, enraged city councils rammed through ordinances declaring their jurisdictions exclusively English-speaking. Anglophones were televised wiping their feet on or burning the fleur-de-lis, and the video clips were replayed endlessly for equally enraged Quebec audiences. Amid the ruckus a filibustering Indian in the Manitoba legislature and the unbudging premier of Newfoundland put the final nails in the coffin.

In the end, the Meech Lake Accord expired in 1990 because of two hold-out provinces representing less than 7 percent of the population. In retrospect, the larger blame was due to Quebec's arrogance, English Canada's mulishness, and the federal government's impotence in controlling events.

The fallout from Meech Lake augured a season of distemper as the nineties began. The central government was not only severely weakened; its leader was sliding in the polls toward single-digit approval ratings, the lowest ever recorded for a sitting Prime Minister. Mulroney had paid a fearful price for having "supped with the devil," as one critic said of his catering to Quebec's nationalists and failing to speak out for a united Canada until late in the day. On the other hand, Quebec, which had supported federation in its critical 1980 referendum and had championed Canada's 1989 Free Trade Agreement with the United States more fervently than any province, now felt let down by the Prime Minister, rejected by English Canada, and no longer welcome in Canada. Backing for the idea of separation rose to more than 60 percent in the province, and a half-million Québécois marchers in Montreal confirmed the sentiment. At the same time, polls showed a majority of English Canadians willing to let Quebec go, and a quarter of them actually prepared to toss the province out summarily.

The abrogation of the Meech Lake Accord also roiled Canada's Native populace, setting off militant protests, road blockades, and a violent stand-off between Indians and authorities at a Quebec town called Oka. In the post-Meech storm, too, regional politics underwent realignment: a stinging protest vote overturned the government in Ontario, ushering in a green New Democratic Party regime; in Ottawa, disillusioned francophones in the Prime Minister's parliamentary caucus bolted from Mulroney to a separatist firebrand, Lucien Bouchard, who reorganized the dissidents into a new party at the federal level, the Bloc Québécois. The rest of the country, Bouchard declared, no longer worked.

Not for Brian Mulroney, it didn't. The country had entered a recession partially induced, many believed, by the tough medicine the Tories had prescribed for Canada's economic ills: a national sales tax, devalued currency, and the highest interest rates in nearly a decade. Even the Canada–United States Free Trade Accord, one of Mulroney's signal attainments, had become a dubious political plus in a nation where every plant closing or transfer of facilities south of the border was now blamed on the accord. The two major political parties were in disarray, a weakened counterweight to the emerging protest parties in Quebec and the West, as well as the stridently socialist New Democrats in Ontario. Mulroney's power base in Quebec was slipping away, lured by the separatists and their siren song of independence. Bilingualism was losing ground across the country; intolerance was on the rise. In early 1993, after yet another failed attempt at constitutional accord, Mulroney threw in the towel and resigned.

After three hundred years of history, Canada, the elegiasts warned, was dying from old confrontations and still had found no road to reconciliation. Whatever national identity it possessed was irrevocably split. It seemed more and more a country of forsaken promises and multiplying divisions.

Bes den heb tavas a golhas e dir.

A man who has lost his tongue has lost his land.

—Eighteenth-century Cornish proverb

"English Canada has closed the gate to Quebec. Must we go on our knees in order to stay in federation?"

—CAROL NERON,
Editor, *Le Quotidien,*
Chicoutimi, Quebec,
June 1992

"My family's been here for one hundred years. Why should I have to bend down to these language laws?"

—MARY LAMONTAGNE,
anglophone housewife,
Montreal, Quebec,
September 1992

3

The Road to Breakup: Canada's Great Divides

Maybe all along outsiders have had the question backwards. Not, How could such a blessed nation break up after so much history? but, How has Canada, born amid dissension and beset with conflict from then on, managed to stay together for so long?

The gristle of nationhood, Sir John Macdonald predicted in the 1800s, would take time to "harden into bone." But even before Canadian nationalism finally became a force in the post–World War II years, some intangible emotion in its people kept the Canadian experience on track through the troubled centuries. For all their internecine disputes, Canadians have felt in their marrows the elemental tug of nationalism, "the primitive stuff of which we are made," as Walter Lippmann once said, "our first loyalties, our first aggressions, the type and image of our souls."

Macdonald as Prime Minister was the first exemplar of that nationalism when he sprang his protectionist National Policy on the federation. Eventually the policy backfired and led to the foreign-controlled, branch-plant economy that typed Canada until a relatively short time ago; American mercantilists, instead of trying to scale Canada's high-tariff walls, simply landed their subsidiaries behind them, the better to service the growing Canadian market. As early as 1871, a Canada First movement was formed by young nationalists in Toronto. The eras of Mackenzie King and St. Laurent witnessed the maturing of Canadian nationalism, at least its English-speaking version, while Diefenbaker and Trudeau presided over the cocked-snoot economic nationalism directed largely at the United States. By the late 1980s, economists and others were dismissing nationalism as obsolescent in an era when the world was fast succumbing to the globalization of economies, rendering borders and flag-waving irrelevant. The real challenge to Canadian nationalism, it was said, was not the Quebec separatists but globalism, and a creeping continentalism that threatened to homogenize the cultures of Alberta or Ontario with those of Texas or New York.

In fact, nationalism is still an essential force to reckon with. While its fever has slackened throughout the world since the decolonizing years following World War II, it retains its potency to galvanize and control events. Violently conflicting nationalisms among the remnants of countries like Yugoslavia and the former Soviet Empire breed civil wars that still necessitate large, established nation-states to help impose order. Multinationals still require governments, backed by national purpose, to defend or advance their corporate interests. Canadians lack no amount of reasons for exercising a nationalism of their own. They lack only a sense of distinctiveness, Quebec excepted, to accompany their pride of country. Canadianism is mercifully short of bombast or petty jingoism. Invariably, however, it takes one reliable catalyst to activate it: the United States.

Canada's history has always been one long struggle against the internal forces of disunity and the external threats to its identity and independence. Its divides are almost exclusively internal: Quebec separatism; regionalism; more recently, its fissive multiculturalism and its endemic economic flaws. But one external divide in particular haunts Canadians and threatens the integrity of their nationalism: the love-hate relationship with their closest neighbor. Canadians' longing to be somehow a part of the American dynamic collides with their fear of being suffocated in America's smothery embrace. The psychological conflict has roiled Canadians increasingly from the 1960s on.

Older Canadians who recall the days of Empire still faintly disapprove of Americans, seeing their society, in the late Edmund Wilson's words, as "devoted to the exploits of a vulgar success, which are impious in both their mutinous origins and their insolence in surpassing the mother country." Middle-aged Canadians of the Diefenbaker-Trudeau eras tend toward schizophrenia: an inferiority complex about competing with America which symbolizes fame, power, and influence, "all the things that shouldn't count but do," to quote the Canadian economist William Watson; and a sense of superiority over America when it comes to moral issues like compassion for the poor or affordable care for the sick. For many Canadians the memories of Vietnam, the rage of America's black underclass, urban riots and violent crime, conjure up a nightmare they want no part of.

Younger Canadians are dead certain they want to be as unlike Americans as possible. They are the ones, many of them professionals, who resent the flight south of Canada's natural resources to American refineries, resulting in fewer jobs at home; who chafe at the fact so many decisions involving Canadian businesses are made in head offices outside their country, in America. It is the young who are fighting to maintain their Canadianism, to be viewed as somehow distinctive from Americans. The historical distinction, observed Northrop Frye, was that the United States was born in a war of independence against a European state and reached maturity in a civil war of its own, while Canada was born out of a civil war between two European states and has been fighting for its independence ever since.

It is a curious psychological struggle for Canadians. Economically, they have prospered beyond their dreams as America's closest trading partner. But they bridle at the suggestion they comprise an energy resource colony for the States. Politically, the Canadian-American relationship is a lopsided affair popularly defined in bestial terms: the Canadian mouse ruefully observing, in Lester Pearson's metaphor, that if it were crushed, it would matter little whether the American elephant "was a rogue or a pet, whether the damage was done by calculated planning or by amiable carelessness." Culturally, the situation for Canadians of a certain sensibility has been wrenching. The pervasiveness in Canada of American culture, from books and films to mass-circulation magazines and television programming, has resulted in the Americanizing of Canadians' tastes and the atrophying of their ability to create a culture of their own. Canada, as the writer Abraham Rotstein observed, bears the signs of a successful lobotomy to which it has voluntarily assented; it has become a society of readers and viewers who occasionally experience the disorientation of not really knowing what country they are living in. In his autobiographical novel, *Come From Away,* David Macfarlane poignantly recounts the preparations for his fellow Newfoundlanders' annual Canada Day fête. In addition to the fireworks and hot dogs, the stars of the patriotic gala were to be the rich, middle-aged members of a famous American rock band. "The only un-American thing about them was the way the Newfoundlanders pronounced their name." The Beach Byes.

For many Canadians, bedazzled by America's pop culture and its yellow-brick road to Croesian riches, the inclination is to sit back and enjoy the ride. The kinship between the two peoples is an almost irresistible force. Twenty-seven million Americans and Canadians, an equally divided number, visit each other's country annually. A half-million visitors from Quebec alone annually flock to Florida's playgrounds where they can enjoy their own expatriate newspapers, TV *française,* and restaurants like Le Roi de la Pizza. The two-way trade exceeds 150 billion U.S. dollars a year, much of it in human talent: American academics dot the faculties of Canadian universities; Canadian stars and journalists inhabit Hollywood sets and TV network news staffs. The trans-border commerce jams bridges and highways from Buffalo and Plattsburgh, New York, to Detroit and Bellingham in Washington. When the Canadian dollar soars, the influx of British Columbians, Quebecers, and Ontarians reaches flood proportions.

In Buffalo's parking lots and public restrooms, Canadian shoppers, out to hoodwink customs inspectors, can be spotted doing quick changes from their old wardrobes into fresh outfits just off the racks. Canadian-American wedding ceremonies are likely as not held in a Buffalo church, with the receptions across the Niagara River in a Fort Erie, Ontario, country club. In Seattle's baseball stadium, half the crowd is Canadian whenever the Blue Jays come to town to play the Mariners. Small gestures of friendship and generosity abound: after Hurricane Andrew devastated parts of Miami in 1992, a Canadian naval unit in the area dispatched sailors and engineers to help in the clean-up; and each year in Boston the city lights two Christmas trees, one from the people of Nova Scotia for the help Bostonians gave them at the time of the 1917 Halifax explosion, the other from the children of New Brunswick for Boston's assistance after a fire nearly destroyed Saint John in 1877.

In these circumstances it is often difficult for Canadians and Americans, alike in so many good ways, to fathom the eternal distinctions between them, let alone the more obvious contrasts. Climate, of course: in winter, so the joke goes, when an American beds down for the night, he contemplates the future of his immortal soul; when a Canadian turns in, he wonders about whether his car will start in the morning. The clichéd border, yes: rivers on the Canadian side flow north toward the Arctic; on the U.S. side they flow south. National habits and outlook, now we're really talking. Introverted Canadians live next to the most extroverted society known to man. Many Americans regard Canada as one vast hunting preserve visited mostly by the Queen and well-heeled sport fishermen. Most Canadians, watching the American presence in their country spread out like some agreeable octopus, regard us as hopelessly self-centered.

Americans glory in the success of their self-made millionaires and bear them no grudge; Canadians envy success and resent the flaunting of it. They save more than we do, and give away less to charity. They dwell in their workable cities, while we mostly labor in ours and cannot wait to escape them for the suburbs. If we decide to work on occasion in a Canadian city, we are apt to find it too clean for our purposes, like the U.S. moviemaker, shooting a scene in Toronto, who ordered garbage strewn around his street set, only to return from lunch to find the street swept clean again. We harass our businesses and doctors with class actions and malpractice suits; Canadians do not. They provide health care insurance for all their citizens; we do not, or at least not yet. In America, people move to where the jobs are; in Canada, they spend a lot of time and money moving jobs to where the people are. Canadians believe they take their politics more seriously: their politicians debate issues in Parliament like Natives' rights, ours schmooze with talk-show hosts and rap singers; their voter participation in elections is indisputably higher.

In Newfoundland, an expatriate from Detroit recalls his former life at home where he kept an attack dog in the kitchen, a 12-gauge shotgun under his bed, and toted a magnum pistol to work; now, he doesn't even need to lock the door. At the same time, Americans work harder than Canadians and are still about 10 percent more economically productive.

We are a competitive, impatient, messianic, hyperactive, overachieving people; Canadians, by and large, aren't.

The contrasts between us did not appear yesterday. They have evolved historically and are imbedded in the way we treat each other as separate peoples, in the way we conduct our more formal relations. The idea that Americans and Canadians are historic friends is, of course, preposterous. Our first three centuries together on the continent have been marked by guerrilla warfare, economic skirmishing, and threats of invasion. Only in the last seventy-five years have we established a reasonably firm friendship and alliance. We are, in the late John Holmes's words, historic enemies who have been tamed and matured into a civilized relationship.

Long before Americans found it chic to patronize Canada, the shoe had been on the other foot. The values of creative democracy and rampant individualism, shaped by the Jacksonian revolution, seemed irredeemably messy to nineteenth-century Canadians reared in the English mode of authoritarian government and conservatism. The wife of Upper Canada's Lieutenant-Governor summed up Americans as "perfectly democratic and dirty." The feelings became mutual and intensified after the Civil War when Americans yearned to take over the whole continent. In 1870, President Grant grumbled that America's three-year-old neighbor was vexatious, unfriendly, and an irresponsible agent of Great Britain. Theodore Roosevelt piled it on with more annexationist rhetoric near the turn of the century. It took the shared experience of two world wars and the Depression to convince Canadians and Americans of the value of collaboration. In the postwar 1940s, as Canada emerged from its womb-with-a-view mind-set, a special relationship developed, thanks in large part to the friendship of Franklin Roosevelt and Mackenzie King.

Professional diplomats are fond of saying that the bilateral relationship functions regardless of what the top dogs think of each other. But if the President and Prime Minister hit it off, anything is possible; if not, the process tends to stall, or worse. The modern history of the relationship is replete with examples. Well into the 1950s personal relations between the President and Prime Minister set a comfortable tone. But from the fifties on, for long stretches, Canadian and U.S. leaders seemed woefully out of sync with one another, a friction of temperaments and style as much as policies. The easy days of Roosevelt and King, of Eisenhower and St. Laurent, were overtaken by a more complicated age. Nuclear arms imperatives and the rude realities of international commerce bred antagonisms that often blazed at the personal level. At a high-level bilateral conference in 1957, a Canadian diplomat had the temerity to suggest that Canada, seeking to loosen its bonds with the United States and diversify its trade, would henceforth be seeking more export markets in Europe. An annoyed Secretary of State John Foster Dulles pointedly reminded the Canadians that had it not been for the U.S. Marshall Plan, Canada wouldn't be able to sell its products to Europe at all. By then, however, Canadians were becoming increasingly sensitive over the extent of U.S. influence on their trade and economy.

The nuclear arms issue in the early 1960s exposed Canada's ambivalence about accepting America's umbrella protection of the continent, as well as the generation gap between the two nations' leaders. When the Kennedy administration insisted that Canada honor its NATO commitments by arming its Bomarc and Honest John missiles with nuclear warheads, a recalcitrant Diefenbaker balked; the Prime Minister was under public pressure not to permit warheads on Canadian soil. But the issue also had its vivid personal contradictions: a glamorous and urbane young President with a French-speaking wife versus an old and cranky Prime Minister who didn't know his bombs from his *bombes*. An exasperated Robert Kennedy told a Canadian reporter that his brother hated only two persons, the Indonesian dictator Sukharno and Diefenbaker. In the end, the dispute cost Diefenbaker his job.

Pearson and Kennedy were far more compatible, the understated Prime Minister better appreciated by the graceful President and his Harvard court; Canadian-American relations flowered again. But when Lyndon Johnson succeeded the fallen President and escalated the Vietnam War, you could hear the clash of personalities between LBJ and Pearson from Texas to Ottawa. The U.S. administration found little sympathy in the Canadian capital for prosecuting the war; the President's men bitterly recalled Britain's Harold Wilson saying once that in times of crisis Canada would give you all aid short of help. When Pearson spoke out, in April 1965 at Philadelphia's Temple University, against the American bombing of North Vietnam, an enraged Johnson took the Prime Minister aside at Camp David and gave him such a lapel-grabbing, nose-to-nose

dressing down ("You pissed on mah rug") that Pearson emerged genu-
inely shaken.

Johnson had yielded the presidency to Richard Nixon by the time the
Trudeau government began its era of economic nationalism in Canada.
Ottawa was also distancing itself from Washington on a host of foreign
policy issues from trade with Castro's Cuba to recognition of Communist
China. Trudeau, snobbish toward Americans and a succession of presidents he considered his intellectual inferiors, became a bête noire in
Foggy Bottom and White House circles. Nixon referred to him on the
Watergate tapes as an "asshole" and threw cold water on the Canada-
U.S. special relationship when he and his Secretary of the Treasury,
blunt-spoken John Connally, initiated their policy in 1971 of imposing a
surtax on foreign imports; that threatened, among other markets, Canada's huge export trade with the United States. Trudeau's court criticized
the Carter administration's abortive attempt to rescue U.S. hostages in
Iran and accused Washington of being caught unprepared when the Sovi-
ets invaded Afghanistan. The nadir in relations came near the end of
Trudeau's term when the Prime Minister's globe-jetting, personal peace
initiative in 1983, to reduce Cold War tensions over nuclear armaments,
was likened by the U.S. Undersecretary of State for Political Affairs to
"pot-induced behavior by an erratic leftie."

Reagan, the latest White House occupant at the time, would never have
publicly said as much himself; still, he barely tolerated Trudeau, and
the gap in bilateral relations widened further during his presidency. The
Reaganauts paid only grudging attention to the bilateral issue that consumed the environmentally conscious Canadians, namely, cross-border
acid rain pollution. The Trudeau government in turn dismayed Washington with its pro-Castro, pro-Mao tilt, its niggardly defense outlays, and
its various actions deemed unfriendly to U.S. business interests. To the
fervently free-market, anti-Communist Reaganauts, Trudeau's policies
seemed almost by design to be Yankee baiting. In fact, the antipathy
was more a collision of strenuous nationalisms, personified by Trudeau's
determination to steer Canada along its own path and Reagan's to make
America "stand tall" again in the world. Almost as soon as Trudeau and
the Liberals were replaced by the eager-to-please Brian Mulroney, bilateral ties mended. Mulroney and Reagan, like a pair of perfectly matched
music hall performers in a soft-shoe number, grinned and glided their
way through "shamrock" summits, signing the far-reaching 1989 Free

Trade Agreement to eliminate all tariffs on goods between the two countries by the end of the century, and settling less momentous issues like
fishing boundaries and the overhaul of NORAD's surveillance system in
the Arctic. Buoyed by an Irish lilt, the Canadian-American relationship
hummed along cheerily into the Mulroney-Bush years, where the personal bonds between the leaders grew even closer.

Mulroney, compared to his predecessors, became almost a fixture at
the White House, he and his family regular guests as well at the Bushes'
summer home in Maine. The two leaders conversed frequently on the
phone, and Mulroney boasted he could reach the President any time he
wanted, "where Trudeau would have been lucky to get past the White
House operator." When the post of United Nations Secretary-General
became vacant in late 1991, Bush wanted to run Mulroney for the job, a
lost cause as it turned out. Canada under Mulroney generally supported
the United States on foreign policy issues despite differences in approach
to the problems of Central America and South Africa. The Canadian
leader was sufficiently obliging to have been dubbed by his critics "the
best Prime Minister the United States ever had." Mulroney also brought
home his share of the bacon, including an acid rain accord that had eluded
his predecessors; it obligated the United States as well as Canada to
reduce the poisonous acid rain emissions that infected Canadian lakes and
forests to so damaging a degree.

The ultimate payoff of the Bush-Mulroney friendship, however, lay in
the trust and candor that accrued between the two men, values that were
essential when they collaborated to guide the Free Trade accord through
its infant years. The tricky process of implementing the accord, dodging
aggressive protectionists and opportunists on both sides, sorely tested the
patience of both leaders.

At one point when disputes were breaking out across the Canadian-
American trade spectrum, and Ottawa was feeling bully-ragged by the
tough-dealing U.S. Trade Representative, Carla Hills, Mulroney picked
up the phone and for thirty scorching minutes read the riot act to the
President. A bewildered George Bush listened as his friend decried what
Ottawa saw as an apparent conspiracy to mount a trade-busting offensive
against Canada, a maneuver that seemed to be orchestrated with the President's blessing by someone near the top of the U.S. government. Canada,
Mulroney raged, had signed the Free Trade accord with the expectation
that the threats and retaliatory measures of earlier years would fade.

"George, I'm taking a Goddamned lot of heat about this," he complained. It was beside the point that U.S. trade officials had for some time been simmering over what they considered unfair trading practices by the Canadians, and were thus ready to take counteractions. The Prime Minister of Canada was being politically embarrassed; the Bush-Mulroney friendship and, by extension, Canadian-American relations, were in jeopardy. It was a question of form and diplomatic nuance, matters beyond the ken of the trade bureacrats in Washington. Shortly, the White House moved into the picture, led by the President's national security adviser. The U.S. Trade Representative's Office was instructed, in effect, to cool it. The top dogs' friendship had prevailed.

Without personal empathy at the pinnacle the Canadian-American relationship might remain one big indigestible stew of unresolved issues, left to simmer indefinitely on the diplomats' stove. It is easily the most intricate, complex bilateral relationship in the world, the areas of mutual interest and conflict—from business and energy to defense and the environment—overlapping and demanding the utmost skill in their management. Yet the relationship much of the time seems less managed than on automatic pilot, the entire machine left to sputter along except when some nuisance part requires emergency repair. For the United States, which has never had a truly coherent Canada policy, preferring to deal ad hoc with issues as they arise, this seems a perfectly acceptable course, the issues being less than life-and-death ones. For Canada, however, whose principal foreign policy preoccupation for more than two centuries has been its relationship with the United States, this is an unacceptable way for two mature nations to run their joint affairs. More demeaning for Canadians are the constant reminders of the relationship's basic imbalance.

As Ottawa sees it, the United States is the fat boy in the international canoe. When he shifts weight, the whole canoe rolls and everyone in it—Canada often as not the first—gets pitched in the drink. Thus, if Washington unloads a retaliatory trade embargo on the Japanese or Europeans, Canada gets hit by the so-called "sideswipe effect," the 1971 import surcharge levy being a prime example. Congress's and the White House's treatment of Canada seems frequently a policy of afterthought, Canadian interests mislaid or forgotten somewhere between the pork barrel dam in Idaho and the perennial Mideast problem. In Ottawa's Department of External Affairs, whole diplomatic and trade sections, filled with seasoned professionals, devote themselves to the U.S. relationship; at the State Department, a bare handful of mid-level officials try with middling success to coordinate the various government agencies whose responsibilities involve Canada. In 1992, when the constitutional crisis was causing turmoil above the border, virtually all the senior U.S. diplomats handling Canada, from key staffers in the Ottawa embassy to the experienced Consul General in Quebec to the Director of the State Department's Office of Canadian Affairs, were routinely rotated to other foreign posts, while the U.S. Ambassador to Canada announced his return to private life. Small wonder there is so little continuity in policy direction or experience among the Canada-watchers in Washington, that the cadre of government experts who truly understand the politics and economic preoccupations north of the border has become all but extinct. "Don't worry," a departing U.S. diplomat told me, "we keep making the same mistakes and it doesn't matter really." But, of course, there could be a price to pay one day for so cavalier an attitude.

The American perspective differs by 180 degrees. A superpower with worldwide responsibilities, the United States tends to fixate on national security issues, while Canada, a middle power with no responsibilities for anyone, busies itself with matters of trade and commerce. Occasionally the areas of priority intersect. Much of the time, though, U.S. policy makers focus on trouble spots like Haiti and Somalia—not exactly comparable to Canada in economic or strategic importance—leaving minor officials to deal with Ottawa's problems. For most of the century, in fact, Washington has treated Canada as a backyard neighbor rather than a foreign power deserving an integrated policy. Washington, a Canadian writer joshed, sends to its embassy in Ottawa only drunks, security risks, and those who want to be near their relatives. For the United States, many of whose diplomats in Canada have been exceptional, the chronic conundrum, contrary to the wits, is the ambivalence of the Canadians themselves, consummate both-sides-of-the-street players. One day, it seems, Canada like a Mafia don wants the full respect due an affluent, power-brokering leader among nations; the next, it craves sympathy and understanding, special dispensations and exemptions from the United States, much like a Third World supplicant. After a while, the Americans tend to tune out.

There is never a serious problem for U.S. diplomats in Ottawa learning the genteel ways of Canadian policy making, no mystery in the structure or process. But for Canadians grappling with Washington's split-level government, lobbying rituals, and social stratification, the process can be daunting. It doesn't help that most of the post–World War II generation of Canadian diplomats and mandarins, seasoned experts on the U.S. division of powers and the Potomac pecking order, have long since retired. Their less experienced successors maneuver hesitantly in a new and jumbled capital arena where executive branch departments fight among themselves for prestigious bits of turf that might entail Canadian interests, while legislative barons preside over a jungle of competing committees and subcommittees, with foreign affairs links, in a Congress shorn of its once familial seniority system. Finding the right ear to bend, the right button to push for action on an issue vital to Canadian interests, necessitates a whole new brand of expertise. Understanding the sources of power for key executive agencies like the U.S. Trade Representative's Office, handmaiden of a protectionist Congress, not the White House, requires new levels of sophistication. By the mid-1980s Canadian diplomats in Washington, tired of trying to decipher the system and of seeing their best efforts ambushed by what one of them called "loose cannons" in Congress, abandoned the quiet diplomacy of earlier days. They took to hiring paid guns, lobbyist-lawyers, all elbows, to help advance Canada's interests in the capital.

At that, misunderstandings, conflicting views, or gross indifference continue to mar Canadian-American relations. Canada's environmental imperatives constantly bump against America's political and economic interests. U.S. authorities were painfully slow to accept Canada's view that the jointly shared Great Lakes were becoming North America's cesspool or that America's midwestern coal-burning utilities were the primary culprits for most of the acid rain pollution that blew across the northern border, rendering some fourteen thousand Canadian lakes virtually fishless. For more than a decade, before both nations finally signed an air quality accord in 1991, acid rain pollution remained the most emotionally charged and disruptive issue between the two countries.

Canada's unwillingness to pull its share of NATO's and the continent's defense load has frustrated Washington for more than two decades. With a policy that seems to enshrine the notion of spending as little on defense as it can get away with, Canada regularly expends barely 2 percent of its gross domestic product (GDP) on the military (versus more than 6 percent for the United States). It has blithely trimmed its force levels to some

85,000 personnel, with the prospect of reducing that number to as low as 76,000 by the mid-1990s; and it ranks just above the duchy of Luxembourg in its overall contribution to NATO. A senior Canadian officer has publicly stated that his nation's armed forces aren't fit for war. There are jokes that Canada would have a hard time invading St. Pierre and Miquelon, the French islands off southern Newfoundland, if push came to shove; that it may be the only country in the Western alliance that wouldn't know if its air space has been penetrated. Washington is not amused.

Even the sweeping Canada-United States Free Trade Agreement (FTA) has resulted less in a warm entwining of mutual commercial interests than a continuance of petty trade skirmishes, and, in Canada, a widening divide between important segments of the populace. While their economy is threatened by other factors, Canadians over the long term stand a better chance with the accord to see their productivity improve, their merchandise trade increase, their industries grow more competitive, and their employment rebound. A nation like Canada—which trades more goods with America than America trades with the United Kingdom, France, Germany, Italy and South Korea combined—can, over time, only benefit economically from an agreement like the Free Trade accord. Yet trade for Canadians, far more than for most people, is a historically potent symbol of their nationhood. Any perceived threat to Canadians' economic independence arouses nationalist passions, which may be one reason why Canada's temperamental chief negotiator regularly took the hide off his American counterpart during the often stormy trade talks leading up to the accord. A sizable majority of Canadians view the Free Trade Agreement, which not only confirms the reality of economic meshing but presages the possibility of political integration down the road, as further endangering their identity and way of life.

In a larger sense the agreement reinforces Canadians' age-old misgivings about American hegemony, their fear of being irrevocably sucked into that orbit. It reminds Canadians all too clearly of America's one-time dominance of their economy, the shame it engendered even as it lined Canadians' pockets and enriched their style of life. The Canadian novelist Hugh MacLennan compared the process to a seduction in which the lady kept murmuring that she couldn't help herself. At one point in the late 1960s and early 1970s, before Trudeau's nationalist measures had taken hold, U.S. investors controlled 97 percent of the capital behind Canada's parents viewing such fare, the pervasive lingo and Americanisms are subtly altering the language of their upbringing, small phrases or words, their cultural fix points. As American arts become increasingly the norm in Canada, many Canadian artists and their work are shoved to the fringe in their own country. A Toronto journalist observed that in his local record store, "Canadian" works rated a special bin along with Ukrainian dances and flamenco guitarists. Canadians, if they care, can occasionally view an honest-to-God Canadian film, though only 3 to 4 percent of screen time in their movie theaters is reserved for that luxury. Of all the fields monopolized by the Americans, cinema is the most conspicuous. It has always been a U.S. fiefdom and fiercely defended. In the early years of World War II, before Pearl Harbor, Canada—already at war—sought to obtain ten minutes of screen time each month to show Canadian audiences promotional films on Canada's contribution to the war effort. When U.S. movie executives balked at the idea, the Canadian government threatened to impose a quota on the number of American films allowed into Canada. Eric Johnston, then head of the Motion Picture Association, rushed up to Ottawa and confronted the authorities. Forget the quota, Johnston pleaded. In return, Hollywood would not only consider granting Canada some screen time of its own, but would arrange for the script dialogue in future pictures to include prominent mentions of Canadian cities. Bing Crosby casually plugging Medicine Hat would do more for the Canadian tourist industry than any quotas, Johnston argued. The Canadians whooped for joy, and caved.

The truth, as evidenced much later, is that the vast majority of Canadians care not a whit about the source of the TV sitcoms and movies that fill their leisure hours. It is the federal government and the cultural establishment that fret about the survival of Canada's arts. Ottawa in the 1970s put a lid on Canadian advertising in U.S. magazines and telecasts distributed in Canada, and for good measure chased *Time* magazine's local operation out of the country. But the U.S. cultural invasion continued regardless. And as Canadians imbibe ever more superficial knowledge about Yankeeland, Americans continue to draw from their own well of amiable ignorance about Canada. At times their unenlightenment is breathtaking.

When President Nixon levied his surcharge on foreign imports in 1971, he was astonished at Canadians' outrage. He hadn't realized that Canada, not Japan, was America's largest trading partner. In a 1991 poll, only 13 percent of American adults surveyed knew who the Prime Minister of Canada was. And when a Calgary newspaperman published as a lark eighty-five things he disliked about the United States, the immediate assumption was that Americans didn't know enough about Canada to list even ten things about it, likable or not. In Canadians' eyes, U.S. gaffes have become intolerable slights. At the United Nations, American visitors habitually confuse British with Canadian diplomats. In Washington, one Canadian government minister was greeted by a State Department receptionist who glanced at his title, smiled blankly and chirped, "Oh, Reverend, go right up, the Secretary's expecting you." And for sheer dumbheadedness nothing has topped the incident before a 1992 World Series game between the Toronto Blue Jays and the Atlanta Braves in Atlanta, when a Marine color guard marched out with the Canadian flag flying upside down.

Mostly, Canadians resent the indifference of the U.S. media, the invariable page-18 treatment they receive in U.S. newspapers even when the Prime Minister comes to town. An American journalist is such a rare sight in Canada that when this writer arranged an interview with labor unionists in Montreal, he was seriously advised he should explain to them he was not a CIA agent in disguise. The problem is insoluble, of course, unless Canadians adopt a soap opera royal family like the British, breed their own Mafia like the Italians, or behave impossibly like the French. If Canada were to become America's deadliest enemy, suggested the humorist Russell Baker, Americans would think about it constantly and relations would be wonderfully improved. Still, some Canadians have a talent for leaving the impression among gullible foreigners that the average Canuck is only a step removed from imbecility. On one U.S. network television show, while an American guest was trying to emend some of the sillier clichés his compatriots held about Canadians, there appeared on camera from Toronto a local wit in a flowered Hawaiian shirt, inviting Americans to come north and visit his pet moose.

The ignorance, the indifference, the cultural and economic intrusions of America tend to drain from the bilateral relationship much of Canadians' natural goodwill and friendship. The creeping "Americanization" of Canada's political institutions, from its initial borrowing of America's federalism concept to its more recent Charter of Rights and talk of an elected Senate, seems an alarming trend to some Canadians. It drives them toward a strident, irrational anti-Americanism that strains relations further. Canada has striven mightily to convince itself of its uniqueness, its un-Americanness. Yet, despite its best efforts, it has had to concede its admiration for, its desire to emulate America in fundamental ways. That has all created a troubling neurosis for Canadians and, for their nation, one of its unbridgeable divides.

Canada's jealously competitive regions have forged another destructive rift.

Regionalism is a common enough feature around the globe, but the sectional divisions in Canada are of a depth and sharpness not found in other Western industrialized nations. The differences at times seem as potent as those in the states' rights debates that precipitated America's Civil War. The struggles over power, money, and territorial rights transpire between aggrieved regions, most of whom have little understanding of each other's problems, and a central government with limited means to enforce its authority. The government in Ottawa, according to the journalist William Thorsell, lacks "the blood of political life, the public brokering of power," a condition which effectively encourages the fevers of regionalism.

By the middle of this century those fevers had already reached an intensity that gave the lie to Lord Durham's one-time view of Canada as only two nations warring within a single state. Canadians have stamped themselves more by their separate origins and cultures than by their common destiny. Politically, the country until recently has divided along the lines of a Conservative West; the Socialist-leaning Prairies, where the new Democratic Party has over the years been a leading force; a Liberal East (Quebec and the Maritimes); and an Ontario that has zigzagged between all three parties. An angry West seeks more influence over Ottawa policy making, while a frustrated Quebec demands more autonomous powers to run its own affairs.

Where cultural factors once drove Quebec separatism, now it is also economic constraints and disparities that lead Quebec and other regions to voice their unhappiness with the status quo. In the West, Vancouver businessmen rail against "discriminatory" bankers in Toronto; Toronto's "Bay Street" has become an epithet comparable to "Wall Street" in the demonology of outlanders. Saskatchewan's farmers rage at their better-off counterparts in Ontario; oil-rich Albertans still brood over Ottawa's expropriation of their resources more than a decade ago. Maritimers, cursed with chronic unemployment and few indigenous industries, fault the government for parachuting new businesses into their region instead of building up local enterprises. Ontarians, always on the receiving end of others' anger, sulk at the widespread ingratitude for their generous share of revenue dispersals across Canada.

At times, surliness can really darken the mood and language of the regionalists. Albertans threatened on their bumper stickers to "Let the Eastern bastards freeze in the dark" during the first winter of Trudeau's hated National Energy Program; the mayor of Calgary referred to his eastern compatriots as "creeps and bums." In Vancouver, an American sightseer accidentally bumps against a local who advises him, "Watch where you're going, Eastern asshole." Quebecers visiting Saskatoon are made to feel as welcome as Martians; and Newfoundlanders shopping in Toronto are apt to experience the same warmth reserved for Orkney Islanders in Harrods of London.

The growth of regionalism and provincial power is not only a historical development, but a response to the federal government's aggrandizement of economic power and the more recent phenomenon of economic globalization. Ever since Canada's birth as a nation, its provinces have tried to strike a different balance of power with the federal government from that originally envisioned by the nation's founders. Early on, Ottawa's legislative authority was severely curbed by Great Britain, while provincial responsibilities were quietly expanded. In the twentieth century the wartime mobilization of federal powers challenged the provinces' expansionary thrust. By 1939, on the eve of World War II, Ottawa collected 39 percent of all tax monies and strictly controlled their disbursement; by 1943, it was collecting 75 percent of the nation's revenues. But after the war the pendulum swung back toward the provinces' advancement. It is a fact of life in Canada that the longer a government clings to power at the center, the more its support erodes in the countryside. Thus, when the Trudeau government moved to exert federal power head-on in the 1970s, the provinces did not back down but instead confronted Ottawa on a range of issues. By the late 1980s, the federal government's diminished capacity to guard the regions from the impact of economic globalization, including sudden changes in international price movements, convinced Canadians of the need to coalesce into smaller factions, regions and provincial governments, in order to protect their economies.

The provinces have thus emerged as formidable rivals to the federal government, probably the most independent and powerful member states of any federation in the world. They comprise a league of semi-sovereign polities that own or claim the rights to every sliver of metal or ounce of "black gold" under their lands or offshore. They largely finance and administer educational, health care and social welfare programs under their aegis, and zealously enforce myriads of rules constraining the flow of people, goods, business services, and capital between provinces. Unlike the states in America, they exercise a stake in international treaty negotiations where their interests are affected; and most of them maintain provincial overseas offices, a larger number, in fact, than those run by the states. On every score the provinces challenge the federal government for efficiency and control in the delivery of services, for meriting the loyalty of ordinary Canadians.

Canada's vital four economic regions stretch east to west from its poorest, earliest-explored Atlantic provinces to affluent, new-age British Columbia, looking to the Pacific for its destiny.

The Atlantic region—New Brunswick, Nova Scotia, Prince Edward Island, and Newfoundland—is a microcosm of Canada's divisiveness. The region's provinces are bound by similar origins (Irish-Scots), common resources (fishing, mining, forestry), and mutually fragile economies. All face the Atlantic. Yet each province is *sui generis,* reluctant to join the others in any viable economic union, loathe even to consider the idea of political wedlock. Three of the provinces dub themselves the Maritimes, regarding Newfoundland as too remote for inclusion. As a quartet, however, they became the Atlantics: mutually bitter over their lot, eternally mired in a dependency syndrome, fearful that separation by Quebec would render them another Bangladesh, isolated from the rest of the country and their lifesaving government dole.

The Atlantic provinces' 2.3 million denizens endure the highest unemployment rates in Canada—as much as 90 percent in some pockets of Newfoundland—the highest tax rates, and a crippling debt service that consumes an exorbitant portion of their provincial revenues. Proud rustics mostly, undereducated and unskilled in modern technology, they cling to the mores and virtues of an earlier century when shipbuilding, fishing, and lumbering made their coffers overflow, when lucrative trade with Britain, the New England states, and the Caribbean crowned their prosperity. That was before Confederation forced them to surrender their trade routes and foreign markets in return for guaranteed access to the new nation's Ontario markets, a guarantee that never materialized. Their shipbuilding industry declined and the new national prosperity bypassed them. Some Maritimers today talk bravely of an economically integrated future; many more remain bitter and unforgiving at the hand history has dealt them, lukewarm at best in their affinity for the rest of Canada.

New Brunswick and Nova Scotia are at least hopeful cases compared to their island cousins. Both were healthy provinces at the time of Confederation, New Brunswick the cap of the New England landmass, Nova Scotia connected umbilically to it. History has bestowed little but the picturesque on Nova Scotia's nearly 1 million people, from the Gaelic-speaking Scots of Cape Breton Island to the German-descended Lunenburgers down the coast. The province, heavily indebted from a succession of budget deficits, is a welfare case, with more than 40 percent of its budget underwritten by the federal government. Its capital, Halifax, financial center of the Maritimes, has figured more in the calamities of the past than in its successes. The city's waterfront was all but obliterated and sixteen hundred Haligonians killed when a French munitions ship blew up in the harbor in 1917, the largest manmade explosion before the atomic bomb. Halifax's one-time primacy as a gateway to the continent, when ocean liners ruled the Atlantic, has been swept away on the contrails of the jet age. Still, Nova Scotia shares ambitious plans with New Brunswick to restructure their economies—attracting new businesses, positioning themselves as specific market and service centers—and move off the dole. New Brunswick, largest of the Maritimes, with a third of its population francophone Acadians, has already made strides in that direction, thanks to an aggressive and frugal young premier, a top financial credit rating, and a bilingual, technologically savvy workforce.

Prince Edward Island and Newfoundland are the Atlantics' certified basket cases: the former, a million-acre, picture-postcard farm run by 125,000 "islanders" who promote only two commodities, seed potatoes and the *Ann of Green Gables* legend, especially beloved of Japanese tourists; the latter, "a monstrous mass of rock and gravel," as an American missionary once described it, peopled, according to lore, by illiterate fishermen who dwell in villages called "outports" with names like Tickle Cove and Horsechops, drink a blinding rum concoction called "screech," feast, when sober, on seal-flipper pies and cod tongues, and otherwise sit around telling dreadful Newfie jokes. Both provinces are, in effect, wards of the state, financially propped up by the government in Ottawa, which regularly injects millions of dollars in transfer payments into their bloodstreams until, as one Newfoundlander put it, the provinces have become addicts. "It's like being on heroin. They send us the money, we fight over it, we spend it." Newfoundland's fishing industry is as depleted as the supply of cod in its seas, most of the labor force idle, with few if any incentives to goad people back to work. The only thing tempering the misery of the hardy inhabitants of Canada's youngest province is their pride in having a recognizable identity, however eccentric. In Canada, that is no small triumph.

Four thousand miles to the west and a cultural eon removed from Newfoundland, British Columbia presents a startling contrast to the Atlantics. It, too, is an extremity, an appendage to Canada rather than part of it. But the similarity stops there.

Once a haven for retired British Army officers and remittance men, British Columbia has been transformed by an invasion of foreign investors and immigrants into the fastest growing, wealth-accumulating province in Canada, third largest in size and population (3.1 million). It is a richly endowed preserve the size of California, Oregon, and Washington combined—a separate region, in fact, with its own agenda, outlook, and colorful politics. The influx of upscale Asians, more than 150,000 since 1987, coupled with a huge intake of eastern and Prairie Canadians, has helped quadruple the province's population over the past half century. Wealthy Hong Kong Chinese, pursuing the Commonwealth connection and exploiting Canada's investment-oriented immigration policies, have swarmed into Vancouver, altering its economic and real estate landscape overnight. The port city, whose population is almost 20 percent Chinese, is referred to as "Hongcouver." It fairly bursts with activity: the building boom has produced blocks of expensive new condos, gleaming hotels, and office towers. In the bustling harbor, hydrofoil ferries and executive seaplanes skim across the waters, while cargoes of sulfur and potash from the Prairies are loaded aboard freighters bound for the dragon-ports of the Orient. British Columbia now exports the bulk of its goods to Japan, the United States, and Europe, with the rest of Canada running a poor fourth. Within a decade the total value of its goods and services, much of it computer technology, has soared, from $48 billion in 1983 to $91 billion by 1993.

The place still has room for its peculiarities. Its premiers have ranged over time from a romantic madman who changed his name from William Smith to Amor De Cosmos ("lover of the universe") to the long-governing W. A. C. ("Wacky") Bennett to the short-lived William Vander Zalm who, in the 1980s, was known as "the tulip premier" for the bulbs he cultivated in his private twenty-one-acre plot, Fantasy Gardens. Tourists, the province's second biggest industry after forestry, savor the wonders of Vancouver's fleshpots, where they can ogle a popular male stripper who reputedly dangles a 40-pound outboard engine from his erect organ. And in the capital, Victoria, a sort of English theme park with bagpipers and pubs like The Waddling Dog, residents a while back confronted a cougar prowling the basement of the grand Empress Hotel.

With such capacity for the offbeat, so vibrant an economy, and so internationalist an outlook, it's not surprising that British Columbia nurtures a separatist strain of its own. Quebecers may still be fighting two hundred years of history, the business elites of Ontario still trying to rub off the encrusted old-boy traditions of Bay Street, but British Columbians see themselves on the cutting edge of the future. Theirs is a separatist mind-set grounded not in bitterness but in optimism, a yearning to distance themselves, economically and culturally, from what they view as a hopelessly ossified, Eurocentric, and contentious society in the rest of Canada. Former Prime Minister John Turner recalls a raucous dinner in 1992 at a restaurant outside Vancouver when one of the businessmen present said, only half in jest, "John, tell us how to cut a deal with the United States. We're ready to join."

East of the mountain ranges of the Cordillera, which isolate British Columbia on the coast, lie the Prairie provinces of western Canada, a regional trove of natural resources whose 5 million custodians carry on their shoulders a chip the size of Labrador. They have all the goodies, but somehow the benefits always seem to land in the laps of rapacious easterners. Not only do Toronto bankers outsmart them and Quebec politicians outhustle them, but their own federal government seems habitually to ignore their interests, treating them like some Rodney Dangerfield in chaps. As far as westerners are concerned, Quebec can separate with their blessing on the condition that it takes Ottawa with it.

Their deeper alienation lies in realizing that, politically, the sparsely populated Prairies—Alberta, Saskatchewan, Manitoba—can never muster a guaranteed bargaining position within the central government, at least under the current system. In a Parliament of 295 members, the Prairies command barely 54 seats; the number of seats representing all of Alberta do not match those from Toronto alone, and at any time Toronto's clout usually overwhelms that of Manitoba and Saskatchewan combined. Central Canada—Ontario and Quebec—has the votes and the seats. Thus on any given issue, western interests can be and often are sacrificed to the political necessities of assuaging Quebec and catering to the business concerns of Ontario. Trudeau's despised national energy policies were seen as proof of that; and, despite a promising start, Ottawa's attitude under Mulroney did not change that much. The West rages at its impotence, its image as a resource-producing region at the service of central Canada. In vain, it has sought to change the system through a regionally oriented, elected Senate. When westerners are elected to Parliament's House of Commons, they often go to Ottawa in such a stew, determined to avenge past grievances, that they fail to wheedle favors for their home districts (ridings) to the extent Quebec's politicians do. In short, westerners play the game with more bile than guile.

Alberta's anger runs especially deep, for it savored good times in earlier days. Of all the provinces, Alberta is the most American: conservative, bronco-busting, Stetson-hatted Reagan territory. Polls show that half the populace identifies more with the western American states than with the rest of Canada, and for good reason. In the opening years of the century, the largest group of immigrants entering Canada were American farmers; about 600,000 of them accepted the offer of free homesteads on the Canadian prairies, sold their farms in the states, and moved north. Many of them settled in Alberta; and many more came later in the 1940s and 1950s when the province became the center of the nation's first big oil boom and pipeline megaprojects. The money gushed in with the oil, skyscapers blossomed in the cities; politicians in the province's capital, Edmonton, cashed in on the windfall and bought a city park the size of Costa Rica. Calgary became the oil capital of Alberta. No one thought the party would ever end. "The oilman here was spoiled," recalls Gus Christopher, a Calgary restaurateur. "He had eleven thousand square feet of office space, plush carpeting, leased Jaguars, a secretary and a receptionist, daily lunches that began at noon and ended nearer three p.m. Hell, he acted like there was no tomorrow." When tomorrow came, and the bottom dropped out of the oil market, the jobs evaporated, the skyscrapers emptied, and Alberta went into a slump from which it has never fully recovered. The province, despite its efforts, has been unable to substantially broaden its economy beyond oil, grain, and gas. Its non-renewable energy resources, meanwhile, have begun to run out.

Things are as bad or worse in next-door Saskatchewan. In the birthplace of socialized medicine, a slow deterioration has set in due to subpar wheat prices, declining agricultural jobs, stagnant population growth, and a public debt that, per capita, is the highest in Canada. Following a trend on the Prairies, many people are leaving Saskatchewan for brighter horizons. Manitoba, too, suffers from depressed grain prices and the demise of Winnipeg as the one-time transportation hub of the West. As in Alberta and Saskatchewan, an increasing percentage of the province's workforce and school population is made up of undereducated aboriginals and foreign immigrants.

Many people in the West increasingly question the worth of remaining attached to Confederation. They profess disgust with a federal government whose policies have kept their energy prices below world levels, have favored Quebec, not them, with lucrative contracts, and have foisted an unwanted bilingualism mandate on them. With diminishing benefits, they argue, westerners might as well go it on their own.

Such talk seems heresy, bordering on the incomprehensible, to those 10 million Ontarians who comprise the richer, more powerful half of Central Canada, that slender urban triangle of a region which accounts for 62 percent of Canada's population and more than 65 percent of its gross domestic product. It, too, is a region divided, for its other half, Quebec, all too clearly understands the language of disaffection. Ontarians, though, are people largely satisfied with the status quo, except for being the brunt of other Canadians' frustrations.

Their province embraces Ottawa, the nation's political center, a city of gray mandarins and dull buildings named for dead knights, and Toronto, focus of the nation's economic power, a city of gold-and-steel financial towers, so highly disciplined and organized that it has been described as New York run by the Swiss. Ontario dominates Canada as no state ever did America and indeed *was,* in effect, Canada until after World War II. Its representatives comprise one third of Parliament. It is the source of half the nation's wealth, generating almost $200 billion worth of goods and services yearly. Ontario is headquarters to the nation's influential newspapers, networks, and publishing firms; it houses most of Canada's manufacturing base and virtually all of its key financial institutions.

As the richest province, it also pays most of the bills. Increasingly,

voices in Ontario question the province's need to continue sugar-dad-
dying its poorer neighbors via Ottawa's equalization payments, which
only adds another wounding note to the national discord.

It is the other half of Central Canada, however, that underlies the discord:
Quebec, the nation's largest and most culturally distinctive province, in
its dreams and historic grievances by far the most troubling of Canada's
great divides.

Quebec's 600,000-square-mile landmass, first settled after 9000 B.C.
in the wake of retreating Ice Age glaciers, is three times the size of France
or Texas and home to 7 million people, 6 million of whom are French-
speaking Québécois long convinced of their separateness as a people and
the dubiousness of their status as Canada's foremost racial minority. The
rest of Quebec's population, anglophones and allophones (whose parent
language is neither English or French), constitutes a minority of its own
that increasingly feels put upon by the province's francophone majority.
Like scorpions in a bottle, René Levesque's phrase, the two rival linguistic forces have mauled each other with mounting venom as disputes over
schooling, services, and other rights have escalated.

The frustration of French Quebecers, quite aside from their weariness
with the ineptitude of the federal government on constitutional and economic matters, is that the rest of Canada seems incapable of appreciating
Quebec's distinctiveness. It is, after all, the only political entity in North
America with a French-speaking majority in charge of its own social
structures and democratic institutions, from its Assemblée Nationale to
its income tax collection system. Alone among the provinces, Quebec
enjoys its own legal tradition, based on the Napoleonic Code instead of
Britain's common law system, runs its own Social Security and public
pension funds, and maintains close to thirty commercial tourism bureaus
in twenty-two foreign countries. It even audaciously designates its premier as "prime minister," an upgrading that has piqued the other provinces. Informally, it considers Quebec City its national capital, not
Ottawa. Quebecers, when not immersed in self-pity, see themselves as a
splendidly unique society: Latin in temperament, European in taste, liberal in attitude, sexier and more sybaritic than their buttoned-up anglo
compatriots, adventurous lovers and epicureans, but still essentially a
cautious people used to walking on ice in winter. That last, as some

Quebecers point out, suggests they will not make the final leap to independence. On the other hand, while 92 percent of Canadians outside Quebec believe marriage is "very important," according to a poll in the early nineties, only 68 percent of those in *la belle province* agree. One can speculate that Quebecers may be as fickle politically as they are maritally.

In Quebecers' eyes, it is demeaning that the rest of Canada knows and understands them so little, on a par with Englishmen's knowledge of Scots. The stereotype of Québécois as grizzled fur trappers in red-checkered lumber jackets may have faded, but their attitude remains a puzzle to uncomprehending anglophones. Quebec, as part of Canada, enjoys one of the highest standards of living in the world, virtual autonomy in a host of social and economic areas, and, unlike the policies of its own language police, no visible oppression from the federal government in Ottawa. Quebecers might acknowledge parts of that impression, but only grudgingly: okay, so they are the richest colonized people on earth. By their lights, they are an endangered species headed for the same fate as the folkloric Cajuns of Louisiana or the white Afrikaners. Their obsession with themselves, their culture and society—Quebec as center of the universe—reflects not only provincial pride but a deeply ingrained sense of victimization: misunderstood, underappreciated, even unloved, in the rest of Canada.

The feeling stems from Quebec's underdog history. French Canadians prefer to feel their entire story has been shaped from first to last by the *conquête* of 1759, that everything that followed has been one long series of other humiliations: the crushing of Papineau's *patriotes* in 1837; Lord Durham's report of 1839, which dismissed French Canadian colonists as "utterly uneducated and singularly inert"; the hanging of Riel in 1885, "a declaration of war on the influence of French Canada," as one Quebec leader raged; the humiliations of military conscription, the War Measures Act of 1970 which temporarily quashed the civil rights of Quebecers during the terrorist crisis that year; the repatriation of Canada's Constitution in 1982 without Quebec's consent; and the repudiation of the Meech Lake Accord in 1990. Quebecers can reach even further back in time, citing the humiliation of the Acadians' expulsion; they can just as easily fast-forward in time to recite the occasional indignities still perpetrated on them by anglo customs officials and store clerks. This is not the stuff of lynch mobs and pistol-whipping southern sheriffs that typified the ordeal of America's blacks. But in its long historical span—more than two centuries of being treated as back-seaters in their own province—it is enough to qualify French-speaking Quebecers as survivors. The British historian Arnold Toynbee, when asked which civilizations might survive a nuclear war, replied that only two societies were hardy enough to endure any calamity: the Chinese and the French Canadians.

The problem is that as their history, their *survivance,* gradually spawned a fiercely passionate nationalism, Quebecers amassed a store of delusionary myths, phobias, rationales, and symbols to embroider their culture of humiliation. Quebec's nationalists have manipulated history to show that the province's failures were always someone else's fault. They argue that their quest for sovereignty only mirrors Canada's own struggle for independence, ignoring the fact that Canada's constitutional fathers granted Quebec the right to be at least culturally separate, which was more than the British had done. Quebecers have indeed toughed out history's defeats, but as orphans of the Conquest they survived, as well, by withdrawing into their shells for two centuries. Even the way they interpret the symbols of their nationalism, like the *je me souviens* slogan on Quebec license plates, bespeaks their ancient resentments: *born French but screwed by the English ever since.*

Out of Britain's attempts to assimilate its French *colons* came the first stirrings of Quebec nationalism. After thousands of English-speaking farmers from Vermont took advantage of freehold offers under the 1791 act creating two Canadian colonies, and poured into the townships east of Montreal, the furious *colons* set up their own newspaper, *Le Canadien,* to propagate their nationalist beliefs. A century later, Quebec nationalism became a bulwark against what the Québécois saw as increasing assaults on their culture within and beyond their province. In 1890, authorities in Manitoba abolished separate state-supported schools for francophones, the beginning of a trend, it was feared, that would whittle away the rights of francophone minorities in Canada. French Canadians found themselves excluded from the great expansionary westward migrations. Nor could they match the numbers of foreign immigrants who swelled English Canada's ranks: few Frenchmen were willing to leave France for the uncertainties of life in Quebec or the Canadian prairies.

Moreover, the migrations of the Québécois themselves in the last half of the nineteenth century undermined many of the traditional beliefs that had defined their culture. Half a million Québécois emigrated to the mill towns of New England in search of jobs; more of them deserted the country life for opportunities in the industrializing cities of their own province, in effect breaking faith with their credo. For the farms and rural parishes of Catholic Quebec had always symbolized a core myth of French Canadian nationalism: virtue flourishes in the countryside; the cities, run by *anglais,* are alien domains of exploitive industry and vice. The literature of Quebec reflects this belief; its heroines are homespun milkmaids who fall for scheming city slickers named Arbuthnot. The myth, of course, serves as a convenient metaphor for Quebecers' anglophobia. Not until 1944 was the first urban novel published in the province.

Slowly, Quebec nationalism altered course to adjust to the new trends. By midcentury French Canadians comprised almost a third of Canada's population, but had barely 10 percent representation in its government and economy: their language, in their own province, was still secondary in the spheres of business and professional success. By the end of the 1960s, as the Church no longer guided Quebecers' social and cultural lives, nationalism increasingly centered on strengthening the Québécois presence in the provincial government and commerce, especially Montreal's business world, as the means to a more durable French-speaking society. From then on, Quebec's nationalists inevitably butted against two powerful forces: the federal government and the English-speaking business establishment.

Ironically, just as positive efforts to loose the province from its shackled past were succeeding, revelations in the 1970s of how Quebec's francophone populace was shrinking caused its nationalism to adopt a more negative role. In the 1840s, half the people in Canada were French-descended; francophones now are only a quarter of the population. Quebec's birth rate, once the highest in North America, has dropped precipitously, to become the lowest in the Western world except for Germany; more ominously, the rate has fallen below its replacement level. Prospects for reversing the trend are poor, as they are for stemming the outflow of immigrants from Quebec, a trend that has intensified over the years. The specter of francophones becoming a minority in their own province, and their economy shriveling up, created a laager mentality among the nationalists. They sought to revive Quebec's earlier *revanche des berceaux,* the revenge of the cradles, by having the government offer parents cash bonuses for each newborn child. The National Assembly ruled that children of immigrants had to be enrolled in French-speaking schools; in some school systems, like Montreal's, more than 50 percent of the student population had become non-French-speaking allophones. Steps were taken by Quebec to gain control of all immigration policies and to francisize the province's businesses and marketplace.

Once the wagon circling and targeting of scapegoats had begun, it was only a matter of time before Quebec's nationalists crossed the Rubicon to become separatists. They backed a stepped process whereby Quebec demanded distinct status in the Constitution and further devolution of federal powers to the province; the plan was to steer Quebec toward a looser economic association with the rest of Canada, then, finally, separation or (more elegantly) sovereignty. In the separatists' scheme, if Quebec's demands were rejected, the province would have to choose between staying with an unaccommodating Canada or seceding. Secession would be the preferred choice. In historical terms anyway, the separatists argued, Quebec's long struggle to liberate itself from the shames of its past virtually dictated an end goal of independence.

For the last quarter of the century, then, Quebec nationalism has focused on that goal—through the emotional years of Levesque; the symbolic elevation of the fleur-de-lis to equivalency with the Maple Leaf; through successive defeats of constitutional proposals that favored Quebec's demands. Gradually the suspicion has grown, not discouraged by the separatists, that no amount of compromise or satisfaction, even if granted by the rest of Canada, will halt Quebec's march toward ultimate separation.

Not even the political clout Quebec has appeared to wield in Ottawa has deterred the separatists. For half the nearly hundred years since 1896 a Quebecer has been Prime Minister of the country, including most of the past half century. Canada's two longest-governing leaders in modern times, Trudeau and Mulroney, were Quebecers; so, under their administrations, were about one third of the Cabinet, the Supreme Court, and the federal public administration. More than fifty thousand Quebecers work for the federal government, and francophones comprise about 30 percent of the civil service. All that has translated into generous federal handouts and juicy contracts for Quebec. Yet Quebec's imprint on Ottawa is seen less as a means of fulfilling the province's desire for greater respectability and power than as a payback for Quebec's vital electoral support in national elections and, more subtly, as a form of bribe to keep Quebec in the federal fold. Quebec's nationalists, sensing facade more than substance behind the impressive French Canadian presence in Ottawa, have turned inward for their cause to Quebec City, seat of the provincial government that has been key to Quebec's renaissance.

There, behind the ramparts of North America's only walled city, on whose heights above the St. Lawrence historic leaders like Montcalm, Roosevelt, and Churchill once plotted the stratagems of war, smaller men wrestle with the political arts of the possible. Three men have dominated the scene: Bouchard, Parizeau and, until recently, Bourassa. Lucien Bouchard has been the most popular politician in Quebec, an intense, impassioned separatist who insists that sovereignty is not negotiable. He has played adroitly on the mythology of Quebecers' injured pride, and, as leader of the Bloc Québécois, has served as separatism's chief proconsul in the federal Parliament of Ottawa. Jacques Parizeau, head of the Parti Québécois and for two decades the driving intellectual force behind the separatist movement, is the patrician-cool opposite of Bouchard, a portly, claret-sipping anglophile with impeccable Savile Row suits and bona fides in the sphere of public finance. When he talks of Quebec separating, it is with such languid matter-of-factness that one envisions the province leaving to do the groceries rather than departing Confederation forever. Robert Bourassa was both the fulcrum for federalist hopes in Quebec and the man at the vortex of the struggle over its future. Until he stepped down as premier in early 1994, wearied by the endless political intrigue and his long bout with cancer, it was Bourassa who had been charged with steering Quebec through the political shoals representing the federalist and separatist factions of his own ruling Liberal Party.

A cool technocrat whose milktoast manner sometimes put off emotional Quebecers (Levesque once called him a walking tranquilizer), Bourassa seldom met an issue he couldn't attack sideways. He was criticized for raising waffling to high art, but his cautiousness reflected the ambivalence of many Quebecers over separation. Bourassa was a survivor, a political escape artist, who had first been elected premier in 1970 at the age of thirty-six, was toppled from power six years later by Levesque, only to regain it in 1985 for another two terms at the top. He was part Hamlet, part Houdini, a doubt-plagued, conditional federalist who saw no future for Quebec outside of Confederation, but who sympathized with his province's demands. "I'm walking a tightrope," he confided, the last time I saw him, looking exhausted. "If I can build Quebec without destroying Canada, I'll have succeeded."

Bourassa had already tasted success in helping lead Quebec out of the economic dark ages. While Lesage and Levesque used the levers of aggressive government intervention to de-anglicize Quebec's economy, Bourassa helped give it a more modern, technological look. Less concerned with ideological nationalism, he sought economic self-sufficiency as Quebec's grail, the true measure of independence if that became the final choice. Even as francophones gradually displaced English-speaking managers across Quebec's business spectrum—by 1988 accounting for 58 percent of the province's executive class, compared to 30 percent in 1959—Bourassa tried to shift the economy from its traditional reliance on natural resources to one more diversified in such industries as aerospace, telecommunications, and computers.

French Quebecers are now largely in charge of their $120 billion economy. They own or control companies that employ more than 60 percent of the province's workforce, up from less than 50 percent in the early 1970s. Francophones run such giant outfits as Bell Canada, the national phone company, and Bombardier, the aerospace conglomerate that also manufactured New York City's subway cars. They manage the huge state-owned enterprises that drive much of the economy: Caisse de depôt et placement du Québec, the biggest pension fund and stock market investor in Canada, and Hydro-Québec, one of the ten largest electric utility companies in the world. They dominate the Montreal Board of Trade where, barely twenty-five years earlier, only English had been spoken in the board's dining room and bar.

The economy that French Quebecers preside over ranks twentieth in the world. It rests on a natural-resource base that includes 75 percent of Canada's asbestos reserves, 40 percent of its iron ore, a quarter of its gold and copper, and a massive chunk of its hydroelectric power supply. Quebec's vast forests account for half of Canada's newsprint production; the province produces almost as much pulp and paper as the United States churns out in toto. Its several hundred computer service firms make it a leader in education software. Some 45 percent of Quebec's gross product is exported, more than three fourths of it to international markets, chiefly America's, and the growth rate of its sales abroad far outstrips the rate of its sales in Canada. The government-industry partnership that accounts for much of the new dynamism—"Quebec Inc."—has helped give the economy a strategic direction and an optimism that has persuaded much of Quebec's business community that separation no longer poses the disaster many feared a decade ago. Some businessmen even see distinct pluses, arguing that separation would make it easier for Quebec to operate as a trading center and would be good for Quebec firms in the long term. This turnaround in the business sector, abetted by English Canada's rejections, has given separatism the credibility and critical boost it needs to pursue its goal through the nineties.

There are still doubters. Separatism is never more alluring than when economic times are flush, and Quebec has its drawbacks. Despite some diversification, its economy is still driven by a handful of big hitters like Hydro-Québec. Its dying but heavily protected textile, clothing, and furniture industries are a drag on progress; so are its militant trade unions and its overpaid army of 340,000 public-sector workers. Its persistently high unemployment rates have exceeded the nation's average for more than twenty years; the Montreal region alone housed more than 200,000 jobless people in the early nineties. Quebec's high school dropout rate (40%) has also exceeded the national average by a wide margin, and its family incomes have been generally lower. Quebecers are among the most highly taxed of all Canadians, and their debt load, as a percentage of the gross product, is one of the nation's heaviest. The province's international debt is one of the world's largest, owned mostly by Americans, and its language requirements can be anathema to potential foreign investors. Japanese executives find it hard enough to master American English, but mandatory French is too much; many of them think twice before deciding to locate new businesses in Quebec.

For Quebec's committed separatists, these are not insuperable drawbacks. They are hardly comparable in magnitude to French Quebec's fundamental disagreements with Ottawa and the rest of Canada. In that context, disagreement is too trivial a word. It is more a total dysfunction of the willpower of two familial races to recognize and give impulse to the ambitions of each other.

Anglophone Canadians shake their heads at the idiocy of a province that would scrap the bounties of Confederation for independence. French Canadians despair at the crabbed notion that their independentist goal involves only economic considerations. The myopia is equally shared. Anglophones mainly believe that Quebecers regard English Canada not as family, but as landlord, not as something they belong to, but as something they negotiate with, as one westerner put it. Quebecers, on the other hand, disdain the very idea of traveling the country, and therefore assume the rest of Canada is nothing but a monolithic conspiracy that speaks with one anglophone voice. With such mutual incomprehension, it is inevitable that the larger visions of English and French Canada clash: what most Canadians envision for Canada in the next millennium is incompatible with the vision of modern Quebec held by that province's francophones. It is not only that Quebec seriously distrusts the federal government's management of the country and views Ottawa as decreasingly useful if Quebec stays in the federation. It is a deeper conflict over the roles of the two governments—the age-old rivalry between two adamant nationalisms, two collectivities, two languages.

The issue of language lies at the heart of the struggle, for nothing touches the essence of Quebecers' culture and identity as language does. Other countries are home to several official tongues, but, aside from Belgium, only Canada is so markedly divided by two languages. In Quebec, alone within an Anglo-Canadian land and inundated by American pop culture, a sense of linguistic siege prevails. More than 80 percent of the populace speaks French fluently as their principal language, but almost half the province's anglophones and more than a third of its allophones cannot. The combined minority of just under 1 million non-francophones, concerned for their own language rights, is a thorn in the side of Quebec nationalists intent on establishing the primacy of French in their community.

It has always been an uphill fight for francophones. The first debate over language, a stormy one, occurred in 1792 when the Assembly of Lower Canada met in Quebec City to determine the status of English and French in parliamentary publications. Canada's Constitution of 1867 expressly protected language rights, providing for the use of French as well as English in Parliament and the federal courts, and in Quebec's courts and legislature. But at the federal level, as it applied to French, the Constitution was often honored more in the breach. Nor, over time, has the constitutionally protected dual school system fared all that well: from 1871 on, provinces from New Brunswick to Alberta and Manitoba bent or suspended the rights of French-language schools under their jurisdiction. It was the conceit of anglo school officials that learning French was about as important as learning to waltz, a slightly sissy pastime of no great weight in the upward mobility of young English Canadians. The language question had class overtones as well: in anglo society, Catholic French Canadians were considered NQOSD—not quite our sort, dear.

In Quebec, as the new century unfolded, the quality of spoken French was deteriorating: workers, operating in a new industrial milieu under English managers, borrowed English words to describe their tasks and spawned the blue-collar dialect, *joual*. French Quebecers, in the decades before the 1960s, were content just to see their language given some presence alongside English in areas such as labeling and packaging. Silently, fuming within, they bore the daily insults of anglophone shop-keepers and plant foremen ordering them to "talk white." The Church was primary custodian of French-language rights; anyone who mentioned the idea of language legislation was thought a bit balmy. The new franco-phone assertiveness of the "quiet revolution" changed all that. In the late sixties, the French Catholic school board of a Montreal suburb attempted to deny English education to its immigrant children. Riots followed and the controversy led to Quebec's enacting a series of language laws that were to turn the province into a virtually unilingual French enclave.

Even as Quebec was proclaiming the supremacy of French—in its gov-ernment, in its schools and the workplace—Ottawa enacted its policy of bilingualism across Canada, making French and English equal and offi-cial as the languages of federal government discourse. The Official Lan-guages Act of 1969 was designed to cool separatist fevers in Quebec by granting special status to francophones outside Quebec. Instead, the Act had the effect of discriminating against anglophone civil servants and politicians, denying them advancement unless they became bilingual. It infuriated many Canadians who regarded the Act as social engineering at its worst; and it made no dent in the armor of Quebec's nationalist *gaule-iters*. They pushed their language offensive even more relentlessly through a series of tough new laws, the most flagrant of which was Bill 101 in 1977. Immigrant children were forced to attend French-language schools only; English-language schooling was restricted to the children of English-educated Quebecers. Companies with more than fifty employ-ees were required to prove they conducted all business, even internal memos, in French. Hardest of all on anglophones was the law forbidding the use of English on commercial signs announcing their services or place of business.

The Quebec government established an entire bureaucracy of surveil-lants and enforcers of its language policies, led by the Minister of Cultural Development, a Cassius-lean and brooding zealot named Camille Laurin. Undercover shoppers roamed through local stores, noting whether the sales clerks greeted customers in French. The antics of the vigilantes, scouring city streets and village lanes for violations, approached the farcical at times. The Office de la langue française pounced on the proprietor of an eaterie who dared slip the words "Open Mon." alongside "Ouvert lundi" on a sign outside his establishment; a local diner, the Victoria Hot Dog Lunch Counter, had to change to the Chien Chaud Victoire. At Montreal's World Trade Center, presumably a magnet for businessmen parleying in various languages, the signs were all in French. And at a winter resort in the Laurentians, safety warnings in English were ordered removed from the ski lifts. The Orwellian zeal to promote Frenchspeak made even the checkout procedure at supermarkets an ordeal for anglophones, who were told by checkers to speak French or else. The climate of Inquisition extended to the schools, where attempts were made to impose the exclusive use of French not only in classrooms but in recreational activities; immigrant students were reprimanded for shooting the breeze in English in their schoolyards.

Enforcement methods ranged from the civil to the violent. Slogans were spray-painted on the premises of anglo violators of the sign law; rocks and firebombs sometimes followed. Fires were set in English-language schools, and one bomb gutted the Montreal offices of Alliance Québec, the 40,000-member lobbying group for anglophone interests. For anglophones, the climate in Quebec, from the mid-1970s through the 1980s, grew increasingly oppressive. As a result, anglophone communities became semi-wastelands, as businesses, jobs, and families fled en masse. Insurance, financial, and other institutions moved their headquarters from Montreal to Toronto. In the fifteen years from 1976 to 1991, an estimated 14,000 management jobs left Montreal, and altogether more than 200,000 anglophones quit the city.

Occasional flashes of anglo defiance became causes célèbres. A nineteen-year-old hockey star, Eric Lindros, threw the Canadian sports world into an uproar when he deserted the Québec Nordiques team, insisting he wanted to play in a city where English was the predominant language. The head of a Montreal shoe company pushed his grievance against the sign law all the way up to the Canadian Supreme Court, which decided in his favor. And an anglophone undertaker, who rebelled at the tongue troopers, took his case to the United Nations, where he won a ruling that the French-only rule contravened international law. The nationalists just circled the wagons closer. The Quebec government announced plans to bar English-language films from the province unless they came with a French-dubbed version. The final straw was its decision to disregard the Supreme Court's ruling against the sign law. Canada's anglophones lashed back. They tore up the Quebec-supported Meech Lake Accord. Twenty-six municipalities in Ontario declared themselves English-only. There were flag-burning incidents, and a Toronto judge stormed out of his courtroom when Montreal police officers handed him an arrest warrant in French. Anglophones and francophones threatened to take to the streets of Montreal. By the early 1990s journalists were warning of open war and the city's becoming a linguistic Beirut.

For all the alarums, Canadians recognize that the language struggles of the past thirty years have achieved some worthwhile goals. Bilingual policies have protected francophones across the country and enriched the lives of many middle-class anglo Canadians. In New Brunswick, where French-speaking Acadians have long been ignored (train conductors used to announce the schedules in English only) and where anglophones fought Acadians in the streets in 1979, bilingualism has become the law of the province, not just a federal policy. In Quebec, the unilingual policy has succeeded in elevating French to the primary language of business and the workforce, thereby restoring francophones' pride and confidence. (Enough confidence, apparently, for the government to back off and permit English words on signs, but only if those in French are twice as big. That concession led the *New York Times* to envisage Quebec's "linguistic cleansers, armed with metric tape measures, calibrating the precise predominance of Voltaire's language over Swift's.") Some in Quebec note the increased use of the intimate "tu" in ordinary discourse between Québécois and draw from that an indication of further bonding against the alien forces of anglophone Canada.

Others see the future through a glass darkly. "A policy of steady expansion of French rights in nine provinces and the steady, progressive destruction of the English-speaking community of Quebec cannot long insure a future for Canada," the Montreal journalist William Johnson has written. "In fifty years, Canada will not exist as we know it."

The separatists count on that happening a lot sooner. Having reshaped

Quebec socially and economically, having won most of the powers they've sought for greater political autonomy, they have smoothly segued from nationalism to the cause of independence. Having survived one history, they are eager to begin another of their own making. Quebec, they assure themselves, is on the cusp of a new world order in which small is better. The times are on their side: more than thirty former colonies have become nations since World War II; and larger states, from Czechoslovakia to Yugoslavia, continue to divide like amoebas into smaller pieces. Half the United Nations members have smaller populations than Quebec. San Marino, a tiny republic in Italy, with barely 23,000 people, has a seat at the United Nations. Why not Quebec? Right next to Qatar in the General Assembly. A sovereign Quebec, claim the separatists, would be the world's eighteenth largest country, with a gross domestic product ahead of Austria's and Denmark's. True, there are few examples of countries breaking up without civil war or some violence. The atrocities in Bosnia and Croatia have been a reminder of that. Eerily, the blood-soaked emblem of the new republic of Bosnia-Herzegovina is the fleur-de-lis.

Quebec's separatists prefer to cite the exception: the peaceful separation of Norway and Sweden in 1905. Besides, the day is past when a rebellious minority in a democratic federation can be forced to remain against its wishes. That is the difference, the separatists insist, between Canada's situation now and America's in 1860 on the eve of the Civil War. The separatist cause has not only dramatically increased its popularity, from less than 10 percent of the Quebec populace in the early 1960s to as high as 70 percent in early 1991; separatism has been riding a momentum propelled by urgency and by Québécois disgust with the rest of Canada. Demography is working against Quebec. Its falling birth rate means that unless it separates soon, its influence in Confederation may shrink to the point where many of its hard-won and singular rights will be contested by the anglophone majority. At the same time, the limitations of federalism and the constrictions imposed by it gall the Québécois, who see their province, as one put it, "strapped to this bloated corpse" of Canada.

What gives the separatist cause its muscle is its political support structure, backed by a history of emotional commitment and single-minded, often brutal, maneuvering for power. Separatism has been institutionalized by the provincial Parti Québécois and the Bloc Québécois in Ottawa;

they have lent the cause important credibility, organization, and a base for strategic planning. The *péquistes,* when not running the Quebec government, form the official Opposition Party, there being no Progressive Conservative party at the provincial level in Quebec. Beyond the party structure are other reliable support groups: academe, the leftist trade unions, the francophone media, the arts, and the province's rural, small-town regions. In the Saguenay, the remote domain that serves as gateway to Quebec's northern reaches, the seventy thousand habitants of its principal town, Chicoutimi, virtually embody the separatist ideal. Descended from French settler stock, their heritage revered as *vieille souche* (old root), they are emotionally a sovereign people already. Canada is a dead-end street to them. "English Canada has closed the gate to Quebec," says the local editor. "Must we go on our knees in order to stay in federation?" Quebec's performing artists, shut out from the rest of Canada unless they perform in English, sing and romanticize the ideals of nationhood into the hearts of young Québécois across the province. It is the generation of twenty- or thirtysomethings that most readily accepts, almost as a given, the notion of Quebec as sovereign.

The passage of youth has changed the dynamics and equilibrium of the separatist cause over the last quarter century. The children of the barricades in the late sixties and seventies are now part of Quebec's business-professional establishment; the separatist sentiments that made their adrenaline flow a generation ago have become quietly ingrained, tempered by maturity and experience. The new generation, less volatile, no longer scourges their professors for assigning them occasional texts in English. Having grown up in a French-controlled environment, they are more naturally, tolerably sovereigntist, resigned to the eventuality of Quebec drifting apart almost *faute de mieux.* They are also willing pawns in the machinations of the separatists who seek to forge a long-term alliance between the youth wings of the Parti Québécois and the provincial Liberal Party. In short, the cause has gained in organizational efficiency and respectability whatever it has lost in passion.

Not all of this has just happened naturally. The separatists have deliberately infiltrated Quebec's school system over the years, ensuring that a generation of young people are imbued with their view of history, a view heavy on the culture of humiliation and Quebec as victim. The conditioning begins at primary school level and continues through Quebec's state-funded junior colleges, the universities and graduate schools. At the University of Montreal Law School in the mid-seventies, the student talk was feverishly political. One graduate recalls the all-night rap sessions that bristled with Marxist rhetoric and calls for promoting the separatist viewpoint at the highest levels of journalism and government. The separatist indoctrination in the schools is still going strong in the 1990s—a litany of disinformation, according to critics—thereby ensuring another generational pass-down.

Some critics of separatism charge that bully-boy tactics are used to repress the federalist, pan-Canadian view. The *péquistes'* vindictive intrigues effectively silence the voices of federalism in Quebec, it is said; those who do speak out risk retaliation in the local media and in their business dealings. Céline Hervieux-Payette, a prominent businesswoman and old-line Québécois, was threatened and denounced as a "traitor" for her outspoken opposition to the separatist cause. "They attacked my integrity and my intelligence," she recalls. Others, like her, stand to lose friends as well as business contracts because of their federalist views.

The separatists remain unmoved. They continue to test their opponents for soft spots and to pursue their goal with a hard-edged scorn for the vacillating. They have stormed into the ideological vacuum created by nearly a decade of bland governance under Bourassa and the Liberals. "When a party in Quebec runs out of ideas and intellectual steam this way, it's over," predicts Parti Québécois vice president Bernard Landry, the man who some believe will one day preside over a sovereign Quebec. The party's strategists have succeeded in shifting their campaign from one of self-centered demands only to a general condemnation of the federal government's leadership, thereby appropriating the grievances of other provinces for their purposes. Now, they follow a strategy of trying to minimize the impact of separation, to counter the Cassandras on the federalist side who warn of wrenching pain and Armageddon if Quebec leaves.

In the separatists' battle plan, the Bloc Québécois provides "air cover" in Ottawa, safeguarding and burnishing the cause as it consolidates its increased political power in Parliament as a result of the last federal election; the plan at the same time has permitted the local *péquistes* to arm their Quebec legions for the provincial election in 1994. That crucial contest has pitted the Liberals against the favored Parti Québécois, fighting on a platform of sovereignty. A P.Q. victory, followed by a Quebec referendum on separation a year later, could mean the beginning of the end of Canada.

Unless, improbably, the English and French of Canada overcome their old antipathies.

They have become, in Ramsay Cook's analogy, "like twin stars rotating around each other, each possessing a gravitational field that encompassed the other, and each unable to break free from the force exerted by the other." Down through history they have been carefully taught not only to ignore each other but, at least in the case of the French, to cultivate through their literature and theater a genuine distaste for the other. Quebec novels resonate with anglophobic themes; Quebec films and dramas are peopled by villains who speak English only. In the 1970s, Françoise Loranger's play *Medium Saignant* included such lines as "I hate them, the English, from the verb to hate, a verb just invented for them." Anglo author Ron Graham took a more detached view in his later book *The French Quarter,* in which he recalled from his youth that French Canadians were "as abstract as the Hindus I read about in Kipling or the Mau Maus terrorizing the British settlers of Kenya."

Western Canada remains terra incognita to francophones; Quebec might as well be Uranus to westerners. "Dealing with Quebec is like trying to communicate through tea leaves and Ouija boards," groused the premier of British Columbia, whose constituents abhor the appearance of French on their cereal boxes. Even the smart young MBAs from Montreal's famed business school, l'Ecole des hautes études commercial, choose to remain in Quebec as big fish in a small pond rather than risk rejection or ridicule in western Canada. There, as one former premier put it, "our folks might not rush to lay out the welcome mat for these apple-smooth cosmopolites from Quebec." Westerners are equally leery of going to a province where they might have to speak with hand signals. One of them informed a friend in Montreal that she was afraid to visit her ("not safe, too many French there").

It's all a bit bewildering to visiting Americans. One tale recalls the black couple from Detroit who pulled their car into a service station in northern Quebec and parked alongside another car with Ontario license plates. The station owner gassed and cleaned the Detroiters' car, all smiles and solicitous to a fault. He took one look at the Ontarians, refused to service them, and, snarling "maudites anglaises" ("damned English"), sent them packing. The black American, incredulous, turned to the owner and said, "This is the first time I've seen discrimination because of the color of my plates."

Nowhere does the English-French divide run deeper than in Montreal, cradle of Quebec nationalism, with its separately entrenched linguistic communities. The bureaucrats in Quebec City, like the provincials in the hinterlands, are already bound to the trappings and compulsions of sovereignty. But in Montreal, where the overwhelming majority of Quebec's 750,000 anglophones live and where cosmopolitan attitudes are cooler toward radical upheaval, sovereignty attracts as much conflict as converts. The holy sites that dominate Montreal's skyline, the soaring cathedrals and churches, "the great grey seminaries and convents stationed like sombre strongpoints across the city," in Jan Morris's description, symbolize the Catholic-French patriarchy whose members, by the thousands, embrace the sovereigntist ideal. In the cafés and boutiques of francophone Outremont, the cause finds countless other fervid adherents, men and women already conversing in a post-Canada frame of mind. But inside the shaded stone mansions of Westmount, bastion of the city's anglophone establishment, sovereignty evokes anger and uncertainty. To the anglophones, the francophones wield their newfound power too excessively, too recklessly.

The divide is not just a matter of ancient phobias and attitudes, of different backgrounds and schooling. It is about mutual obliviousness and misperceptions on a colossal scale. Compared to the psychological distance that separates Catholic and Protestant families living chock-a-block in the same shabby spaces of Northern Ireland's Belfast, the cultural chasm between Outremont and Westmount is, if anything, wider. One community imagines the other as a *joual*-gabbling, priest-ridden culture of the soutane and the chalice; the other envisions a society composed of gin-sipping Colonel Blimps and colorless accountants in three-piece suits. One sees a paranoid enclave of language bullies and muggers of the anglophone patrimony; the other sees something akin to the fortress white Rhodesians, a privileged sanctuary of anglos who have lived all their life in the second most important French city in the world and who, for the most part, have never read a French newspaper and would prefer never to have to. "They don't understand our language concerns and we don't understand their feelings," says a leading Westmounter. An Outremont journalist stares at the cigarette in his hand and confesses, "I'm fifty years old and I don't have a single English Canadian friend in this city, my home. I've never been in the home of an English Canadian, or they in mine. I don't know what they do, what they eat, what they read, what they watch on television."

Between the two solitudes, resentments are as vividly personal as they are political. Anglos complain that they showed good faith by voluntarily attending or sending their children to French-immersion classes in the seventies, only to have French-language laws rammed down their throats in the eighties. "My family's been here for a hundred years," says Mary Lamontagne, a modish young anglophone married to a francophone investment banker. "Why should I have to bend down to these language laws?" The anglos fear for the future of their health services, their English-speaking hospitals and schools, as well as the cultural institutions their community founded and has sustained through the decades. They fume at being denied good jobs in the civil service and public sector because of language shortcomings or their sheer un-Frenchness. Poised for another mass exodus if Quebec separates, they resent the thought of having to liquidate their assets and put up "For Sale" signs on their lawns. "I was born and bred here," says one, "but at a certain point, you get fed up fighting for your rights." With portents of convulsion in the air, the anglophones of Montreal now watch and wait, many with their belongings already packed, *en standby,* as one real estate agent puts it in his best franglais.

For many francophones, a final anglophone exodus from Montreal will come none too soon. It will be like losing the estranged aunt who always stayed locked in her bedroom, anguishing about her lost youth and the neighborhood going to pot. Francophones turn a deaf ear to anglo complaints about having to forfeit their rights; they observe that the anglos, with a state-supported network of English-speaking facilities at their beck, are arguably the best-treated minority on earth. Old humiliations still rankle: the name calling and taunts from anglophone children in earlier schooldays; the shame of once having had to anglicize their names in order to get hired for grunt jobs in the mines up north or to join the Army; the shakedowns by surly immigration officers at Toronto International Airport when a returning traveler exercised the right to answer questions in French. Michel Tremblay, Quebec's celebrated playwright, is unforgiving toward anglophones: "They lived here, a minority, but didn't respect the majority enough to learn its language." Pierre Le Fevre, a financier, remembers how he grew up hearing the parents of his anglophone friends tell their children, "Learn a little French, enough so you can talk to the servants."

It's especially cutting that so many English Canadians, enamored of France, its châteaux and cuisine, seem contemptuous of French Canada and its mores. The arrogance and indifference are powerful incentives for those seeking independence. "It's better than remaining a kept woman, especially if the pimp no longer cares," cracked the francophone publisher of a leading Quebec daily. Only the brute politics of language enforcement gets the anglos' attention, the separatists feel. English Canada will never respect Quebec's demands unless there's "a knife at its throat," warned one of them. Another added that the knife to the throat isn't enough: a little blood would have to start spilling before the anglos realize Quebec is serious.

Neither English or French Canadians, locked in the time warp of their antagonisms, fully appreciate that the last decades have brought a new divide to their country, one that may someday displace the obsessions of language and separatism. It has become one of the centerpieces of Canada's discord, bearing the clunky title "multiculturalism."

It has been around since the first aboriginals, who had crossed the Bering Straits from Asia to North America, were joined twelve millennia later by the immigrant progeny of Northern and Eastern Europeans, by Loyalists from America, and, full circle, by modern-day Pacific Asians. Pierre Trudeau is credited with institutionalizing multiculturalism in Canada in 1971, making it a policy whereby Canada's numerous cultures would be protected, promoted, and financed by the state. It was considered a wise move for several reasons: multiculturalism, as a third force, would help dissipate Canadians' fixation with the French-English quarrel; it would show up America's melting-pot practice (no one in Canada would have to be "melted"); it was good politics, buttering up all those ethnic bloc votes for Trudeau's Liberal Party; and it broached the arching theme of "unity in diversity"—that the nation could best be held together by recognizing the claims of its different cultures.

In retrospect, multiculturalism should have been quietly acknowledged, but never enshrined with fanfare as national policy. It has made a lot of Ukrainian folk dancers in Saskatchewan and Inuit soapstone carvers in Baffinland happy; it has enhanced Canada's world image as a tolerant,

inclusive society. It has also enraged French Quebecers, who see themselves reduced in status to just another ethnic minority. It spurs Canada's
disgruntled Natives to press their claims with unmitigated zeal. And it
provokes all sorts of other special-interest pleaders, some of them dubious, to demand their place in the sun. It has invited established Canadians
to distance themselves from a common identity; for new immigrants, it
vitiates any coherent Canadianism they might aspire to. Canadian identity
is always a nebulous proposition, but official multiculturalism fragments
it further. By encouraging hyphenated Canadianism, keeping the nation's
ethnic enclaves ethnic, multiculturalism threatens the chances of Canada's immigrant cultures ever coalescing to produce something distinc-
tively Canadian. Every sizable minority shouts and jostles for a seat at
the political table, the cacophony engulfing whatever unity process is left.
Ethnic diversity as a credo is not the answer to a unifying nationalism.
Where the national identity is already weak, as Britain's *Economist* has
warned, multiculturalism is more likely to lead to breakup.

Canada's 1.5 million Natives are at the vertex of the multicultural
divide. Neglected and abused by history, they have become victims of
the gulf between themselves and the rest of Canada, a gulf in some ways
more unbridgeable than that between French and English Canadians.
Once, they were valued wartime allies and economic helpmates of the
British and their Canadian colonists, enlivening the early fur trade, siding
with the British in the Revolution and War of 1812. Thereafter, when
they had lost their usefulness, the Natives were subjected for a century
and a half to a succession of laws that effectively stripped them of their
hunting lands, their political and economic autonomy, their identity.
Their traditions were outlawed, their ceremonies and dances, the drum
and the pipe; they were told to cast aside their spiritual talismans, the
sacred sweetgrass and sage. There were no Wounded Knees or migratory
"trail of tears" as in America, no blood-hunts for the warrior likes of a
Sitting Bull or Geronimo. In Canada, it was callousness, not genocide,
that stripped the Natives of their lives and culture.

As the British tried with the French in Quebec, so Canada sought to
assimilate its Natives starting in the late 1800s. Having confined them
under the Indian Act to reserves held in trust by the federal government,
Canada compelled the Natives to enroll their children in special schools
run by the Church. Memories of the so-called "residential schools," some
of which operated through the 1960s, still sear the consciousness of

Toronto is a babble of accents—Guyanese, Latvian, Maltese, Chilean; taxpayers' notices come in four languages besides English: Italian, Chinese, Portuguese, and Polish. More than 60 percent of the city's 3 million people boast non-English backgrounds. One fifth of Montreal's populace are immigrants, more and more of them French-speaking Haitians and North Africans. Along the city's thoroughfares, Muslim butcher shops vie for space with Laotian tearooms and Filipino bakeries. The Prairies are dotted with the Ukrainians' onion-domed Orthodox churches. In Vancouver, Sikh temples stand alongside the parishes of Chinese, who now comprise a third of all new immigrants to the city. The Mounties are admitting turbaned recruits to their ranks.

The Canadian mosaic sparkles in its diversity, on the surface anyway. The immigrants have fashioned their own success stories, from fortune-making real estate developers to theater-chain impresarios to politicians who have become Governor Generals of the realm. In Saskatchewan, the premier, Roy Romanow, recalls his Ukrainian parents, the mother who conducted her business without knowledge of either of Canada's two official languages, the father who died never knowing more than a hundred words of English. In British Columbia, where the province's Lieutenant-Governor (representing the Queen) has become the first Chinese-Canadian ever to hold the post, rags-to-riches tales are as plentiful as fortune cookies. One immigrant, grown rich from his garment factory, planned to return to Hong Kong and build a sumptuous mansion for himself and his two sons and their families. Advised this wouldn't necessarily please his offspring, who'd grown accustomed to their adopted country, the man sold his factory for $100 million and divided the sum equally between his sons who, in turn, invested their father's gift in a new development north of Vancouver called Whistler, destined to become one of the premier international ski resorts in North America.

Until recently most Canadians have welcomed the new immigrants, the dynamic they bring to a country long defined by its anglo-European establishment. The elites of that old structure, the Canadian publisher Conrad Black, has charged, have produced "an uncompetitive, slothful, self-righteous, spiteful and envious nanny-state." The new immigrants can do no worse. Still, the uneasiness grows. If the nation's established groups—the descendants of British, French, and continental Europeans—have yet to coalesce harmoniously, the new potpourri hardly bodes greater comity. For Quebecers, the immigrants threaten what is left of the old anglo-French compact under which Quebec rated special attention. Uptight English Canadians, watching the new ethnics pursue their old-country customs and nonchalantly dismiss fears of being co-opted by the Americans, question the Canadianism of the newcomers, their commitment to keeping Canada whole and out of the American orbit.

The new immigrants may show their faith in quiet ways: a century before, when a Chinese died in Canada, his friends had him cremated and sent the ashes home to China; now, there are stories of immigrants digging up and cremating the remains of their parents in Hong Kong, then bringing the ashes with them to Canada. Such displays make little impression on Canadian public opinion. A survey in late 1993 found Canadians in a growingly hostile mood toward immigrants. The nation's bend-over-backward immigration policy has turned sharply restrictive: the new policy aims at selecting "quality" immigrants rather than approving every visitor who may tear up his or her identity papers en route, then request political asylum. The tightening rules coincide with signs of resurgent racism in the land.

Despite its liberal reputation and its empty spaces crying to be filled, Canada has never been quite the exemplar of tolerance it credits itself with being. During World War I it interned thousands of Ukrainian settlers in the West because, by historical mischance, they carried Austrian passports. It did the same in World War II to some twenty thousand Canadians of Japanese ancestry living in British Columbia. It has followed the U.S. pattern and, through immigration and employment practices, discriminated against Asian Indians, its own Natives, Jews, blacks, and the luckless Chinese. In earlier times, Canadian authorities imposed a "head tax" on Chinese immigrants, denied them certain jobs, and forbade them, as occasional employers, from hiring white women. In Vancouver, it is said, the locals of another era tied Chinese coolies together by their queues and tossed them from cliffs into the sea. Blacks were kept out of Canada on the laughable assumption that they could not stand the fierce climate. The historian Pierre Berton recounts how the immigration commissioner for western Canada paid one medical inspector in Manitoba a fee for every black he rejected. In smaller ways, immigrants with unpronounceable names from Eastern Europe and the Mediterranean have also felt the lash of racism: in Canada today some adult children of first-generation Slavic immigrants actually do not know their national origins because their parents were too scarred by the past to tell them.

Canada, unlike America, has no prominent history of slavery, lynchings, or urban race riots on a massive scale. But the anti-immigrant mood has given rise to racial incidents across the country, with premonitions of worse to come. In Vancouver, it is still "racism with a whisper," as one Chinese executive phrased it: limited entrée to social clubs or civic boards, quiet resentment at any flaunting of new immigrant wealth. In Ottawa, Toronto, and Montreal, the racism is of another sort. Gangs of neo-Nazi skinheads prey on elderly Asians and dark-skinned teenagers in the shopping malls of the federal capital. Crowds rampaged through downtown Toronto in May 1992, protesting the fatal shooting of a black man by police, the eighth such incident in less than four years. In Quebec, home to mass influxes of francophone immigrants from North Africa and the Caribbean, tensions between the newcomers and local Québécois have already led to stone-throwing, window-smashing skirmishes on the streets of Montreal.

With immigrants arriving daily from countries like Senegal, Morocco, Vietnam, and Haiti, the black community of Montreal has grown to nearly 10 percent of the city's population. Blue-collar Québécois feel their jobs threatened by the immigrants; Montreal's nearly all-white police force evinces little affection for the volatile Haitians. People talk worriedly about the "German factor," referring to the racial violence directed at foreign immigrants in that country. Some in Quebec believe the new tensions are potentially more explosive than those between English and French Canadians.

Canada's social and political discord is no isolated phenomenon, but inextricably linked to the failings of its economy.

The racial, linguistic, multicultural, and regional divides all exacerbate the nation's economic problems, just as those problems fuel the political and social tensions. Economic concerns—massive debt, joblessness, excessive taxes, a feared decline in living standards—have driven Canadians to disturbing levels of stress and anger. By the same token, ceaseless entitlement demands, federal-provincial power spats, the costly burden of dual government, all have propelled the negative economic trends. As much as anything, the bottom-line struggle between the forces of the economic status quo and those of painful reform constitutes Canada's fifth great divide.

Canada's stand-patters, the we're-all-right-Jack brigade, point to the obvious: a nation ranked thirty-third in population boasting the world's seventh largest economy. It has unparalleled natural resources. In national wealth per person, Canada has ranked second among the world's industrial countries, just behind the United States. A prodigious trader, it is the world's second largest exporting nation after Germany. In rankings by *Fortune* magazine of top non-U.S. companies, Canada could claim more than three times as many entries as Italy and almost as many as France. It has a relatively youthful population, enviable proximity to the world's richest market, a projected growth rate in 1994 that would be the strongest of all industrial nations, and a future in the next millennium that includes a predicted gross national product of nearly $1 trillion.

The reformers base their appraisal on Canada's recent economic history and evidence of severe structural weaknesses. Even with recovery from recession and a political armistice, they say, the nation is headed for a steep dive in international prestige and its Cadillac style of living. For more than a century Canadians have allowed their economic direction to be set, first, by Great Britain, then by the United States. They have prospered in an economic hothouse, their markets sheltered and their federal government rushing to the aid of every provincial or private enterprise wobbling toward bankruptcy. Since the mid-1960s, successive governments in Ottawa have built an unprecedented pyramid of debt, bailing out eminently drownable projects and satisfying countless demands for regional development and make-work programs. Canadians, who sometimes have trouble differentiating between their entitlements and their productivity, increasingly consume more than they produce. They also pay themselves extraordinarily well. The economy coasted through the 1970s on windfall profits from the Mideast oil shocks that rocketed up energy prices. Even in the 1980s, with revenue losses from collapsing world oil prices already eating into its fat, Canada enjoyed the second highest growth in the OECD. All the same, the economic pie has not grown as fast as Canadians' appetite, a fact that became painfully apparent when recession struck in the early 1990s.

Amid wasting unemployment rates (11% plus) that resulted in huge losses in annual output and threatened to become long term, amid permanent plant shutdowns in the prized resource sector, amid record-high bankruptcies and plunging corporate profits, Canadians knew something terrible had gone wrong with their economy even if they were unsuspecting of the deeper causes. Public confidence hit new lows; foreign investors sat on their wallets. In late 1992, Standard & Poor's of New York, the corporate rating organization, downgraded Canada's $10 billion foreign currency debt to a lower category, a signal embarrassment.

Recession, like malnutrition, has exposed the weak limbs of Canada's economy. The globalization of investment, accelerating technological change, and the Free Trade accord with America has magnified them. Canada, with its withering branch plants and trickling east-west trade flow, is dangerously vulnerable to the tectonic shifts and competition of the new age. Its economy has been revealed as a second-rate industrial one with, until very recently, a dismal record of productivity growth and an addictive dependence on foreign technology. Its sky-high interest rates encourage further foreign indebtedness; its exorbitant wages and labor costs make it difficult for manufacturers to compete and augur the exodus of many of them to the United States. The cost of capital remains higher in Canada than in most other competing nations. So does the potential cost of its high school dropouts, who are leaving at a rate estimated to be the equivalent of 100,000 a year. As the Harvard Business School's Michael Porter observed in his devastating 1991 study, Canada has become the custodian of an ill-educated workforce, antiquated labor-management relations, historically weak competition laws, and trade barriers between its provinces that have long since dulled any notion of vigorous domestic rivalry.

The central and weakest limb of Canada's economy has been its productivity, the determining factor in how people's incomes and living standards progress. Canada's productivity performance was the worst among major industrial powers at the beginning of the nineties: its ranking in productivity growth over a thirty-year span nudged the bottom of the charts among the two dozen OECD countries. Only in 1992 did Canada's manufacturing productivity finally make an encouraging spurt—a jump of 4.2 percent, or five times the average annual pace of the previous seven years. The contributing factors in that record stand out like diseased joints in need of urgent medication.

Canada's class-riven labor relations are burdened on either side by sluggish institutional practices and reflexes invariably attuned more to concerns over equality and security than hard work and competition. The climate of hostility between old-fashioned management and the clamorous unions leads to strikes and other disruptions that at one time, between

1973 and 1982, caused Canada to lose more working days each year than any other industrialized nation except Italy. The scale of work stoppages has seriously hampered productivity growth and appalled international observers, who not long ago consigned the country's retrograde labor-management relationship to the backlots of the developed world.

If Canada's unions seem frozen in an "I'll-get-mine" mentality, much of its business leadership is rutted in parochialism and smugness. Management has become part of the suffocating concentration of wealth in Canada, where a handful of powerful families and conglomerates control about a third of all non-financial assets. The men who run things comprise a clubby old-boy network where the trusting handshake has counted for more than global insight or sophisticated skills. In such a tight community, bound by tradition and exclusivity, frauds of the magnitude of America's junk-bond and savings-and-loan scandals are less likely; unfriendly corporate takeovers are considered poor form. But neither is there much dynamism, initiative, or smart risk taking. The average six-tyish executive in Canada, one critic has charged, has a global view bounded by Wall Street, Palm Springs, and Miami Beach.

Canadian managers tend to be less well educated than their counterparts elsewhere, and that deficiency traces right down the line through the workforce to the high schools. One reason close to 600,000 jobs were vacant in Canada in the early nineties was the lack of sufficiently trained manpower to fill them. Canadian industry spends less than half as much effort training its workers as U.S. industry, a fifth as much as the Japanese. The shortage of skilled labor in a variety of occupations, chiefly technological, stems from the fall-off in enrollments in advanced training at the university and post-university level. Some top Canadian companies predict serious shortages of engineers in the years ahead. In the high school system, about 30 percent of the students never bother to graduate. The gaps in Canada's learning culture are such that 38 percent of the population can barely get through commonplace reading tasks, while about 30 percent of high school graduates cannot meet most normal reading demands or follow a simple sequence of numerical exercises. Unless the figures improve, some experts warn, Canada will produce more than a million illiterates during the 1990s.

The lapses in mathematics and science training have already reduced Canada to a society of "technological illiterates," according to critics. Not only is much of its workforce unprepared to handle complex jobs in the new age, but Canadian industry lags behind other nations by at least half a decade in investing in and applying state-of-the-art technology. One 1991 survey ranked Canada last among leading OECD countries in exploiting new technologies. Only a small fraction of Canadian manufacturing firms have any real research capability and the large majority employ not a single engineer.

Canada's spending on research and development is a pittance, the lowest as a percentage of its national wealth of the Group of Seven industrial nations. The result is a country that, technologically speaking, has found itself lumped with the likes of India, Mexico, and Ireland. The lack of adequate research and development has led to a brain drain of some of Canada's brightest and most ambitious professionals, who are lured south by promises of working with the latest technology in a more innovative environment. Countries like Canada that are unable to successfully create and develop new technologies, concludes the journalist David Crane in his compelling book, *The Next Canadian Century,* face declining wages and living standards—in other words, will get poorer. The Conference Board of Canada has warned that unless Canada improves its technology as well as its productivity, within thirty years Mexico will overtake it to become America's foremost trading partner.

As Canada struggles belatedly to adjust to the new technological imperatives, it is watching the traditional source of its prosperity, its natural resources, begin a slow sunset. Nearly half of Canada's exports have customarily been natural-resource-based goods. But as foreign investors shift their attention to service and high-tech industries, old standbys like steel, mining, fossil fuel, and forest products find themselves beset by weak markets and increasingly tough global competition. Petroleum producers are stuck with basement prices for their wares, auto parts manufacturers are shackled to the doubtful U.S. auto industry, and machine-tool makers face slumping markets. In a country whose citizens are perhaps the world's most profligate users of energy, oil supplies are rapidly depleting, production has been declining at about 4 percent annually, and reinvestment in oil exploration and development is shrinking. The exhaustion of Alberta's conventional oil reserves is in sight; frontier oil resources in the Arctic are still light-years from commercial development. Trends indicate that before the turn of the century Canada will be a net importer of oil. The mining industry, custodian of what Stephen Leacock once described as "a store of minerals and metals that Pluto himself might envy," is virtually comatose. It has been crushed on all sides by unstable prices, signs of resource depletion, crippling regulation and taxes, delays due to environmental concerns, and uncertainty about the outcomes of Native land claims. Some mining firms have already high-tailed out of Canada, bound for more promising places like Mexico and Chile. Forestry, the nation's largest employer, has become a metaphor for Canada, one of the industry's top executives opined in late 1992: it is simply dying.

Canada has become a nation not only in danger of seeing the benefits of its natural resources dribble away, but one in which the natural talents of its people and its basically frugal economic values have been too often compromised or squandered by the policies of its political leadership.

The federal government stands accused of having sapped the competitive drive of Canadian industries over decades of nannyism. It has imposed national standards on everything from income support and bilingual signs to the quality of milk. Government-regulated prices have proliferated. Government efforts to farm out manufacturing development to the lesser regions have resulted in all manner of inefficiencies. The federal Unemployment Insurance scheme, which until a short while ago permitted many Canadians to work for as little as ten weeks and reap the benefits for forty-two weeks, has bred a class of habitual loafers. Too many government-owned Crown corporations are cited as inefficient, undercapitalized, overpriced, and unresponsive—feedbags for the political faithful, as one critic put it.

Nor are Canada's provinces models of prudence or vision. Always, the aim has been to employ, protect, cure for short-term satisfaction, with little regard for long-term consequences. In the Maritimes, a structure of inordinately high wages for arguably skilled workers has discouraged new businesses from starting up. In Newfoundland, preoccupation with maintaining jobs at all costs has turned the province's sick fishing industry into a virtual social welfare net, when more than anything the industry needs to be downsized and retooled to compete with aggressive foreign fleets. In Saskatchewan, the government has supported a $1.5 billion health care budget and more than 130 hospitals for barely 1 million people. The system perpetuates itself through heavy borrowing, but is manifestly unsustainable.

The provinces' multifarious barriers to domestic trade have comprised one of the worst structural failings of the Canadian economy. The process to finally remove those barriers may be nearing completion, but meanwhile there have been more constraints on the flow of capital, labor, and goods between the provinces than between the countries of the European Economic Community. A former Canadian Ambassador to Washington observed that his countrymen have freer trade with the United States than they do between their own provinces. Everything has been affected, from beer to bricks. Beer could be sold only in the province where it was brewed (to protect small local breweries), so the Maritimes' popular Moosehead export, for example, could until very recently be quaffed in Manhattan but not in Montreal. In one Quebec town, across the river from Ottawa, officials ordered the new sidewalks upheaved because they'd been laid with bricks made in Ontario. The provinces engage in preferential hiring and procurement practices that favor locals over outsiders even when the latter offer lower bids on a contract. Minerals mined in Saskatchewan must be processed there; in Alberta, half the members of a corporate board have to be residents of the province. The patchwork of provincial regulations and different licensing standards is a nightmare for industries like telecommunications, financial services, and transportation. A mechanic in Vancouver might not be able to ply his trade in Winnipeg; companies have found it easier to truck goods from Toronto to the Mexican border than to make the run across Canada. All told, the roughly five hundred interprovincial trade barriers have cost Canadians $6.5 billion a year.

The absurdities are no less in the tangle of overlapping programs and duplicative responsibilities created by the federal and provincial governments. In their separate drives for power, both entities have accrued such costly bureaucracies that providing public services in Canada has become a frequently chaotic exercise in frustration. Many departments like labor, manpower, energy, and the environment operate at both levels of government. Prime ministers' federal cabinets, which have varied recently between twenty-five and forty members, are apt to be duplicated and occasionally exceeded in each of the provinces. As a result, no one can be sure which level of government is supposed to be delivering what service. Businesses as well as outside investors bear the costly burden of having to deal with multiple layers of government, fill out multiple sets of forms, and figure out how to meet the often incompatible objectives of federal and provincial bureaucrats. Federal intrusion is rampant. Quebec and Ottawa have clashed over manpower-retraining strategies for failed industries in the province. If Alberta seeks to build a dam that affects rivers running through Indian lands, it brings the Ottawa bureaucracy down on its head. A mining company in Ontario might get the province's nod to open a couple of new coal pits, only to encounter demands from Ottawa for a separate environmental review study. The situation is guaranteed to send investors reeling and deter local economic expansion.

None of the structural failings, however, approaches the enormity of Canada's debt problem. Over a relatively short twenty-year span, the federal government, which once operated one of the soundest economies in the world, has run up a succession of budget deficits that by 1992 marked Canada as the world's second largest debtor (after the United States). Its current federal deficit of $31 billion exceeds America's, per capita, as well as the rest of the industrialized world. Its total debt burden is so high, so crippling as a percentage of its national wealth, and so fast-growing that it almost assures the necessity of an international rescue operation before the decade's end.

Canada's federal debt, in U.S. dollars, has ballooned to more than $354 billion and its provincial debt to $112 billion for a total of $466 billion as of December 1993. The provinces by themselves are now borrowing in toto more than the federal government, with their share of the total annual public-sector deficit now more than 40 percent. Most of Canada's debt is held by American and Japanese bondholders, and that foreign debt alone, $228 billion, as a percentage of the gross domestic product, is the industrial world's highest—five times that of the United States—and the fastest growing. It means, of course, that a larger proportion of what Canada produces each year goes to foreign creditors instead of being used for its own needs or to create new wealth. For example, the $35 billion or more that Ottawa paid annually during the Mulroney years to service the national debt exceeded the cost of all its social programs in any given year. The most frightening statistic, though, is that the overall net debt burden has now risen to more than 90 percent of Canada's GDP, with more than $1 of every $3 in federal revenue going to pay just the interest on it. Any government that lets its public debt exceed 50 percent of its GDP, argue some business leaders, is basically bankrupt. Canada is literally borrowing funds to pay the interest on previous borrowings, and the law of compound interest is starting to eat it alive. It is also diminishing investors' confidence: within a short time, the federal government and the debt-ridden provinces will face trouble borrowing on the international markets. That point has become known ominously in Canadian economic circles as "hitting the wall"—the final crash in which the nation's economy, like a high-speed car with no effective brakes, strikes the once immovable wall of worldwide faith in Canada's ability to muddle through.

Foreign investors have long stayed clear of Canada's equity markets, withholding or sending elsewhere the sort of risk capital that financed new plants and forward-looking research. Now they watch disapprovingly as Canada's interest rates mount faster than its economy grows, the rates spiraling upward in order to keep luring the capital Canada needs to meet its debt obligations. It is a course akin to one followed by the dog who expired in pursuit of its tail. Experts like Harvard's Michael Porter doubt whether Canada can upgrade and lift its economy out of the debt hole soon enough without a massive shift in Canadians' attitudes, namely, their old aversions to rumbustious competition. Some Canadians, despairing of redemption, see the debt mess as grounds for the richer provinces and Quebec to conclude that federalism is no longer profitable. With fewer federal benefits in the offing and no end of federal borrowing in sight, some provinces have more than enough incentive to prepare exit papers and skip out on paying their share of the debt.

The way out of the morass is not to print more money and risk hyperinflation nor to deflate the economy and court a depression. Higher taxes offer no escape either, unless the government wants open rebellion. Canada already shoulders a heavier taxload than its major trading partners, including the United States, and the load keeps growing. Its personal tax rate is among the highest of the industrial nations, its citizens afflicted by an array of federal, provincial, goods-and-service taxes that soak up 20 percent of the average family income and 40 percent or more of the average wage earner's. Half the provinces levied tax increases in 1992. In one, Ontario, the tax bite on businesses is typically 20 to 30 percent higher than in comparable American states. The impact of all this is predictable: falling consumer demand, a burgeoning underground economy based on illegal bartering, and the exodus of small to medium-sized companies, many to relocate across the border in the United States.

If economic health is essential for its future, then Canada is living on borrowed time. Failure to reform its economy and start living within its means presages the inevitable unraveling of its welfare and healthcare programs, eventually perhaps its whole social system. Failure to keep intact its political order, under which its economy can function normally, invites more serious economic harm. Either way, Canada is increasingly imperiled.

On October 26, 1992, Canadians voted on a constitutional package that many believed represented the country's last chance to save itself.

The historic vote on the Charlottetown Accord was the culmination of two years of sulk and rage since the collapse in 1990 of the ill-fated Meech Lake Accord. Rejection of that pact had soured Canadians on the constitutional process. Many found it a costly and distracting bore, even though it involved the political life or death of their country. Others viewed the process as self-destructive: Canadians really got along fine in practice, if not in theory; it was when they began writing things down on tablets that trouble started. Unfortunately, the original tablets and their runes no longer applied to modern Canada, and the nation, after all, did need a workable constitution. Meech Lake had failed, the politicians were persuaded, because it focused too heavily on Quebec's demands. The new talks, held in Charlottetown and Ottawa, became known as the "Canada round" for their emphasis on addressing the demands of other parts of Canada. The man appointed by Prime Minister Brian Mulroney to orchestrate the talks was Joe Clark, a former Prime Minister, a westerner, and one-time political adversary of Mulroney's. The premier of Quebec, still smarting from Meech Lake's demise, boycotted the talks.

With Bourassa absent from the table, Native and western leaders rushed to fill the vacuum and push through their own demands. The Natives' chief of chiefs, Ovide Mercredi, stood in the dust of the road leading to the conference center and stopped every premier's limousine to inquire of its occupants why he and other Natives leaders weren't included in the talks; shortly, they were. The westerners flogged their proposal for an elected Senate and found in Albertan Clark a silent friend. At the same time, Ontario and Quebec's proxies fought for recognition of the original compact between Canada's two founding peoples. At one point, as demands and counterdemands threatened to render the discussion unmanageable, a disgusted Mulroney reportedly told a participant that Clark couldn't lead "a one-man parade" down Main Street. Just as the talks stalled in confusion and "we saw the apocalypse coming," as one of the premiers later confided, enough additional compromises were fashioned to save the agreement. The result, after six months of arm twisting and deal cutting, was an accord that presaged drastic overhaul of Canada's Constitution and government system. The package—approved in late August 1992 by Ottawa, all ten provincial and two territorial governments, as well as four Native organizations—had something for nearly everyone: an elected Senate attuned to regional interests, additional specific powers for the provinces, and recognition of Quebec as a "distinct society" as well as of the principle of self-government for Canada's aboriginals. All the accord needed was the public's approving pat.

Over the next two months before the national referendum, every other political faction or interest group sharpened its knives and weighed in on the issue. By the time the campaign officially began in late September, opponents of the Charlottetown Accord had already declared their colors: the rapidly growing western Reform Party; Quebec's separatists and the powerful youth wing of the province's Liberal Party; major organizations representing Canada's women, the elderly, the mentally and physically disabled, all of whom felt their interests had been ignored in the constitutional talks; and millions of other Canadians who thought the process had become hostage to every special-interest group except left-handed dentists. Some opinion shapers, recalling Winston Churchill's classic put-down, dismissed the accord as one large pudding with no theme. Then Trudeau delivered his lightning bolt on the pages of *Maclean's* and *L'Actualité* magazines, condemning the separatists as "master blackmailers" and the accord as the first step in the dismantling of Canada.

The "No" side was already in high gear by the time the "Yes" campaign, backing the accord, got off to a slow and comically inept start. Its opening rally in Quebec featured a giant banner proclaiming in huge block letters "YES" in English only. The premiers, who had assembled and endorsed the deal, proved to be inert salesmen for it. Most of them returned to their provinces and sat on their hands, leaving Quebec's Robert Bourassa and the hapless Prime Minister to spearhead the "Yes" campaign. Mulroney, whose credibility at that point was said to be only slightly higher than Saddam Hussein's, invited more scorn than support for his cause. When Joe Clark predicted that a "No" vote would result in sovereignty for Quebec by the year 2000, and Bourassa warned that without Quebec there would be no Canada, many Canadians took the doom-saying to mean the accord was headed for the deep. Their worries triggered a massive sell-off of Canadian bonds and securities in the weeks preceding the referendum. Even the Toronto Blue Jays' World Series victory two days before the vote couldn't save matters.

The overwhelming "No" vote crushed the Charlottetown Accord and with it any serious hopes of reconciling the nation's conflicting interests. The electorate decisively repudiated Canada's political leadership. In polling booths from Moncton to Medicine Hat, angry housewives and ranchers settled their scores with "Lyin' Brian" & Co.: Mulroney was judged to have been responsible for persuading twice as many Canadians to vote against the accord as for it. The voters branded the accord as hopelessly indigestible and potentially disintegrative. They rebelled at the Halloweenish scaremongering and the know-it-all establishment. The urban intelligentsia voted "Yes," the countryside resoundingly "No." The rest of the divisions fell in place. Quebecers and Ontarians voted against the West and its design for an elected Senate. Westerners said no to "distinct society" status for Quebec. British Columbians mooned the rest of Canada. Everyone stuck it to the Natives. They reacted with the fury of a people spurned, threatening more Okas and widespread civil disobedience. In the end, everyone lost on that October day in 1992. Almost everyone.

Amidst the carnage of failed hopes, Quebec's separatists celebrated. The death of the Charlottetown pact was yet another rejection of Quebec as well as of constitutional unity. But it spurred the separatists to new heights of defiant rejoicing over the inevitability of their cause. In a downtown Montreal disco palace, festooned with "NON" placards, hundreds of flag-waving, chanting Québécois jammed a klieg-lit auditorium the night of the big vote. As a huge screen flashed the final vote tallies, cheers erupted from the boisterous crowd and a great choir of voices filled the smoky air with the separatist anthem, *"Gens de Mon Pays."* A burst of pyrotechnics engulfed the stage in flashing lights, smoke and whorls of sparklers. Pounding steel drums mixed with the cheering to create a pandemonium of sound that was atavistic, almost feral, in its intensity. Out of the tumult, armored in a gray double-breasted suit, emerged the triumphant separatist leader, Jacques Parizeau. The thunderous approbation seemed to bear him almost weightlessly from the stage into the arms of his delirious followers surging across the auditorium floor.

In the aftermath of the Charlottetown debacle, Canada lay politically prostrate, exhausted and drained by the ordeal. Solutions deemed work-

able had been turned to dust. What remained, as the crestfallen Prime
Minister acknowledged, were the grievances and unattained aspirations
of the nation, the bitter divisions and warring camps.

A plague of despair seemed to grip the land. Charlottetown was "one
of those rare historical moments that will not come again," *Maclean's,*
Canada's weekly newsmagazine, intoned. In less than a decade the nation
had experienced three tragically missed opportunities to resolve its constitutional crisis: repatriation in 1982; Meech Lake in 1987; Charlottetown
in 1992. With each miss, Quebec had been spurned by the rest of Canada,
moving the province another step closer to abandoning federation. The
federalism embodied in the Charlottetown Accord, which tried to reconcile the irreconcilable, was "truly deceased," the editor of *Le Devoir*
wrote. The statecraft employed in constitutional reform had become a
scrum in which petty politicians tried to broker among immutable claims.
The mainstream political parties and their beliefs were in danger of reced-
ing, of becoming, like Ottawa itself, increasingly marginal to the local or
regional interests of ordinary Canadians. Having repudiated its political
establishment at the polls, the country seemed to be casting itself adrift
from those institutions and faiths that had anchored its past. Canadians
had allowed themselves to be brought to the brink of their own destruction. They were, in the words of one prominent nationalist, sleepwalking
toward extinction.

More of them talked privately of either leaving Canada or making sure
their funds did. A leading business executive in Edmonton confided he
was seriously thinking of taking out all his money and parking it in a
U.S. offshore fund to support his family and grandchildren. German and
U.S. bonds looked increasingly alluring as hedges against a perilous
future. Quebecers favored a series of preferred shares that traded in U.S.
dollars on the Montreal and Toronto stock exchanges, valuable offsets
against a plunging Canadian dollar if Quebec separated. Other Quebecers, rich entrepreneurs in their sixties, were by late 1992 already reducing
their financial exposure in Canada, moving a quarter or more of their
accounts out of Montreal and into blue-chip Wall Street banks. One real
estate development trust, owned by a half-dozen families in Toronto and
Montreal, started moving more than $12 million of its assets into a U.S.
holding company. The executive heading the trust feared that when Quebec separated, things would collapse as swiftly as the Berlin Wall had.

Outside the country, investors had already slowed their buying of

Canadian bonds. Japanese, who held about one quarter of Canada's federal and provincial government bonds, were on edge over the growing foreign exchange risk due to Canada's troubles. Germany's Deutschebank advised its clients to curtail their holdings in Canada until the political and economic crisis had cooled. Across the southern border, Canadians had begun to increase their already sizable deposits in the banks of border towns like Plattsburgh, New York. Business properties and vacation homes in U.S. border areas were selling to Canadians at an unusually brisk pace. American executives and federal officials jogged themselves to a state of high alert. On Wall Street, analysts reported that a number of state governments had already put their Quebec investments on hold; some were selling their Quebec bonds and buying Alberta paper instead. In late 1992, when Merrill Lynch sent out a conference call to assess the Canadian crisis and its impact on U.S. markets, more than 150 investors joined the nationwide hookup, the largest conference call in the company's history. In Washington, a very senior policy maker at the State Department pondered the impact of a breakup of Canada, with Quebec, then British Columbia and Alberta separating. He concluded it would pose an almost unthinkable question for the U.S. government: Faced with similar internal strains in the United States, what if California or Texas or Alaska were to go?

After Charlottetown, Canadians sensed that the familiar Canada of the past was all but buried. They could not return to the old ways of running their country, yet they were too traumatized to think about new moves to preserve the union and stave off separation. The nation drifted on uncertain currents, heading for falls unknown.

The year 1993 passed fitfully. That September, Robert Bourassa announced his retirement as Quebec's premier, setting the stage for the province's Liberal Party to anoint a new leader, Daniel Johnson, the unimposing president of Quebec's Treasury Board. In October, the Toronto Blue Jays won their second straight World Series, jolting the country into a brief spasm of national pride. Then the carnage of the federal elections shocked it back into reality, the results mirroring the nation's implacable divisions.

The elections pitted Brian Mulroney's incumbent Tory successor, a testy woman of modest accomplishment and uncertain vision, against the

Liberal challenger, a veteran Quebec-born politician who had few if any original ideas and more than occasional trouble making himself understood in either French or English. Kim (née Avril Phaedra) Campbell, Canada's first woman to reach the top, would not be quite its shortest-lived prime minister, but from the beginning her chances of staying on were sorely burdened, if not doomed, by the Mulroney legacy. Campbell's personal popularity with the voters could never overcome the low esteem in which they held her predecessor and her party. Her lackluster performance in the fall campaign against the politically savvy Jean Chrétien led to the worst defeat of a major party in Canada's history. The Tories plunged from their powerhold of 157 seats in Parliament to a rock-bottom two seats, reducing the party, in the words of one of its key strategists, to a "guerilla insurgency" movement. The leftist New Democrats, with no clear message to offer the voters, saw their status as Canada's third main party evaporate as their representation in Parliament was cut from forty-four to eight seats. The triumphant Liberals increased their standing by nearly one hundred seats, winning in all ten provinces—a feat not even Pierre Trudeau had ever accomplished. The populist Reform Party and its autocratic leader, Preston Manning, swamped all opposition in the big western provinces, roaring into Ottawa's House of Commons with fifty-two seats and a corralful of momentum and prestige, just behind the surging Bloc Québécois. The message of Reform's historic breakthrough was that Canadians increasingly wanted their representatives more accountable to their constituents than to their parties.

In one massive vote for change, "yesterday's man," as his critics had dismissed Jean Chrétien, became the new hope for Canada. A shrewdly disarming striver who grew up in poverty, the eighteenth of nineteen children born to a machinist in Shawinigan, Quebec, Chrétien cultivated his folksy habitant mannerisms as he moved from the family's tar-paper dwelling through law school, into politics, and up through the ranks of the Liberal Party. Even as he gained respect for his successes, he could never quite escape looking like the driver of the getaway car, as one wit put it. In fact, his crooked smile and mangling of English syntax, partly the result of a paralyzing birth defect, became emblems of a rough-hewn charm and integrity that helped propel Chrétien through virtually every important ministerial post in the Trudeau government before he finally won the Liberal leadership in June 1990.

Chrétien's broad experience in government, his clear mandate from the voters, and his sense of calm authority suggested real hope for his prime ministership. Approaching sixty, he was, as one Canadian observed, "an old horse who's been around the track and won't panic in the stretch." Like Mulroney, Chrétien is a master of the deal, a politician who, as the saying went, knows how to "skate." The question in the wake of the elections was whether Chrétien would push beyond the dealmaking to exert real vision and power in the struggle to keep Canada whole, in furthering the larger interests of not only his own country but North America as well. On that score there was limited cause for optimism.

Chrétien's Liberal Party was said to be less ideological and more pragmatic than it had been under Trudeau, but the party still harbored a sizable interventionist and nationalist wing. The new Prime Minister would not tear up the 1989 Canada–U.S. Free Trade accord, as he had once pledged, but he and his Liberals still talked vaguely of trying to renegotiate specific parts of it that continued to cause Canada trouble. At the same time, Chrétien was fond of pointing out that he had no interest in going trout fishing with the U.S. President, as Mulroney did with Bush, lest he end up as the trout. Canadian-American relations were entering a new era.

The elections, by conferring on Ottawa five political parties, underscored Canada's jarring break with tradition: the two established national parties, the Liberals and Progressive Conservatives, could no longer accommodate the country's regional and ethnic tensions under their wide umbrella. Moreover, the fractured makeup of the new Parliament envisaged the sort of cacophonous political center that could render the nation ungovernable, a further spur to Quebec's leaving. The newly empowered regional parties had little affinity for the new Prime Minister. The Reformers distrusted his party's centralism and economic direction—in particular, Chrétien's pledge during the campaign to put Canadians back to work via a costly public works and jobs creation program. The Bloc Québécois detested Chrétien for his unabashed federalism, never forgave him for ridiculing the separatists at the time of Quebec's 1980 referendum and for helping engineer into law, as Trudeau's Minister of Justice, the 1982 Constitution Act over Quebec's opposition. To many Québécois Chrétien had evolved from his Shawinigan days into little more than a political Judas, a contributing factor to his becoming the first Liberal Prime Minister ever to win office without a majority of the seats from Quebec.

In the post-election cauldron of late 1993 Canada's future seemed doubtful as ever. The economic situation was daunting; to substantially reduce the debt and slash in half the nation's 11.6 percent jobless rate before the end of the decade was a tall, if not impossible, order. Prime Minister Chrétien and his Liberal Party, the *Wall Street Journal* warned, "represent the last chance for Canada's government class to show that it can run an economy somewhere other than into the ground." And the political wolves were circling. The next election in Quebec might well restore the Parti Québécois to power, and the referendum a year later confirm the mood to separate. The country could be lurching toward breakup by 1996 or sooner.

Or, mindful of Canadians' stubborn instinct to grab for the life belt one more time, a different plot-line might unfold.

PART II

SCENARIO FOR THE FUTURE

Decentralization. A shift of the onus for having to answer for mistakes from head office to the field.

Restructuring. An attempt at self-redemption, in which everyone and everything is moved up, down or sideways, and then given a new name to see if the firm works better that way.

—From *White Knights and Poison Pills,* a dictionary of business jargon

"Always, we seem to be blocked. In my heart I don't see anything but separation for us."

—GEORGES POIRIER, Quebec steelworker, June 25, 1992

4

Last Try
for Nationhood:
Crossing the Desert

The last scheduled event in Canada's quarter century of constitutional strife, the 1994 provincial election in Quebec, came and went without cataclysm.

The nation's partial recovery from the 1990–93 recession had restored a measure of relief, particularly in Quebec, where unemployment had begun to recede and new business ventures in technology were slowly recharging parts of Montreal's economy. The Parti Québécois and its separatist vision remained fixed in the public's consciousness. The separatist leaders, repeating their performance of two years earlier, had mounted the stage of the Metropolis Café & Disco the night of the provincial vote and electrified the *péquiste* faithful once again with the blazing rhetoric of "sovereignty tomorrow and forever." Still, the election results seemed less compelling to Quebecers than the urge to exploit the improving economic climate and restore business confidence to the point where separation could be effected with maximum support and a minimum of financial distress. For the time being, Quebecers shelved their separatist

compulsions and contemplated new strategies for the further empowerment of their province.

In the National Assembly, *péquiste* leaders began quietly feeling out
their Liberal Party colleagues on how to restart, at a propitious moment,
the political process to acquire fresh powers for Quebec within Confederation. At the same time, Bloc Québécois operatives in Ottawa began contacting Members of Parliament from the other big provinces on the same
issue, but including them as potential beneficiaries as well. If nothing
else, the failed constitutional talks had revealed the depth of frustration
among the richer provinces at having to carry the poorer ones indefinitely
on their backs, at their limited say in how their tax revenues to Ottawa
got distributed. In early 1995 Quebec, in league with Ontario, its largest
trading partner, and the other big revenue producers, British Columbia
and Alberta, began considering a scheme whereby Ottawa would agree
to transfer more federal powers to them. The four-way arrangement
would serve to keep Quebec in Confederation without making it appear
the province was getting preferential treatment; it would also markedly
reduce the federal government's intrusive clout.

For the next three years, the thrust of this scheme was never far from
the minds of provincial strategists as Ottawa and the provinces, for the
last time, tried to stake out common ground on which to unify the nation.
This time the game was no longer constitutional reform, but a full-court
political press to reconfederate Canada and restructure its flawed economy. It was a daunting task propelled by the realization, finally, that
Canada could not survive much longer with its political and economic
house in such disarray. While the process moved simultaneously on two
fronts, it was the economic restructuring talks that commanded most
immediate attention.

By spring 1996, when the National Commission to Rebuild Canada held
its first meeting in Winnipeg, the country's economic baseline had
already shown some signs of marginal improvement.

The Commission's economic task force, composed of business, labor,
and government leaders, could point to federal tax reform and other initiatives that since the mid-1980s had helped to restore a modicum of
competitiveness, speed the privatizing of Crown corporations, and ease
the deregulation of certain industries like transportation. Some manufac-

turing companies had started to make far-sighted investment decisions in research and development as well as North American expansion; others had taken steps to get leaner and more efficient. Canada's resource-based economy already appeared to be shifting toward the production of more refined value-added goods. Many of the new immigrants were coming equipped with valuable entrepreneurial skills. The Free Trade Agreement, for all the grief it had initially caused, had increased Canada's access to the vast U.S. market.

Large shadows remained, however, clouding the economic future. Canada was still trying to live down the international embarrassments it had suffered in the early nineties when, among other things, the *World Competitiveness Report,* an authoritative scoreboard of three dozen industrial economies, had dropped Canada from fifth to eleventh place, while Standard & Poor's had downgraded its foreign currency bonds. Canada's climate and restrictive immigration policies impeded the massive population increase it needed in order to broaden its tax base. In a world where capital was becoming ever scarcer, Canada had yet to figure a way to attract enough of it for its needs. (Rent Ross Perot, someone suggested.) There was still too much complacency, "Canadians have to get off their butts, get off the federal teat, and get to work," advised the chief executive of one of the nation's biggest industrial conglomerates.

The national smugness recalled the old Chinese proverb about how to take revenge on one's enemy: Introduce his son to opium to dull his ambitions, then tell his parents what a fine son they had so they could continue living in their dreamworld, and finally offer the son an extra harem to exhaust any lingering yen of his to succeed. Canadians, it was suggested, were letting the good life, no longer affordable, do them in.

The broad outlines of restructuring the economy were clear. Governments at all levels had to pay down their deficits and curb the monster debt; no longer could they throw money at questionable megaprojects and make-work schemes. Business needed to think and plan globally, designing more competitive products for international markets. Tax-averse Canadians needed to recognize the virtue of tax revenues spent on long-term investments like public education and job training. Canadians in general needed to face the reality that economic equality among regions was a chimera, that if Newfoundlanders wanted to live well like British Columbians, they would have to leave their rock for Vancouver; people had to move to the jobs and resources, not the other way around.

If Canada was indeed a Garden of Eden, it needed its weeds pulled and the plot replanted to survive. And the first weeding should center on the federal government. The Commission's task force recommended a drastic downsizing of the bureaucracy, eliminating or amalgamating its multiple departments and agencies which, in total, far exceeded the number in the U.S. and British governments. Ottawa needed to do less and do it better, to spend smarter and encourage greater private-sector competitiveness. It needed to cut back on its costliest social welfare programs, from Unemployment Insurance to health care, and it needed to apply some common sense about paying social benefits to Canadians who didn't need them and providing social services gratis to those who could afford to pay for them. Universality was not one of the Ten Commandments.

As for the millions of dollars lost through the duplication of federal and provincial government programs, as well as interprovincial trade barriers, the task force moved to hasten the final elimination of the overlap and barriers, replacing the latter with a long-overdue economic union that would reduce the cost of interprovincial transactions and promote the free flow of goods and services. Beyond that, the task force called for more imaginative industrial development in the regions. Borrowing a page from Michael Porter, it proposed that governments stop subsidizing inefficient industries in a region, and, instead, reinforce established clusters of promising local industries. It urged the provinces to coordinate their technological and productive strengths, to forge strategic alliances among provincial utilities or medical centers, for example.

Business and industry, said the task force, needed recharging across the spectrum. First off, they had to alter their relationship with the government, insisting that Ottawa no longer substitute federal programs for private-sector initiatives, that it scale back such traditional aids to industry as subsidies and guaranteed procurement. Also, it was past time for industry to develop global strategies; 70 percent of Canada's manufacturers served no export markets. The task force plan called for business and industry to devise a strategy that would double the number of exporting firms in order to capture a larger share of global trade and investment. Other parts of the plan exhorted the private sector to join with government in financing the start-up of more medium-sized, technology-driven businesses geared to producing "niche" or specialty products for export, from automobile accessories to surgical instruments. Above all, business needed far more inspired productivity and marketing. All too uncommon

in business circles was the kind of scene that occurred at one 1992 conference of executives in Montreal when the newly introduced conference
chairman, a food and candy CEO, trotted to the rostrum, lugging bags of
chocolate bars and packaged cheese which he proceeded happily to hawk
in lieu of delivering a welcoming speech.

The task force reserved special attention for the problems of Canada's
debt, its unemployed, and its shortcomings in research and development.

The forecast was for continued large welfare rolls because so many
jobs had been permanently lost during the recession of the early nineties,
when companies not only cut production but closed down. In Ontario
alone, government figures had shown that more than 60 percent of laid-
off employees had worked for companies that no longer existed. One of
the task force proposals mandated that a substantial portion of the savings, incurred through downsizing the federal government, be funneled
into a pool whose funds would underwrite a long-term program to create
jobs and retrain the unemployed. The task force also proposed new initiatives to fill the gaps in research and development, science education, and
technological training. Among them: a concerted effort to expand the
use of information technologies by annually increasing the number of
computers and software in schools; an interprovincial campaign to coordinate national education standards for more effective testing and evalua-
tion of students' skills; and a program of actively involving businesses at
the postgraduate level to ensure that research and training at university
centers was more relevant to commercial needs. The task force unanimously recommended draconian measures to reduce the national debt and
consequent high interest rates: the amount of federal and provincial debt
allowed would be limited to each government's capacity to service its
debt; a constitutional limit would be placed on the level of indebtedness.

Two years later, as the economic task force wound up its deliberations
in Toronto, it concluded that unless action was taken on its proposals,
Canada was fated for even more fragmentation. The economy in its present state was not sustainable, a condition that endangered the sustainabil-
ity of the nation itself.

The National Commission's political task force, which convened later
in 1996, faced a more potentially explosive challenge in designing the

reconfederation of Canada: how to fix the nation's shaky political power grid without blowing out the whole system.

Power flowed from Ottawa to the regions through a complex of grid lines bearing federal transfer payments, social and health services, development programs and authorizations for this or that local initiative. Of late, the grid lines had gotten scrambled, thanks to a power overload caused by conflicting federal and provincial signals. A radical overhaul of the system might save it from a disastrous flameout. It also risked severing delicate transmission nerves and weakening the system beyond repair. The task force engineers faced the unpleasant job of performing on Canada what they dubbed the "Humpty-Dumpty" option, breaking up the national grid, then reassembling it along different lines. It was that, or let the whole system—and nation—sputter out completely.

Canada was clearly overgoverned and undermanaged. In the climate of the task force's deliberations, some devolution of federal powers seemed inevitable, even acceptable. National unity, for many Canadians, had come to seem more a disposable abstraction when compared to the dismal reality of Big Brother in Ottawa. Unlike Americans, Canadians didn't necessarily see themselves as one people; they felt uneasy with the compelling undertones of the U.S. Constitution with its "We, the people" striving for "a more perfect union." The big resource-rich provinces of Canada had come to regard themselves as virtual nation-states within confederation, forever clashing with a federal government unable to satisfy their varied economic needs. Ottawa, they felt, had turned the original intention of federation on its ear by commandeering taxing powers that had formerly belonged to the provinces, then consolidating its control and imposing uniformity across the board. The provinces were only turning the clock back to its right position: it was time to return responsibility and accountability closer to the people. The centrifugal forces militating for a reconstituted Canada, thus, had logic and historical plausibility on their side.

Having agreed that the current federal-provincial structure had outlived its effectiveness, the task force confronted two basic choices for reassembling it: Either reconfigure the Canadian federation into a community of regional states, or decentralize it.

The first option appeared the easiest to negotiate, a cleaner, more natural division of the country into five regional units: Quebec, Ontario, Canada West, Canada East, and the Territories / First Nations. Canada West would constitute a loose amalgam of wealthy Alberta and British Columbia, plus the ailing prairie provinces of Manitoba and Saskatchewan. Canada East would embrace the four Atlantic provinces. The Territories / First Nations would comprise the Yukon and Northwest territories, the huge region that was home to so many of Canada's Natives. Ontario and Quebec, unique in their size, influence, and cultures, qualified as separate regions. The brainchild in part of a university scholar, Thomas Courchene, the plan envisaged a Canada of the next century in which the regions would assume far greater powers than the old provinces, an association somewhere between the European Community model and Switzerland with its autonomous cantons. Ottawa would remain the seat of government, but confined to a relatively few responsibilities like foreign affairs, monetary policy, and maintenance of the economic union; it would transfer to the regions enough taxing authority to finance whatever powers the regions chose to exercise.

Canada as a confederation of quasi-sovereign regions, sharing common trade and social interests, had merit on several points: it signaled the abatement of regional bickering with Ottawa; it relieved the debt-burdened federal government from further transfer payments and costly development programs which the regions could administer more efficiently; and it represented an accepted model of governance already functioning in other parts of the world. When the regional concept had been first broached at a First Ministers conference in 1969 by the current premier of British Columbia, the unpredictable W. A. C. ("Wacky") Bennett, there'd been titters among his fellow premiers as Bennett unrolled a map of Canada with redrawn borders. He was almost laughed out of the conference. This time, at least, attention was paid.

The idea, however, did not bear up to close scrutiny. It turned out to be a prescription, in Canada's case, for potentially worse economic and political instability. Ottawa's capacity to aid the less fortunate regions would be curtailed, its expenditures by 1998 shrunk to below a fifth the size of total provincial expenditures; the impact would devastate the economies of Canada East and the prairie provinces. Regionalization would likely weaken the political party system by substituting for the federal Parliament a more diffused central authority run from the regions. With half as many political entities as before, and a marginalized federal government, the new federation would be subject to tensions arising from some regions seeking special trade advantages with the United States or among themselves: an Ontario-Quebec deal, say, that would rile Canada West. Nor would the First Nations, the Indians and Inuits, fit tidily into any one region. They would continue to agitate for self-government across the spectrum, just as Quebec would probably insist on retaining more areas of jurisdiction than the other regions.

The basic inequalities of regional Confederation—the combined population of Canada East, for example, was barely 24 percent of the population of Ontario—condemned it as a viable choice. In the end, the Commission's task force rejected the idea and turned full focus on the possibility of decentralization.

Many thought Canada was already halfway there. Some form or another of decentralization had been part of its history and psyche since shortly after its birth when Quebec and Ontario complained in the early 1890s about having to subsidize the poorer provinces, "the shreds and patches of Confederation." Marshall McLuhan in 1966 had heralded the coming of decentralization throughout the world and declared it wouldn't spell the end of Canada. The process had been helped along in the 1980s by such underlying trends as the information revolution, economic globalization, and, in Canada, the widespread fiscal crisis. From the Maritimes to British Columbia, the move toward fuller decentralization had growing appeal among Canadians disenchanted with Big Government. It seemed a relatively painless way to achieve a better-coordinated distribution of powers between the two levels of government. The key challenge was always how much power Ottawa could afford to surrender without sacrificing the core revenue and authority it required to govern effectively.

Quebec, for its own designs, was happier if Ottawa could *not* govern effectively, and was therefore one of the strongest advocates of decentralization. The province's governing Liberal Party in 1991 had adopted a report recommending such a massive shift of powers to the provinces that the federal government would have been left with few sole jurisdictions other than defense, criminal justice, customs and tariffs, management of the debt, and the nation's waterways. Five years later, Quebec's emissaries were back at the bargaining table, demanding the transfer from Ottawa of exclusive jurisdictions in a range of areas from communications to urban affairs, a sort of "Charlottetown-plus." Quebec had no need to browbeat the task force members—separation was always the implicit threat if Ottawa and English Canada hung tough—and, in this case, Quebec had allies everywhere to help champion its cause: decentralization was Canada's panacea of the decade.

No need to redraw the map and tribalize the country into separate regions; it was simply a matter of switching grid lines and readjusting the power flows. Anywhere from a quarter to a third of all federal spending could be shifted to the provinces, it was estimated, and the result would be manifold efficiencies, cost savings, and the prospect of a more market-sensitive federation. Provincial and local governments, after all, were closer to their market areas, able to adjust their commercial policies faster and with more savvy. Devolution, according to a key study, would tighten the link between voters and the tax-and-spend process, thereby enhancing political accountability at both levels of government. One enthusiastic decentralizer wanted to jump ahead with more direct action. "If they dropped a bomb on Ottawa tomorrow," said a former anglo business journalist, "it would free Canada from its federal government, which it doesn't need, and liberate the provinces to flourish on their own."

A number of the larger provinces urged the task force to recommend that Ottawa grant them expanded taxing powers, more control over natural resources and immigration, and more autonomy in the field of culture and communications. The provinces wanted their own say on the disposition of income security (pensions, family benefits), on health care delivery, environmental policy, and labor manpower training. Less immediately, they wanted exclusive authority in the areas of housing, urban affairs, mining, forestry, recreation, and tourism, the so-called "six sisters" that the federal government was actually not all that loath to part with.

In December 1998, the political task force submitted to its parent commission a report which recommended turning over to the provinces most of the important federal powers they had sought, except for communications and cultural policies. In Ottawa's eyes, those were vital to a perception of national cohesion. The report spelled out clearly the primacy of the provinces in specific areas. It recommended certain financial and power-sharing guarantees for the weaker provinces, and it included a carefully hedged proposal for granting more autonomy to Canada's aboriginals. The report managed to do all this without so much as a hint of the months of billingsgate and table-pounding that had attended the controversial deliberations. The task force's final vote tally on the report was not published, nor were any dissenting views recorded. The report never once openly stated in plain language its decision to decentralize the nation. It never even mentioned the "d" word.

In May 1999, amid nationwide preparations to celebrate the new millennium, the National Commission to Rebuild Canada approved the reports of both its task forces, then solemnly announced them to the press and media.

The ensuing firestorm built slowly, but when it reached full intensity a month later in the black-fly heat of early summer, Canada knew its last try for nationhood had been a dreadful miscalculation. What conventional wisdom and the polls had recorded did not begin to reflect the hidden depths of emotion so many Canadians felt about the basic integrity of their government. The dryly confident analyses of economists and academics had overlooked the raw fears of countless citizens who relied upon the security of Ottawa's aid and protection.

Within forty-eight hours of its nationally televised press conference, the National Commission to Rebuild Canada was buried under an avalanche of phone calls, faxes, and telegrams—sixty thousand or more—from every corner of the country. The vast preponderance deplored the recommendations of the task forces. The opposition was directed mostly at the political report and its thinly veiled call for decentralization. From the six "have not" provinces of the Atlantics and Prairies came a swell of angry reaction damning the Commission for a report that in effect condemned Canada to "death from a thousand cuts," as one Newfoundland editor put it. In Manitoba, the leader of the provincial Liberal Party foresaw a nation so decentralized that no national political will would be left—"and when there's no political will," she warned, "there's no nation."

The proposed changes were faulted for endangering the success of the economic union long sought by economists and the federal government. Decentralization of Ottawa's powers would lead to wide disparities in the standards and quality of public services, it was charged. The federal government's diminished role in transferring payments and taxing income would effectively end its function as mediator of equity among Canadians; it would undermine its longstanding ability to smooth out distortions and stabilize the economy. As the richer provinces assumed more jurisdictional powers, they would insist on more taxing authority to administer those powers. That would lead to a decrease in the federal government's tax revenues which, in turn, comprised the pool of transfer payments bound for the poorer provinces. Ottawa would be reduced to little more than a central post office for distributing fewer and fewer funds. That specter chilled not only workers and elderly people in most of the provinces, but also the country's labor unions and their political parent, the New Democratic Party. Their voices had not prevailed in the closed-door deliberations of the task force, but now Labor and the NDP vented their concerns openly.

They were joined by leaders of the First Nations, who realized belatedly that a strong, cohesive federal government, not near-autonomous provinces with their own agendas, would more likely honor treaty commitments to the Natives. Canada's sizable corps of nationalists, led by the activist Council of Canadians, turned their energies from berating the Free Trade Agreement to assaulting decentralization as the ultimate vehicle of Canada's destruction. Even the usually passive business community, alerted by the Canadian Manufacturers Association and the prestigious Business Council on National Issues, took up cudgels against the decentralization plan: under it, businesses would have to cope with a whole clutch of bureaucratic decisions levied by all levels of government. It even dawned on some of the larger provinces that a decentralized Canada would not fare that well in international transactions. As a former Canadian Ambassador to Washington warned, "You don't have to be a rocket scientist to figure out what kind of leverage Alberta would have in winning a trade dispute on its own with the United States."

Newspaper pundits and the foreign press inveighed against the conclusions of the National Commission. Canada, advised *The Economist,* would become the first post-modern nation-state "with a weak centre acting as a kind of holding company" for a few limited federal activities. The thrust of editorial comment was that while decentralization might suck out the poison in federal-provincial relations, relieving the nation temporarily, it would do little to strengthen and preserve Canada for the long haul. The liberated provinces would soon discover they had far fewer shared concerns than differences. In a basically cohesive nation like the United States, decentralization of political authority might work. In a fragmented nation like Canada, it was a prescription for ruin.

The political outcry reduced the Commission's economic report to secondary billing, eventually entombing it in a standing committee of the

House of Commons. There was no sense debating its sensible but tough measures in the middle of the storm over decentralization. It was becoming clear, as well, that many Canadians would continue to resist the economic medicine they needed, that within the federal bureaucracy there was insufficient energy and will to undertake serious economic renewal unless the full blaze of parliamentary and media attention forced action. But that blaze was now consuming the political arena, fanned by the hot winds of five contentious parliamentary parties. And in the midst of the tumult raged the representatives of French Quebec, maddened that their strategy to weaken and wrest more power from Ottawa via devolution-for-all had backfired.

With rotating teams of speakers, the fifty-four-member caucus of the Bloc Québécois tried to commandeer the crucial debate on reconfederation that summer in the House of Commons. Through the steamy months, as the debate ground on and Members' vacation plans evaporated, Quebec's MPs, along with a posse of die-hard westerners, pushed all the buttons, from impassioned filibusters to blustery threats, to persuade Parliament of the virtues of decentralizing. As their momentum ebbed, the debate took on cooler tones of desperation. The Bloc Québécois moved from defending mass devolution to making one final lunge for power on behalf of Quebec. All the old, previously rejected demands were methodically retabled: recognition of Quebec as a distinct society, the right of a constitutional veto, special powers to preserve the francophone culture. It was as if Quebec wished to record for posterity one last time, in detail, its accumulated rejections—testimony that might be offered in a future court of world opinion when Quebec was asked why it had deserted Confederation. The spate of eleventh-hour demands met an icewall of silence in the House.

At that point the debate crossed the line from rejection to a last attempt to salvage some shred of comity, to avoid if possible an ugly exit scene. But even the separatists' silken re-argument for sovereignty association between Quebec and Ottawa collapsed amidst snickers from the anglophone benches. Canada, the Prime Minister affirmed from the well of the House, would not be treated as "a cafeteria" from which Quebec could pick the choicest economic dishes while ignoring the less appetizing political ones. Sovereignty association was a non-starter, the House declared in a raucous voice vote, as the packed galleries cheered. And that was it. The members of the Bloc Québécois caucus rose from the benches as one and filed grimly from the chamber. Anglophone MPs, shocked by the suddenness of the debate's end, sat mute and deflated in their seats. Outside the chamber, a Bloc Québécois strategist sucked quietly on a Gaulloise. "Eh bien, c'est dommage," he said to no one in particular. "Now Quebec must act on its own."

The following day, a clear September Friday, the stillborn report of the National Commission to Rebuild Canada was sent to the parliamentary printer to be enshrined and forgotten in a green leatherbound volume of some 1,200 pages. As scores of MPs departed for delayed vacations at lakeside cottages in the Gatineau Hills or in fishing camps along the trout streams of New Brunswick and Alberta, the government of Quebec announced it would immediately launch a debate on the sovereignty issue in its National Assembly, to be followed by a provincewide referendum. A cold front of resignation moved across the land. In Quebec's francophone media, the defeat of the reconfederation package was judged to be the final repudiation of sanity by English Canada, the jeering dismissal by Parliament of Quebec's demands the crowning humiliation. Rejecting sovereignty association, *La Presse* snapped, was tantamount to saying that English Canada no longer needed Quebec's market. Rejecting the proposed restructure of Canada's economy virtually assured that the global economic community would soon pass Canada by. There was no future left for Quebec in Confederation; like Garbo, it wanted to be alone. The National Assembly had already begun drafting a declaration of sovereignty in anticipation of the debate's outcome. Canada, as Charles de Gaulle once said of France when it suffered through a barren patch of history, was "crossing the desert."

The debate began October 1 and was over in three weeks. It could have been over much sooner, given the damn-and-be-done-with-it attitude of most of the 125 members of the National Assembly. But protocol for so historic a proceeding mandated formal elaboration of the passage from province to nation, a minuet appropriate to the self-esteem of the Assembly. Inside the turreted Assembly building, in the Renaissance-style chamber with its blue carpeting, the President from his paneled throne solemnly reavowed the principles of sovereignty: Quebec's right of self-determination, its authority to impose its own laws, levy its own taxes, ratify its own international treaties, retain its current borders. The last was a *cri de défiance* against any attempt to redraw Quebec's northern borders on behalf of its secessionist Natives. Legal preparations were necessary to transfer to the Assembly all federal jurisdictions and powers applicable to Quebec, ending the Canadian Constitution's sway within the province. A Quebec constitution would be drafted for the new state.

What debate there was halfheartedly addressed the financial costs of separation. Those would be worked out later in negotiations between Ottawa and Quebec, although it was assumed that a sovereign Quebec would right off face up to $150 billion in public debt, including its share of the federal government's indebtedness plus what monies the province already owed; and there were other hidden costs and liabilities Quebec might have to assume. The doubters in the Assembly gradually subsided. Government whips acknowledged the high costs, but argued convincingly that a sovereign Quebec would no longer have to help subsidize Canada's poorer provinces or pay its share of interest on the national debt. Quebec's tax revenues henceforth would be used solely for its own benefit.

On October 22, the National Assembly unanimously approved the standing order for Quebec's sovereignty and declared the province officially independent. The declaration would be formally ratified five months after a referendum had been held to confirm it. The referendum was set for the following January 1, the first day of the new millennium.

In the interim, English Canada and the international community wrung their hands in the media. There were warnings that Quebec's unilateral declaration of independence (UDI) invited a free fall of the Canadian dollar that even 35 percent interest rates would not arrest. There would be panic among international investors unsure about Canada's ability, without Quebec, to pay the interest on its debt, a quarter of which was held abroad. Legal scholars pointed out there was no constitutional provision for UDI, that there could be no lawful secession without the federal Parliament's consent: Quebec's action was, in effect, treason.

It was the kind of bald secession, one editor wrote, that would bring such federal retribution down on Quebec—trade sanctions followed by a series of shutdowns of federal facilities—that the breakaway province would be on its knees within days. There were the usual drumrolls about civil war. *National Geographic* reprinted an open letter, written by its editor a quarter century before, in which he prayed the day would never come when "a Canadian prime minister must decide, as Abraham Lincoln had to do, whether to preserve a country by force of arms." The response from Quebec was not reassuring. One separatist spokesman suggested that the first thing a sovereign Quebec should do would be to sink a ship in the middle of the St. Lawrence channel, cutting off passage to Toronto as well as to Detroit and Chicago.

In Washington, where Quebec emissaries had tried for years to establish a back-channel relationship with U.S. officials, the State Department kept a respectful distance from any new attempts by the renegade province to get prematurely chummy. The United States still held out hope for a last-minute reconciliation in Canada. Aware that the quickest way to unite Canadians was to threaten them, some officials briefly considered issuing a statement warning that the political crisis to the north constituted a threat to North America's general stability. In U.S. border communities the apprehension was palpable. Plattsburgh's *Press-Republican* newspaper warned that the local retail market, 40 percent of which was comprised of Montreal shoppers, would be "sliced and diced" if Quebec's post-separation economy floundered under the weight of transition costs. At the same time, some bankers and realtors reported an upsurge in inquiries from Quebecers about moving investment funds south to banks in Plattsburgh and Massena, New York, or relocating small businesses across the border within commuting distance of Montreal.

The investment community moved smartly to offset any losses resulting from Quebec's departure. Canadian Bond Rating Service, an agency based in Montreal, placed Quebec's treasury bills, debentures, and loan guarantees, as well as billions of dollars in Hydro-Québec bonds, on credit watch. Japanese institutional investors prepared to cut by one quarter the 15 percent share of their portfolios made up of Canadian bonds. In New York, Merrill Lynch's Debt Markets Group got ready to join other U.S. investment majors in a widespread sell-off of a sizable piece of the Quebec government debt held by foreigners, mostly Americans. The Quebec-U.S. bond spreads had begun to widen markedly, enticing investors to cash in. Over the next two months, $3.5 billion worth of Quebec bonds and cash investments were unloaded. The market, at least, had discounted the impact of the coming referendum.

The results of the referendum on January 1, 2000 were surprising only in the magnitude of the pro-sovereignty vote: nearly 80 percent of the 4 million votes cast. For the next five months a select committee of the

National Assembly labored over a dozen or more drafts of the proposed constitution before signing off on the document that would guide the new nation to maturity.

On June 1, 2000, at a glittering night session in the gilded Assembly chamber, the government of Quebec formally ratified the results of the referendum and approved its new constitution. The ceremony, conducted solely in French, was attended by representatives from some sixty nations, among them the approving heads of state of the world's other francophone countries. A cluster of ill-at-ease junior envoys from Ottawa, London, and Washington, D.C., observed the proceedings from a far corner of the newly installed Diplomatic Gallery at the rear of the chamber. As the president pronounced Quebec officially the world's newest independent nation, members of the Assembly, perspiring under the glare of the television lights and chandeliers, pounded their oakwood desks in a delirium of joy. One of them, carried away by the moment, grabbed the fleur-de-lis flag flanking the president's throne and held it aloft, waving it in rhythm to the desk-pounding and chants of "Vive le Québec libre!"

Next day, the moving vans lumbered down the streets of Westmount and into the anglophone townships east of Montreal. In the border towns of Ontario, New York State, and Vermont, banks reported a shortage of safety deposit boxes for the personal savings, heirlooms, and jewelry of thousands of Quebecers fearful for their future.

"As a general rule, a newcomer should not make a noisy entrance."

—Louis Balthazar,
Professor,
Université Laval, Quebec

"Once you take a slice out of the heart of the country . . . and it finally dawns on people the enormity of what has been done, then all kinds of passions are unleashed."

—Prime Minister Brian Mulroney,
CBC-TV interview,
December 1991

"Once things start to come apart, they move very quickly. Events take on a life and character of their own. The unraveling moves fast and unpredictably."

—Gordon Ritchie,
former federal official

5

Adieu, Québec: Bitter End of the Dream

Three weeks later, on June 24, 2000, the date of the annual St. Jean Baptiste *fête nationale* honoring their patron saint, the French-speaking citizens of sovereign Quebec uncorked the greatest celebration in their history.

The impact of Quebec's separation on the rest of the country had been not one of relief, but of profound shock. Canadians had dared the unthinkable to happen, and when it did, millions of them had trouble accepting the enormity of it. They felt psychologically bereft, then betrayed, then in time deeply resentful at what they had lost. The exuberant partying across Quebec that June day only fed their resentment.

From the crowded ramparts of old Quebec City a joyous, full-throated roaring swept across the waters below where a score of tall ships—replicas of Cartier's fleet that had sailed up the St. Lawrence four centuries earlier—paraded down the narrows under a flawless summer sky, their canvas billowing, deck cannons thundering in triumph. On the Plains of Abraham, celebrants prepared to light the traditional giant "bonfire of joy." From Trois Rivières to the Gaspé, fleur-de-lis pennons fluttered from every housetop. In the churches, special masses were offered in honor of independence and St. Jean, in that order. In the town squares people joined hands, then sang and wept their way through the stirring verses of *"Gens de Mon Pays."* Some, filled with cheap booze and old rancors, belligerently cheered on public burnings of the Maple Leaf.

Montreal hosted the mother of all blowouts. Jubilant thousands thronged the streets, chanting: "Un pays! Un pays!" Organizers of the festive picnic in Jarry Park that noon dispensed four tons of shrimp and Magdalen Islands lobster, along with pork brochettes, corn on the cob, and thirty thousand slices of pizza. Surfeited, the crowd of one hundred thousand or more swarmed from the park and down the three-mile stretch of Rue St. Denis, where they jammed the sidewalks and cafés as the parade got under way. Hundreds of fleur-de-lis banners and blue balloons trailed from windows beneath the mansard roofs of the small stone houses and shops. At the intersection of St. Denis and Sherbrooke Street East, where French Montreal begins, cheering celebrants overflowed the balconies of apartment buildings. The fleur-de-lis was everywhere, emblazoned on a million T-shirts, spray-painted on the thighs of teenage girls, the theme even of an aerial billboard borne by a quartet of sky divers floating above the multitudes. The parade, a grand swirl of costumes, bands, and floats, swept by. Then suddenly the clangor ceased and the street became a surging sea of blue. Thousands of *péquistes* and union workers, holding aloft tiny blue-and-white flags, filled the way, their ranks swelled by a ragtag army of other marchers: chattering housewives with babies in strollers, young lovers arm-in-arm, one-legged men in wheelchairs, rheumy-eyed *anciens* who had dreamed as boys of this day. It seemed as though all of French Quebec was marching.

That evening, as fireworks exploded over Mount Royal, the new nation's first Prime Minister, a graying Lucien Bouchard, delivered an uncharacteristically somber inaugural address from the balcony of City Hall in Montreal's historic old sector. Thirty-three years before, from the same balcony, Charles de Gaulle had electrified the audience with his bumbling call for a "free Quebec." On this night, the immensity of what Quebec had done seemed to sober many in the huge crowd listening to Bouchard. It was as if they and he understood that the end of Quebec's history of humiliations also marked the beginning of an uncertain new chronicle in which the opening chapter promised few rainbows.

Across Montreal, that June day, in the city's English-speaking districts, a different somberness pervaded the shops and boardrooms, the fastnesses of Westmount. Those who had not joined the initial anglophone exodus kept to their homes and television sets, bystanders transfixed by the spectacle in Outremont and City Hall, so stunned and dispirited that even the expectation of Canada Day a week hence, Canada's annual two-cheers-and-a-pint for nationhood, held little prospect for a happier mood.

It would be months before the full impact of Quebec's withdrawal could be assessed. For now, it was clear that Canada had lost its most culturally distinctive province and more than a quarter of its tax base. Financial markets remained relatively calm, although major investment decisions regarding Quebec were postponed indefinitely. In the period of uncertainty ahead, Canada could anticipate either increasingly higher interest rates or a flight of foreign investment funds. Both parties, Canada and Quebec, could anticipate turmoil in the transition period: new treaties and defense arrangements had to be negotiated, legal authority reallocated in the courts of Quebec, the transferral of thousands of mostly francophone federal workers in Ottawa and Quebec worked out.

It was equally clear that once the partying had stopped, Quebecers faced infinitely more pain than just their hangovers. In addition to assuming a share of Canada's federal debt and paying off its old provincial debt, Quebec would have to take over at some point Ottawa's Social Security and pension payments to Quebecers; further, it would be held liable for a range of damages and compensation to individuals and companies financially stricken by Quebec's separation. The total transition cost to Quebec would, by some estimates, reduce its economy as much as 10 percent in the short run, 3 to 5 percent over the longer term.

Quebec's fall from grace in the international markets would compound the cost. For months before the final act of separation, the markets had been penalizing the Quebec government as a borrower, forcing it to pay a higher premium on its bonds. That, plus the reluctance of investors to finance new enterprises in Quebec, spelled an outflow of dollars and potential jobs that could only stunt the new nation's economic growth. Quebec stood to forfeit more revenues and jobs if Canadian financial institutions pulled their head offices out of Montreal—top executives, after all, didn't usually reside in a foreign country—or resident foreign subsidiaries left because sovereign Quebec didn't constitute a big enough market for them.

Quebec's weak, labor-intensive dairy and textile industries, traditionally subsidized by Ottawa, would force the new nation either to continue the costly subsidies on its own or to drastically rationalize the industries and absorb the costs of thousands of unemployed workers. Other job losses would occur in the shakeout of the federal civil service, the military, and imperiled local resource industries like pulp and paper manufacturing. Nor would there be any more higher-than-average unemployment benefits from Ottawa to soften the blow of Quebec's higher-than-average unemployment. Quebec could rely henceforth on no further payments whatsoever from Ottawa and the richer provinces. Quebec had always been a net recipient of the rest of Canada's largesse, paying less in federal taxes than what it got back in benefits. When the paymaster in Ottawa had reduced those benefits in the lean decades of the eighties and nineties, Quebec had considered leaving. Now it had to pay its own way.

Quebecers would have to adjust to paying far higher income taxes than they were used to, as much as a 30 percent increase across the board, in order to maintain the level of services they had enjoyed under Confederation and to compensate for the loss of federal payments. They could also expect steep rises in their phone rates, gasoline prices, and in other areas where Quebec had previously shared costs with other provinces. All this, before they had even sat down to negotiate the terms of the divorce settlement.

That was almost bound to be a messy affair. Too many loose ends had been left hanging before Quebec finally slammed the door.

Both sides knew beforehand that the division of debts and assets and territorial jurisdictions would be fiercely contested, that there would be fights over the issues of currency and the free movement of goods and services between the two countries. No one underestimated the atmosphere of revenge and bloody-mindedness. No one, however, had fully gauged the complexities, the difficulties in even defining the issues, let alone agreeing on the logistics of the negotiations. It took two months just to decide the makeup of the negotiating teams and to agree that they would meet, in alternate months, in Ottawa's Conference Center or in a suite of rooms in Quebec City's hulking Château Frontenac. The talks began early in August.

When it came to assigning Quebec's debt obligations, the negotiators dumped the Kiss Principle ("Keep it simple, stupid") and promptly fell to wrangling over which formula should apply to Quebec's portion of the Canadian public debt. The formulas ranged from Quebec's share of the value of federal facilities inside its borders (18%) to its share of Canada's gross domestic product (22%). Quebec's starting position was the 18 percent formula, unacceptable to Canada, which insisted Quebec should be responsible for a figure equal to its portion of Canada's population (26%). That obligation, if accepted, would have amounted to nearly $100 billion. Coupled with Quebec's $40 billion provincial debt and another $60 billion owed for the expansion of Hydro-Québec's vast facilities at James Bay, the total debt of $200 billion would have forced Quebec into crippling interest payments and deficits from the start.

Sovereign Quebec had no legal obligation to assume any part of Canada's debt, as its negotiators pointed out at the start of the talks. It risked censure and loss of credibility in the international markets, however, if it failed to pay an appropriate share. More immediately, if Quebec refused or dragged its feet, Ottawa might threaten to renege on its debts to individuals and institutions in Quebec. The trump cards were not on Quebec's side, but neither would it accept a suicidal debt share. The talks proved a bitterly frustrating exercise for both sides.

How to dispose of Canada's federal assets in Quebec was even more snarled an issue, involving everything from government office buildings to more than 125,000 square miles of federal lands. There were financial assets like bank deposits, circulating currency, and the big Crown corporations; and non-financial assets like airports, bridges, highways, military installations, and government research laboratories. There was valuable real estate like national parks and the St. Lawrence Seaway which cut through lower Quebec. There were "movables" like Coast Guard vessels, Canadian National Railway locomotives, and Air Canada jetliners. The whole pot was worth anywhere from $5 billion to $25 billion, according to which estimate best suited the interests of the adversaries.

Quebec's approximate stance was: We'll take it all. According to international law, its negotiators argued, Quebec automatically, and without compensation, became the owner of all federal assets on its soil the moment it became sovereign. If that wasn't acceptable to Canada, Quebec would assume a share of the assets equal to its quarter share of Canada's population. If that didn't fly, at the very least it should take over the properties of all Crown corporations operating exclusively in Quebec.

The Canadian negotiators listened with mounting incredulity.

The currency issue, Swahili to most folk, involved matters of sovereign power and survival that made these talks as emotional as any. Quebec might one day issue its own paper *louis,* but for now it sought the security of its traditional currency, the Canadian dollar. Quebec argued it should wield full power over financial institutions inside its borders, but share a common currency with the federation it had deserted and, by extension, share control of Canada's central bank and the formulation of monetary policy. Once on its feet, the new nation could print its own currency, pegged to the U.S. dollar, a move which might destabilize the Canadian dollar, among other things. The Canadians' disbelief turned to anger: once again, it was coldly stated, there would be no sovereignty association, no monetary union. Quebec could use up its existing Canadian currency, then stew in its own *louis.*

While the divorce talks stuttered along, Quebec's two established minorities, its anglophones and aboriginals, pondered a grim future. Both peoples feared the vitiation of their cultures under a sovereign francophone regime; both now harbored secessionist dreams of their own.

Quebec's remaining 600,000 anglophones were already a community in decline, their numbers continuing to drop substantially each year with little hope of replenishment; the authorities, to protect the French culture, had sharply limited immigration by anglophones from other parts of Canada. The irreversible decline was the product of a falling birth rate, a heavily aging population, and the departure of thousands of young anglophones over the years. In the early 1990s, more than 40 percent of the 18-to-24-year-olds had told poll takers they didn't expect to be living in Quebec by the millennium. Now, the remaining anglos saw more of their elementary and secondary schools closing doors for the last time, the institutions they'd founded—from McGill University to Montreal's Museum of Fine Arts—francisized or fading from lack of financial support.

A decade earlier, after separatism had gained respect following the Meech Lake debacle, a few English Canadians had impolitely suggested that Quebec would come to be regarded as "an enemy" after secession. That feeling became prevalent in the late months of the year 2000. In Alberta, the gas companies agreed to slap an extra duty above the world price level on the natural gas they piped to Quebec. Some of Quebec's export goods got a rough reception in anglophone stores, like the costumed Québécois dolls that ended up in broken pieces. In the West, bilingual cereal boxes were knocked off market shelves. Quebec's anglos feared that the ruling francophones would be even more dismissive of their rights, especially language rights. Some anglo communities that had long enjoyed exemptions from Quebec's language laws braced themselves for harsh new restrictions as their population numbers slipped. In Quebec's principal English-speaking regions—western Montreal, the Eastern Townships, and the Ottawa Valley—there was serious talk of seceding and carving a new Canadian province out of southwestern Quebec. The people of these regions had voted overwhelmingly in the referendum against sovereignty and for the right to remain in Canada. Now, their leaders said, they would follow the example of West Virginia, which in 1861 had elected to peel off from its parent state and stay with the Union when Virginia joined the Confederacy. The government in Quebec City dismissed such talk, curtly reminding the anglophone minority that it did not constitute a "nation" and that only "nations" had the right to leave a sovereign country.

This was news to the aboriginal nations of Quebec, especially to the Crees in the northern two thirds of the country, and to the dominant Mohawks who inhabited the peripheries of the Montreal region. Quebec's 62,000 aborigals had no interest in separating from a Canada whose government had at least tried to make amends for past faults. There was little rapport between the Natives and the non-Native people of Quebec. Aboriginals had difficulty with the French language; most preferred to speak English. Quebecers gave Native issues a low priority, generally believing the tribes got too much aid from the federal government. A strain of casual racism colored parts of Quebec society. For years, one of the National Assembly building's entrances, near which stood an artwork depicting a traditional Indian family, had been routinely referred to as "la porte du sauvage."

Resentment of Quebec's Natives had built up over the past decade. A Manitoban Indian leader's eleventh-hour tactics helped derail the Meech Lake Accord which Quebec had championed. Native demands had preempted those of Quebec's during the Charlottetown negotiations. The violent stand-off at Oka in 1990, between Mohawk warriors and Quebec's provincial police, had cast local authorities in an unfavorable light and deeply embarrassed Quebecers. Later, the blocking by Crees of Hydro-Québec's expansion at James Bay in northern Quebec had pricked Quebecers' pride in their showcase state enterprise and cost Quebec's undernourished workforce thousands of new construction jobs. Ever since Oka and the collapse of the Charlottetown Accord, frustrated Natives had peppered Quebec and the rest of Canada with highway blockades and ugly confrontations. The situation in Quebec's Mohawk reserves along the Canada-U.S. border had deteriorated; increased arms and drug smuggling had made them powder kegs ready to explode at the first serious provocation. Now, in the wake of sovereignty, the Natives were not only pressing their right to secede from Quebec and rejoin Canada, but insisting that history and law favored their claim that the northern lands should go with them.

The issue of redrawing Quebec's boundaries was provocative but not grounds in most cases for urgent discussion. Quebec's anglophones had a marginal case at best for forming a new province. The demand by some elements in Canada for a land corridor south of the St. Lawrence that would connect Ontario to the Maritimes was strictly back-burner; so was Quebec's claim to Labrador, the forbidding landmass it had held before the Conquest and which Britain had finally awarded Newfoundland in 1927. The border dispute affecting the Native territories of northern Quebec, however, was an altogether different issue: the lands in question— some 410,000 square miles, or about two thirds the size of Alaska—were not Quebec's by historic right.

The so-called "Ungava Territory," first settled by aboriginals, had been part of the vast northern Rupert's Land that was operated for two hundred years by the Hudson's Bay Company under Britain's aegis until 1870, when Canada bought it. The Ungava Territory was transferred to Quebec in 1912 with the clear assumption that Quebec would remain a province. A sovereign Quebec now, the Natives argued, was bound to return Ungava to Canada. The territory had not been part of the Confederation bargain, and now that that bargain had been abrogated by Quebec, Canada had the right to resume jurisdiction. To Quebec, the idea that its seventeen thousand Crees and Inuits could pack up and take two thirds of its territory with them was preposterous. The issue was non-negotiable.

The underlying reason was the crucial Hydro-Québec facility at James Bay. If Hydro-Québec was the linchpin of Quebec's economy, generating 95 percent of the country's electrical power, its sprawling complex in the

La Grande River basin near James Bay was the jewel of the company's operations. La Grande's drainage basin, more than twice the size of Switzerland, contained the world's fourth largest hydroelectric complex, and its three generating stations provided more than 10,000 megawatts of power.* (Six additional stations were slated to produce another 5,000 megawatts sometime before the year 2005.) James Bay provided a safe, clean, renewable source of energy to Quebec, and to much of New England and New York State, which found that buying Quebec's electricity was a good deal cheaper than building their own power plants. James Bay not only electrified Quebec City and Greater Montreal, but helped light up parts of Boston and Providence and keep air conditioners humming in Hartford and Manhattan. Under a long-term contract to make power available to America's Northeast during the summer months, Hydro-Québec accounted for nearly 10 percent of the region's combined electricity needs.

The cost of building the La Grande complex had been appropriately monumental. From the day in 1971 when Quebec's premier, Robert Bourassa, had announced the "project of the century," through the completion of its first phase thirteen years later, sixty-eight workers had died in construction accidents, and Hydro-Québec had run up debts totaling nearly $70 billion. More than fifteen thousand workers had labored to excavate five reservoirs, totaling in area the state of Connecticut; built more than forty miles of dams and dikes to divert three other rivers into La Grande; and blasted out what was billed as the largest underground power plant in the world, more than 400 feet down, a third of a mile long and large enough to accommodate two football fields. The fill used in the effort could have built the Great Pyramid of Cheops eighty times over.

From the start, the ten thousand Crees in the vicinity had opposed the project. They had lived, hunted, and fished in the valleys and kettle ponds and black-spruce forests of this sub-Arctic wilderness for five thousand years. They feared the consequences of so vast a technological disfiguring of their lands, a giant engineering experiment on an ecosystem thought to be comparable in importance to South America's rain forests. Early on, the authorities believed they had bought off the Crees and Inuits with a generous agreement in 1975, which gave the Natives a cash package that would eventually total $300 million, while granting them hunting

---

* A megawatt is a million watts, enough to light ten thousand 100-watt light bulbs.

and fishing rights to 29,000 square miles of land, an area nearly the size of England.

The Natives grudgingly signed the accord, ceded rights to most of the northern territory, saw their standard of living measurably improve in some respects, and watched their ancestral hunting lands disappear. As La Grande's reservoirs filled and the valleys became lakes, the habitats of beaver were flooded out. Rotting vegetation in the reservoirs released levels of mercury that poisoned the whitefish, pickerel, and lake trout that over centuries had become the main source of protein in the Crees' diet. The rivers which had been drained, diverted, and made to run backwards were no longer familiar to the migrating herds of caribou, ten thousand of which perished in the raging waters of one in 1984. Fears mounted that the ecological tinkering, the massive changes in water flow, would jeopardize the welfare of other creatures like shellfish, polar bears, and James Bay's ringed seals. Environmentalists predicted disaster. Meanwhile, dietary deficiencies, alcohol, and drug abuse ravaged the local Native communities. Then, Hydro-Québec announced further plans for an ambitious expansion of its James Bay facilities: the Great Whale Project.

In January 1992, Matthew Coon-Come, Chief of the Crees, journeyed 1,500 miles to New York City to protest the expansion before an audience of lawyers and environmentalists in the great hall of the city's Bar Association. The Natives had barely had time to heal their land from the impact of La Grande's first phase, he said, before this new multi-billion-dollar project was unveiled, promising more flooding and disfigurement. A few months after Coon-Come's eloquent cri de coeur, the state of New York canceled a $17 billion long-term contract with Hydro-Québec and the Massachusetts legislature tabled a bill prohibiting the investment of state workers' pension funds in Hydro-Québec bonds. Angry Quebecers blamed U.S. environmental lobbies, but targeted their real fury on the Natives for having beached Great Whale. The resentment festered over the next eight years, even after Great Whale had been resuscitated and the expansion rescheduled. By then, the desperate Crees were arming themselves with more than eloquence.

By April 2001, nine months after they had started, the negotiations in Ottawa and Quebec City had slowed to a crawl. They had settled into a

routine of nitpicking and bargaining ploys that resembled a Middle Eastern bazaar. Quebec refused to accept a share of the Canadian debt
exceeding 20 percent. The haggling over the division of assets had
become mired in technicalities; Canadian authorities refused to hand over
a number of federal installations until agreement had been secured. Quebec had not budged on the Ungava border issue, and some Canadians
were unwisely talking of unilaterally reasserting jurisdiction over the territory. The currency discussions, always sensitive, had become a suddenly compelling issue.

Quebec's separation had splintered the delicate Canadian financial system along both nations' borders, reducing the ability of banks and savings
institutions on either side to diversify their loan risks across what was
once the entire country. Canadian and Quebec regulatory agencies were
at odds. Money was seeping out of both countries, as investors wavered.
But Quebec stood to lose the most soonest. It held almost a quarter of
Canada's money supply, and much of it, particularly the smaller bills,
would shortly wear out. Only the Canadian government could replace the
old currency, and it was in no mood to do so. Sharing its currency and
monetary powers with Quebec would invite instant opposition from Canada's provinces; it was unrealistic to think the two nations could meet the
requirements of a shared currency by cooperating on public spending,
tax, and interest-rate policies. Without supervisory authority over Quebec, Canadian institutions were at risk if a major Quebec corporation or
industry went bankrupt without warning. Quebec continued to press its
case for a common currency, but refused to cede control of monetary
policy to Ottawa. Ottawa balked, and its negotiators warned that if Quebec persisted, Canada might recall its existing dollars in Quebec and
place restrictions on the export of Canadian currency. The negotiations
collapsed in an orgy of recrimination. Talk of Quebec's establishing an
independent currency began to leak out.

It was not the option Quebec had sought. A separate currency would
cost the new nation an estimated $1 billion a year and lead to further
disputes with Canada over exchange rates. Once the decision had been
forced on it, though, the *péquiste* government of Quebec plotted a high-
risk course to exploit its independent currency to the fullest. It prepared
to adopt its own devalued dollar, or *dollard,* and to address its first priority of full employment by deliberately invoking an easy-money policy.
At the same time, it decided to peg the *dollard* to the Canadian dollar at

a level that clearly favored Quebec's exports to Canada at the latter's expense, a move calculated to enrage the remaining provinces. In Quebec City there was some satisfaction gained from the spite; the consequences, however, were almost predictable. Foreign investors, skeptical of Quebec's new discounted currency and the effect of its planned policy of inflation on price stability, consulted their tea leaves, then acted. Over the next six weeks, before devaluation took effect, the investors withdrew several hundred millions of dollars from their Quebec accounts for redeposit in Canadian and U.S. institutions. Within a short time the liquidity reserves of Quebec's financial houses were exhausted, and the new nation faced a credit crunch that threatened to squash its economy before it had even gotten its legs.

The crash of the currency talks spread to the other negotiations. Differences over the amount of debt Quebec should assume had narrowed to a few points, but was stuck at about 21 percent, still too low for the Canadians, who finally, in disgust, called for a lengthy recess. The division of assets was far from resolved, as the negotiators fought over every specific facility and shard of real estate. There was no give on the northern border dispute; in mid-May, Cree and Inuit representatives stalked out of the talks and pledged they would boycott them indefinitely. In Quebec's francophone media a swelling chorus of commentators condemned the snail-paced negotiations, the mean-spiritedness of the Canadians; polls and letters to the editors reflected the growing frustration and anger of Québécois over the lack of progress. The Toronto newspapers and networks berated Quebec's have-our-cake-and-eat-it arrogance, the surrealism of its negotiating positions. In Quebec City the anger coursed through the chambers of the National Assembly and through the winding streets of the Old Town. It pulsated among the drinkers in the cafés along the Grande Allée, where one could hear the curses muttered against the anglos, against the Natives, against the greedy bureaucrats in Ottawa. Against the whole damn conspiracy to undo the achievement of Quebec's independence.

By late May the divorce talks had lapsed into the ugly slanging of mediators who sense failure. It was at that point that all the old warnings about Canada's twin linguistic minorities, the anglophones of Quebec and the francophones of greater Canada, came into agonizing play. The Canadian historian Desmond Morton had once called the existence of these hostage populations, so vulnerable to the intolerance of their majorities, the single most explosive element in Canada-Quebec relations. Now, the majorities threw caution to the winds.

Across Canada provincial legislatures, acting with Ottawa's unspoken assent, disbanded French-speaking services for francophone communities from Ontario to Alberta. What had once been a gesture of inclusiveness toward Canada's francophones was now regarded as an obsolete financial burden, unrequited by a Quebec no longer even *en famille*. In Quebec, the nightmare of every anglophone became reality. Maddened by the failure of the talks, by the economic misfortunes they ascribed to Ottawa's obduracy, by the rampant exodus of anglophones and their investments, Quebec's authorities called down a torrent of repressive new laws on the remaining anglos. First, they toughened the language laws of the workplace, forcing the smallest of anglophone businesses, those with as few as ten employees, to conduct their affairs in French. Then, they extended the directive to schools and universities, forbidding English to be spoken even in social discourse or at play. Finally, they began removing the rights of anglophones to receive English-language services in hospitals, banks, and other institutions. That was when the first whispers of violent retribution began to circulate.

In a country known for its international peacekeepers, citizens talked openly of public disorder escalating into civil strife. Violence was hardly a Canadian hallmark: less than a hundred persons had lost their lives in domestic political conflicts since Confederation. But violence in Canada had its own history replete with fatal riots, strike beatings, separatist bombings and kidnap murders, armed confrontations and blockades by angry Natives. Much of the violence in the previous century had occurred in Quebec, which twice in a twenty-five-year span had had to summon aid from the Canadian Armed Forces. Canada's reigning spectator sport, ice hockey, thrived on mayhem. Back in 1977, when the newly elected Parti Québécois was stirring the separatist pot to a boil, a classified U.S. State Department memorandum had warned of rash acts by radical factions in Quebec and noted that "The possibility exists for anglophone violence in the Montreal area as a reaction to new restrictive language laws." The *New York Times*'s James Reston did not rule out "the possibility of dismemberment of Canada or even civil war."

By late 1991 the issue had gained sufficient currency to merit warnings from at least one premier and a former commander of the Canadian Armed Forces. In Toronto, a conference of historians and academic strategists had coldly assessed the military implications of Quebec's separating. Armed conflict was not only possible but highly probable, one of the participants predicted. Another doubted the loyalty of French Canadian military units, which comprised more than a quarter of the federal forces. An American expert foresaw that the U.S. Army might have to come to the aid of Canada's depleted forces if they were unable to contain spreading violence in the aftermath of separation.

Ten years later, three conclusions were indisputable: Of the world's 21 million people who had died in violent conflicts since 1945, the great majority were victims of some form of nationalist struggle for independence. Civil war or strife was the norm when nations fractured. And Canadians and Quebecers had no rights to immunity.

In early June, the Canadian Armed Forces Command sent a special cable to all Canadian Forces headquarters in the country and abroad. The wording in parts was almost identical to that in a cable which had been sent a decade earlier by the Command at the height of the constitutional conflict: "The role of the Armed Forces will be a silent one. Our only involvement will be to assist the police and associate agencies in the maintenance of law and order, should that be necessary."

The silent role was appropriate to a military that had shrunk to barely 65,000 men and women by the year 2000 and which, in Quebec, was a federal asset already riven by doubts about competency and allegiance. The Regular Army forces numbered no more than 18,000 personnel—the Toronto-region police force had more men available—and the 80,000 or so federal reservists, or militiamen, were only marginally trained compared with, say, the U.S. National Guard. The problem was not just the weakened condition of the Canadian Forces; one senior officer said they were incapable of managing multiple and simultaneous internal threats. The whole question of loyalty—whether to Canada or to sovereign Quebec—permeated the French-speaking ranks of the military.

The issue was acute in Quebec, where the French Language Units of the Canadian Forces had become a self-contained organization that included a military college, two air bases, and most of Canada's mobilization stores, as well as 5,000 militiamen and the 4,500 regular troops of the 5th Brigade at the Val Cartier Army Base outside Quebec City. The militia was riddled with partisan enthusiasts, mostly young and volunteers; the use of these raggedy cadres in deadly tense situations posed incalculable risks. The Brigade, francophone from top to bottom, boasted the Royal 22nd Regiment known as the "Van Doos" (for *vingt-deux*), the military's first all-francophone unit eighty-five years earlier. The officers, some of whom had had to anglicize their names when they joined up, wondered how they would react in confrontations with fellow Québécois, many of whom they had gone to school or college with.

It was assumed the 5th Brigade could be rushed to support the three main police groups in Quebec—the Royal Canadian Mounted Police (RCMP), the Sûreté du Québec, and the Montreal urban police—if trouble started spreading in Montreal or elsewhere. But the RCMP, a federal force, was already disbanding its headquarters and pulling out of Quebec, along with the Canadian Security Intelligence Service. The Montreal police were a questionable asset, largely white-francophone, intensely disliked by many of the new Haitian and North African immigrants. As for the 4,500-member Sûreté, Quebec's provincial police, its reputation for brutality dated to the 1950s when its head-cracking enforcers had acted as Premier Maurice Duplessis's personal goon squad. It was big on billy clubs and gratuitous battery, roundly hated by Quebec's Natives, especially the Mohawks.

The most militant of Canada's aboriginals, the Mohawks, like the Crees and other tribes of the First Nations in Quebec, believed themselves a distinct society with the right to self-government. On a handful of reserves along the St. Lawrence near Montreal, the Mohawks defiantly conducted an illegal cross-border traffic in deadly arms, drugs, and cigarettes. They did so with virtual impunity from the undermanned border authorities. They frittered away their earnings on liquor and the lures of the cheap bingo palaces and illegal gambling casinos that dotted the reserves. They cursed their lot and brooded over the memory of Oka, a decade earlier.

Oka was burned into the consciousness of every member of the Mohawk Warrior Society: a symbol of the white majority's insensitivity to the Indians' past, the brutality of Quebecers and their police. When the town of Oka had attempted in early 1990 to expand a nine-hole golf course into an ancient Indian burial ground, enraged Mohawks on the adjoining Kanesatake Reserve had thrown up barricades to halt the work, shutting off access to one of the major bridges that link the shore communities of the St. Lawrence with Montreal. The Sûreté, with their assault rifles and tear gas, had descended on the Warriors, followed by a Canadian Army regiment. The subsequent eleven-week stand-off had resulted in the death of a police officer, the beating of Indian women with rifle butts, and the intimidation of Mohawk children and their elders by a stone-throwing white mob as Sûreté officers stood by.

The Oka spectacle had drawn a rebuke from the United Nations human rights committee and outrage from tribes across Canada. Quebec's Crees had pledged that any armed attack on the Mohawks was considered an attack on them. The Mohawks and Oneidas of southern Ontario quietly began to arm. Oka became a model and rallying cry to those hotheads among the Natives who had become increasingly difficult to control. In British Columbia the Toosy Indians, angered by provincial rulings against their land claims, blocked federal military maneuvers in their vicinity. In southern Alberta one hothead, Milton Born With a Tooth, had begun organizing acts of sabotage with bulldozers. Across the border in New York State, the Senecas had watched the drama at Oka and launched their own skirmishes against the authorities, protesting efforts to tax their gas and cigarette sales; at least four state troopers had been hurt in clashes with the Indians.

In the summer of 2001, ferment among the Natives was spreading. Fearful Quebecers, who perceived the Natives' quest for self-government in terms of armed revolt and land grabs, called for reinforcing the Sûreté with more arms and officers. With the RCMP gradually abandoning its duties assisting the Sûreté around the Mohawk reserves in Quebec, and the Canadian Army there a divided and uncertain foreign force, Quebecers demanded a stronger paramilitary force of their own. The current Sûreté was no match for even one well-armed Mohawk reserve.

Such was Akwesasne, a sprawling six-mile-long strip of woods and shantytowns that straddled the borders of Quebec, Ontario, and New York State. Akwesasne lay just southwest of Montreal in a pocket of the St. Lawrence Seaway where the international bridge links Cornwall, Ontario, to Massena, New York. Over the years the bridge had been occasionally blocked by Indians angered at the traffic congestion caused by shoppers in search of bargains below the border. On the U.S. side of the bridge a major aluminum plant provided jobs for many of the twelve thousand Mohawks on the reserve; on the Canadian side a pulp and paper plant offered work as well. Too many of the Indians, however, found the lucrative cigarette-smuggling business irresistible. Efforts in 1994 to curb the illicit trade through tax changes had proved short-lived; the trade had gradually renewed itself. By the end of the decade, contraband cartons of cheap American cigarettes were once again selling out on the black market in Canada. The Mohawks spent their bountiful profits enhancing their equally lucrative drug trade and their stockpile of arms.

The money went to equip a drug-running fleet that competed in swank and speed with those of the Caribbean cartels. The Mohawks raced their cocaine across the reaches of the St. Lawrence in everything from sleek Catalina Chris-Crafts to a second-hand minesweeper, purchased as U.S. military surplus. The money also went to pay for averted eyes and turned backs at the border posts. And if bribery and elusiveness didn't always work, overwhelming firepower would. The Mohawks' smuggling of arms was massive, brazen, and responsible for an armory of Kalashnikov assault rifles, American-made shot guns and 9mm pistols, M-50 and M-60 machine guns, armor-piercing grenades and grenade launchers— "enough fireworks to start World War III," according to one of Akwesasne's fifteen patrol officers. The Indians, many of them Vietnam vets, were adept at converting semi-automatic weapons like the Russian-made AK-47 rifle into fully automatic weapons right on the reserve. A favored weapon of convenience, acquired through a South African pipeline, was the *qwash,* a crude zip gun made from rubber tubing and springs. The arms had already led to killings on the reserve. The Indians at Akwesasne and other reserves were also gathering, ominously, huge stocks of military food rations in the event of another protracted siege.

The arming of the Mohawk reserves had become so blatant and intimidating, the weapons moving on trucks driven by armed Warriors from the New York State side of Akwesasne to the Canadian side, that unarmed customs officers more often than not perfunctorily waved the trucks through. Out on the St. Lawrence, the nights were punctuated by gunfire between rival smugglers, sounding at times "like a war zone," according to river residents. The Mohawk thugs held increasing contempt for the police, who generally were loathe to make narcotic busts on the reserves for fear of igniting an ever more combustible situation. So the arms kept flowing: to protect the drug and cigarette trade; to bolster the Indians' claim to total sovereignty on their reserves; and to ensure that their lethal armories were ready-perfect for that day when the First Nations decided either to enforce their demands for autonomy in Quebec or fight for their right to remain Canadian.

For much of June, Quebec and Canada, limp from the exhaustions of fruitless negotiating, seemed to bask in the loveliness of late spring and early summer. It was as though the warming sun and freshening showers could somehow dry out the hatred and wash the slate clean for a new beginning; as though the gripping beauty of the Laurentians, the placid meanderings of the St. Lawrence, could almost lull away the forebodings of convulsion.

Small things happened at first, the sort of blips that wouldn't draw much attention in the media: scattered incidents of hooliganism in Montreal's west end; in Westmount, loaded moving vans defaced with obscene graffiti, their tires occasionally slashed; in the townships, unreported break-ins of anglophone homes and businesses, a string of seemingly unrelated arsons; everywhere, a rising tide of mutual insults and barely concealed menace—against anglophone shoppers and merchants in Quebec, against Acadian families in New Brunswick, against the residents of francophone pockets across Canada, like Winnipeg's St. Boniface suburb or Vancouver's tiny Maillardville. The anglophone merchants of Quebec, tired of having their storefronts forever scarred with *péquiste* slogans or worse, banded together in an armed protective association. Montreal's seething Haitian and North African communities formed a militant alliance to boycott francophone stores and realtors that condoned discriminatory practices. The immigrant street gangs, spoiling for a fight with anyone in authority, pooled their muscle to organize a combined crew of enforcers throughout the city. All across Quebec people brooded, hoped for the best, and armed themselves.

A faction of the *péquistes* made their own preparations. Since the mid-1990s the Parti Québécois' radical wing, small in numbers but fierce in its fanaticism, had been quietly infiltrated by a group steeped in the arts of agitprop and terrorism. Its leaders were *provocateurs* and sometime bomb makers, trained in Libya; one or two were retirees from the old Bader-Meinhof gang in Germany. Their followers, fewer than a hundred, had taken special oaths of fealty and bore tiny fleur-de-lis tattoos below their right armpits. Throughout the spring, they had been secretly scouting the vulnerability of Canadian government installations in the Montreal area.

Canada's security forces readied for the worst, impeded by uncertainty as to which facilities belonged in its or Quebec's hands, which units would act reliably in Canada's best interests if the military was needed. By some quirk of politics or expediency, most of Canada's military supplies had ended up in Quebec. In the late 1980s, as Canada's military structure continued to dwindle, Ottawa had decided to consolidate its scattered ordnance depots in one area. Given Canada's NATO and NORAD obligations, it had made sense at the time to center the depots in Montreal, with its access to the St. Lawrence Seaway and bridge links to the United States. The move was encouraged by the defense minister of the day, a Québécois who liked the idea of extending jobs to his Montreal constituents and maybe giving Quebec an edge in building up its own armed forces should the province ever separate. Ottawa now faced the unsettling prospect that should civil strife escalate into military conflict, the Canadian Forces would have to fight their way into Montreal in order to retrieve much of the ammunition, weapons, and combat vehicles needed for their troops.

By the middle week of June, the talks on the division of federal assets having collapsed, Ottawa had become resolute in its refusal to hand over the majority of Canada's federal installations in Quebec. The exasperated authorities in Quebec City therefore ordered that water and other services be shut off to such key facilities as Dorval International Airport, Montreal's main post office, and the Canadian Broadcasting Corporation's radio and television center.

This new turn of the screw prompted the government in Ottawa to announce its intention to protect all Canadian citizens in Quebec from any threats to their safety or loss of property, and to safeguard all federal installations as well. Emergency rations, power generators, and fresh water supplies were rushed to the beleagured facilities. Ottawa's National Defense Headquarters ordered Navy and Coast Guard ships deployed in the Gulf of the St. Lawrence to protect federal property in ports along the river and to stop and search suspicious vessels in the area. The United Nations Security Council was advised of the crisis, while the U.S. State Department received twice-daily reports, including the suggestion that authorities curtail all travel to Quebec and beef up state police detachments at key border points. At the Port of Montreal—terminus for ocean-going ships and a small city unto itself with its own security force—surveillance was increased, the chain-link fences enclosing the terminals patrolled by extra guards and attack dogs. To Pointe Longue, the Canadian Forces' main ordnance depot on Montreal Island, a small cadre of English-speaking militiamen, armed with M-16 rifles and concussion grenades, was dispatched for round-the-clock guard duty.

Canada's Land Force Command in Montreal alerted Valcartier's 5th Brigade as well as the Communication Command Headquarters at the St. Hubert Air Base across the river. It also mobilized in the Montreal area two anglophone militia units, the Black Watch Royal Highland Regiment and the Canadian Grenadier Guards; a third anglo militia group in the townships, the Sherbrooke Hussars, was placed on semi-alert status. All leaves were canceled, the units revved up to a state of high readiness. The rest of the twenty-five militia units in Quebec, nearly all francophone, were purposely not mobilized. Ottawa considered the risk too great. There had been reports of infiltration by radical *péquiste* elements bent on persuading the young militiamen to defect to Quebec's side.

The show of force by Ottawa succeeded in cooling tempers in Quebec City. The Quebec government's plan to dispatch Montreal police and Sûreté officers to take control of the hold-out Canadian facilities was shelved. Quebec as a sovereign nation could have legitimately challenged Canada's mobilization of its regular and reservist forces in Quebec. But the swiftness of Ottawa's action had caught Quebec off guard, even temporarily cowed it. Quebec had no military presence yet, other than a dozen or so naval vessels under construction, plus the potential of one day converting the francophone militia units on its territory into a professional force. For the time being, any power confrontations were best saved for dealing with rebellious Natives or unruly anglophones.

The episode, however, signaled the relative impotence of the infant nation, further bruising Quebec's pride and incensing its more militant nationalists. It was seen as yet another humiliation, fodder for agitators whipping up the bitter passions that always attended the annual St. Jean Baptiste Day parade scheduled a few days hence, on June 24, 2001.

Police intelligence had picked up rumors of possible trouble erupting in Montreal's English-speaking sector. The night before the *fête nationale* officers had gone from door to door in Westmount, advising residents to lock up or leave town for the day. In the city's downtown shopping area the morning of the parade, immigrant gangs were already out on the streets, swilling a homemade Haitian brew from brown paper bags. The anglophone Merchants Rights Association (MRA) had planned to defy the police ban on other demonstrations that day by staging its own protest march down Sherbrooke Street. Some of the marchers packed leaded blackjacks for protection; a few, ex-Army officers, carried Browning service revolvers tucked inside waistbands.

The crowd that swarmed out of Jarry Park that day, high on shrimp and beer, was a different crowd from the year before. Since early morning it had been worked up by sound trucks cruising through Outremont, blaring patriotic slogans and anti-Canadian invective. *Péquiste* orators at the picnic had unleashed more tirades, blaming the woes of the past year on the intransigent anglos next door, inflaming francophone emotions to new heights. The parade floats, too, differed from the last time, their historical motifs running to humiliation and revenge: a mock execution of John Bull by a firing squad of costumed French *colons;* a fleur-de-lis pennon crushed between a giant Maple Leaf and Union Jack. The crowd jostled the few anglo spectators visible along Rue St. Denis, chanting, "Québécois to the streets! L'Etrangers on the sidewalk!" When the last float had disappeared up the parade route, scores of club-wielding Québécois toughs spilled into the street and headed in the opposite direction. At the intersection of St. Denis and Sherbrooke they turned right, picking up more followers, the crowd gradually assuming the shape and mood of a mob. "À l'ouest!" a vast shout went up. "À l'ouest!"

The MRA marchers, sallying down Sherbrooke Street from the west end, heard the shouts and slowed their pace. The shouts also reached the ears of Haitian and Senegalese gang members who had convened earlier that morning in Parc Lafontaine a few blocks east, where they'd continued to drink and harass celebrants bound for the parade. Now the gangs poured out of the park and raced along the opposite side of Sherbrooke Street, yelling epithets at the francophone mob, flashing an occasional bayonet or dirk. Close by McGill University's gray-stone music building, in front of which a statue of Queen Victoria blandly surveys the thoroughfare, the three mobs converged. The melee moved quickly from fists to clubs to knives, then, fatally, a dozen shots. The rioting surged west along Sherbrooke. The police, more than half of them still back on the official parade route, were outmanned by the rioters who now numbered in the hundreds. The MRA marchers dispersed and fell back in confusion toward their sector, the francophone mob hard on their heels, bludgeoning anglo stragglers along the way. Police reinforcements chased the gangs down the byways off Sherbrooke and into the narrow streets of the Old City, where a shower of Molotov cocktails rained down on the cops from the upper windows of the immigrant ghetto homes.

The rioters lashed out at the most conspicuous symbols of anglophone prestige along Sherbrooke Street, smashing the show windows of the Ritz Carlton Hotel and Alcan's tony headquarters into rubbled heaps of glass. By the time the mob reached the first row of shuttered Westmount mansions, the local police and Sûreté had thrown up barricades, while the Black Watch and Grenadier militia units had wheeled into position several armored personnel carriers with machine guns mounted on them. Behind the barricades, infuriated MRA marchers screamed curses at the francophones, while distraught Westmount matrons remonstrated with Sûreté officers for having lost control of events. A CBC television camera caught a beefy Sûreté cop, grimacing in frustration, at the instant his nightstick laid open the skull of one shrieking woman. The image flashed across TV screens that evening from Vancouver to St. John's, and in the squalid encampments of the James Bay Crees and the Mohawks of Akwesasne.

Sherbrooke Street was a scene out of Sarajevo: bodies, congealing pools of blood, overturned cars, strips of torn clothing, the wail of ambulance sirens charging the late afternoon air. The toll was inconceivable to Canadians: eight dead, 110 injured, 230 arrests. The dead included four francophones, three MRA marchers, and a Montreal police officer.

The next day, June 25, as the city recoiled in shock, roving gangs of immigrants continued their assaults and looting in the eastern end; harried police reported more than two dozen injuries to francophone residents. The Sûreté reported scattered violence in a number of Montreal suburbs and riverside communities. In mid-afternoon the city was rocked by two explosions coming from the vicinities of Point Longue and the air base at St. Hubert. The evening television news showed huge palls of smoke hanging over what had been the ordnance depot; three deaths were reported in the St. Hubert bombing. By 8:00 P.M. the first of two infantry battalions from the 5th Brigade had reached Montreal's northern outskirts. An armored regiment was en route.

On the third day, thousands of Outremonters streamed into Montreal's

Paul Sauvé Arena for a rally in memory of the francophones who had died in the rioting. Afterwards, they gathered behind police barricades at the other end of Sherbrooke, taunting and hurling paving stones at the anglophone militiamen guarding McGill and other properties in the area; more arrests, more injuries. Sûreté intelligence was now reporting that the violence had spread to Trois Rivières, Shawinigan, and Ste. Hyacinthe, where a militia battalion of the "Van Doos" had burned their uniforms and defected en masse to the Quebec government. There were unsubstantiated reports of lynchings of anglophones in several remote towns of Quebec's western interior.

The brushfire had spread by the fourth day to the Eastern Townships, where clashes between anglos and francophones strained the limited capacity of the Sherbrooke Hussars. Tire-burning blockades, hit-and-run bombings, and break-ins roiled across the townships from Granby to Drummondville. A few miles south, in the border hamlets of northern Vermont and New Hampshire, extra detachments of state police moved in to reassure the inhabitants. In Montreal, city officials hastened to condemn the Haitian community and the Merchants Rights Association for triggering the violence on St. Jean Baptiste Day, ignoring the role of the francophone mob. The air was rife with venom and calls for reprisal.

In Ottawa, the Prime Minister publicly deplored the tragedy even as military advisers warned against the government sending additional federal forces to Quebec. Canada's small and thinly stretched army was needed to quell any violent reactions on its own soil; the talk-show lines from coast to coast were already shrill with threats to savage the French-speaking minorities outside Quebec. The 5th Brigade would have to handle matters on its own, and already it was stretched to the limit. One battalion was keeping the lid on Quebec City and the northern reaches. The other two battalions and an armored regiment were trying to restore peace to Montreal, where scattered rioting persisted. Late on the fourth day came word that Akwesasne had exploded. Two thousand Mohawk Warriors, many of them drunk or drugged out, were rampaging across the international bridge, overturning cars and beating the occupants. Customs posts had been set afire, at least three inspectors killed.

The 5th Brigade's armored regiment rolled south that night out of Montreal, racing to intercept a fifty-truck convoy of Mohawk Warriors threatening to attack the pulp and paper plant on the Canadian side of the reserve and to blockade all highways and bridges in the area.

Matthew Coon-Come was meeting with Cree elders from the nine Native villages in the James Bay area when the first word came of Mohawk casualties at the Akwesasne Reserve. Before midmorning of Day Five of the Quebec crisis, seven Mohawk Warriors were dead, cut down by 50-caliber machine guns from the 5th Brigade's APCs or crushed under the treads of the armored regiment's 50-ton Leopard tanks. A force of 3,500 RCMP, Sûreté, and New York State police officers, backed by the Brigade's armored unit, had managed to secure the international bridge and other access routes after a three-hour pitched battle with the Mohawks. The reserve had been cordoned off, all vehicular traffic redirected except for the steady stream of ambulances that raced in and out of Akwesasne, bearing many of the estimated 350 injured Mohawks to nearby hospitals. By the time the Cree elders at James Bay had decided late on the fifth day to activate their plan—"Operation Almighty Voice"—the casualty count at Akwesasne totaled twelve dead and nearly five hundred injured. Two of the dead and more than a hundred of the injured were police officers felled by Mohawk arms.

The Crees were now joined with their brother Mohawks, as they had pledged all along. A press release from the First Nations declared Quebec's Natives were acting unilaterally to assert their independence and avenge the bloodshed at Akwesasne. Operation Almighty Voice, months in preparation, would send an indelible message to Quebec and the outside world.

On the moonless night of Day Six, an assault force of three hundred Cree braves from the tribes of the Great Whale–Opinaca river region descended on the La Grande complex. They had driven in their pickups from their villages to the staging area at Chisasibi at the mouth of La Grande Rivière. There, the head shaman had blessed the mission and a chief elder had fired up the warriors with the tale of Almighty Voice, a Swampy Cree of the Canadian prairies who in the late 1890s had killed a North-West Mounted Police officer, then fled into the Saskatchewan hills with a price on his head. For more than a year Almighty Voice had eluded the authorities, a symbol of defiance among his people, before the police hunted him down. When Almighty Voice died in a hail of bullets in 1897, it marked the end of that century's Native resistance in Canada. Now the warriors of the new resistance dabbed symbolic spots of the legendary Cree's blood on their foreheads, checked their weapons, and moved silently out of Chisasibi on foot.

They trekked east along the river over the rocky outcrops of the taiga, through the low jack pines and dwarf larches, heading for the La Grande-2 facility, crown jewel of the Hydro-Québec operation. The warriors were armed with M-1 carbines, sawed-off 12-gauge shotguns, and assorted handguns. They carried aerial maps and blueprints of La Grande-2, sections of heavy-duty nylon rope, Motorola walkie-talkies, and 1,000 pounds of Semtex plastic explosive. They had Almighty Voice in their hearts and in their minds the knowledge that La Grande-2 was lightly manned, mostly remote-controlled, and that the coming days in New York City and America's Northeast would be among the hottest on record for early July, with electric power demands at their peak.

Sometime after midnight the Crees penetrated La Grande-2's thinly secured outer perimeter, cutting communications lines before any alarm could be given, then split into three raiding parties. One party headed for the south section of the main dam, which held back the waters of LG-2's largest reservoir. The reservoir covered more than 1,000 square miles of what had once been choice hunting grounds and held enough water to drown the entire state of Rhode Island. The explosives planted there by the Crees had the potential to destroy enough of the dam wall to deplete large parts of the reservoir and submerge most of the land below it. A second party of braves made for the giant spillway, a canyonlike staircase of huge terraces over which drained the excess waters from the reservoir. The aim was to set off a secondary explosion that would release an even greater torrent of excess waters to abrade and erode other sections of the dam further downstream. The main Cree party raced toward La Grande-2's underground control center and powerhouse at the heart of the complex.

They commandeered the elevators leading down to the vaulted cavern that housed the system's sixteen massive turbines along with its microwave communications network and electronic monitoring devices. While specially trained sappers laid the puttylike Semtex along the orange equipment cabinets above each turbine, other warriors overpowered the surprised dozen or so engineers manning the consoles that directed the flow of hydroelectric power from the plant to client users. The rest of the plant personnel were rounded up from the machine hall and the adjacent surge chamber, bound and removed from the premises. All sluice gates and electrical control panels were wired with explosives, also the circuit breakers and switches for the power generation system. The raiders and their prisoners rode the elevator back to the surface, quickly vacated the complex, and rendezvoused with the other raiding parties at a prearranged spot safely distant from the complex. There, a little after 1:00 A.M., the Crees detonated their explosives by remote control.

In that instant, much of the can-do pride of corporate Quebec disappeared in the conflagration at La Grande-2. Thousands of megawatts of electrical power stopped surging down the high-voltage transmission lines from James Bay to the U.S. border. Within minutes Montreal, Quebec City, and large sections of Boston, Hartford, and Providence went black. Nothing moved through the wrist-thick cables that draped the steel towers stretching from Massena south to the major junction point at Utica, then along the Marcy-South line past Cooperstown and across the Hudson to Poughkeepsie, thence through Fishkill and into the metropolitan New York area. New Yorkers, in the small hours of that morning, were not yet aware of the misery ahead, a breezeless day of record heat, unrelieved by the air conditioners sitting powerless in their homes.

Hours after they'd blown up La Grande-2, the Crees issued a joint ultimatum with the Mohawks and other First Nation tribes, demanding that Quebec recognize the Natives' independence and the right of the northern tribes to transfer their Ungava Territory back to Canadian ownership. If Quebec failed to meet the Natives' demands, it could anticipate further sabotage and unrest.

On the seventh day of the crisis, the government in Quebec City was under siege from its Natives, north and south, from its outraged anglophone populace, and its estranged immigrants. The exhausted security forces could no longer cope with the widespread violence. There were no units to spare to send north to subdue the Crees. The 5th Brigade had its hands full restoring order at Akwesasne and keeping the other Mohawk reserves from blowing, mopping up the isolated rioting in Montreal, patrolling the still volatile townships, and holding the fort in Quebec City. The Sûreté was fully engaged in containing unrest in the smaller cities along the north shore of the St. Lawrence. The new nation was not about to request more troops from Canada and risk a likely rejection from Ottawa. But there was always Washington.

For months the Americans had watched the eerie scenario unfolding to their north. In the fifth-floor suite of the State Department's Office of Canadian Affairs, officials convened urgent meetings with the other Washington agencies in the Canada loop, from Commerce to the Treasury Department. The original concern had been for the safety of American nationals and property in Quebec that might become terrorist targets. Now, as the situation in Montreal and along the New York State border rapidly deteriorated, the Americans feared for the safety of such vital interests as the St. Lawrence Seaway and, in the wake of the La Grande-2 bombing, their shared NORAD facilities in Quebec.

After brief consultations with Ottawa and a cursory nod to Quebec, the Pentagon ordered the Army's 10th Mountain Light Infantry Division at Fort Drum, New York, to roll north across the border to relieve the 5th Brigade at Akwesasne and the other Indian reserves, and, if necessary, mount a show of force across the river from Montreal. It was a small incursion, but effective. It gave the Quebec government some badly needed breathing room, allowing elements of the 5th Brigade to pacify the northern Crees; it shut down the Mohawk insurrection and helped cool the street skirmishes in Montreal. Of course, Ottawa professed displeasure that the Americans had seen fit to intervene and Quebec publicly expressed its indignation. Privately, everyone was relieved to see that, as always, the surest way to deflect internecine strife in Canada was to have the Americans charge in. Washington, not the Natives, became the new bête noire.

Within seventy-two hours the violence had largely subsided, the Quebec government had begun negotiating a deal with the Natives, the 10th Mountain Light had returned to its barracks in Watertown, New York, and millions of North Americans could begin to calculate what the unprecedented ten-day spasm of violence had cost all parties.

Hospitals in Quebec reported a total of twenty-eight deaths and nearly seven hundred injuries attributed to the political violence. Property damage was estimated at more than $1 billion. Business losses ran in the hundreds of millions of dollars. The loss of investor confidence worldwide was incalculable. So was the loss of face in Ottawa and Quebec City at having in effect had to invite U.S. intervention. Offers from Washington of standby financial aid to Quebec only deepened the resentment among francophone nationalists.

The immediate financial impact reflected concern that the upheaval in Quebec might spread throughout Canada. No serious reprisals had been attempted against the francophone communities outside Quebec; the few isolated blockades and acts of sabotage by militant Native warriors in British Columbia and Saskatchewan had been contained by the RCMP and local police. But the veneer of civility, so prized by Canadians, had been irreparably shattered, and with it much of the faith of a watching world. The Canadian dollar had nosedived below the benchmark 80 cent (U.S.) level, and the Bank of Canada was scrambling to shore up its value by buying millions of "loonies" (the Canadian dollar coin bearing the image of a loon) and increasing the interest rate by nearly 3 percent, the largest one-time jump ever. Nervous money was fleeing the country at a gallop. The soaring interest rates threatened an inflationary explosion.

Canada's financial markets were in turmoil. The day after the Montreal riots, the Toronto Stock Exchange had closed at its lowest level since the Depression. In the "deposit houses" in Toronto and New York City, where billions of dollars crossing the border in instantaneous transactions are cleared and settled, the giant computers whirred and choked on overload, as investors by the thousands transferred funds out of Toronto banks into U.S. holding companies and offshore accounts. The Department of Finance in Ottawa dispatched senior officials to key money markets in London and Tokyo to try to reassure investors. There was fear that without significant increases in interest rates, an all-out repatriation of funds from Canada could occur shortly. Speculators were already marking down the value of corporate Canada by 7 percent or more. The urgency to stabilize panic flows before Ottawa's and Quebec's huge foreign currency debts were downgraded off the charts consumed the moneymen in Montreal and Toronto. Still, the Canadian dollar kept falling, and the markets were nearing a meltdown as scorching as the summer heat that first week of July.

The morning after the St. Jean Baptiste Day riots, within minutes of the opening bell at the Toronto Stock Exchange, chaos had swept the third floor of the RBC Dominion Securities building in downtown Toronto, where seventy-five traders in fixed-income deals manned their computer pods in the bullpen area. The RBC traders, normally unflappable in their striped shirts and suspenders, played in one small corner of the $500-billion-a-day international currency market. But on that day and succeeding days they must have felt as though the whole market had come down on their heads. The computer banks, with direct lines to designated brokers and major RBC clients—managers of pension and mutual funds, insurance company directors, provincial government treasurers—were spitting out "sell" orders in unprecedented volume. Across the country, holders of Canadian bonds clogged the phonelines to their brokers on Bay Street, who in turn fired off "sell" instructions to the RBC traders via computer or vocally through the special "shout boxes" atop every terminal. The frenzy that crisis week had almost overwhelmed the small band of traders and their Bond Automated Trading System, known affectionately as Bats.

In the vast fixed-income trading room on the seventh floor of Merrill Lynch's world headquarters in Manhattan's World Financial Center, the pandemonium was only slightly more controlled. In this room, crackling with intensity and barked commands involving fortunes, more than four hundred traders, sales specialists, and syndicate handlers daily transacted billions of dollars in trade of U.S. Treasury notes and corporate bonds, preferred shares, commercial paper, and foreign corporate bonds. Canada alone accounted for 30 percent of the action in the international fixed-income sector. Merrill Lynch was not only king of the Wall Street brokerage houses but, along with First Boston, one of the biggest underwriters of Quebec bonds in the U.S. market. Back in 1970 it had enjoyed, in traders' jargon, one of the "blowouts" of the decade when Hydro-Québec had issued its first bonds for the construction of the La Grande complex, and the issue had been bought out within minutes. Now La Grande was dust and American and foreign investors were swamping Merrill Lynch's traders with requests for bids on their Hydro-Québec bonds. In the uneasy aftermath of the bombing at James Bay, Merrill Lynch made a considered decision to refuse bids on some $3 billion worth of Hydro-Québec bonds offered, thereby knocking about 9 percent off the company's total market value. It was a blow not easily forgiven by Quebec.

The traders on the seventh floor, harried men and women with nicknames like "Rocket" and "Wedge," knew the unsettling figures on Canada and Quebec as they related to Merrill Lynch's clients: more than $200 billion worth of Canadian bonds held by foreigners, about $65 billion by U.S. investors; more than $20 billion of Quebec government and Hydro-Québec debt held in U.S. dollars. Now, as they wolfed down lunch snacks at their consoles, their eyes glued to the blinking yellow numbers reporting the plunge of Canadian exchange rates and bond values against other currencies and bonds around the world, the traders assessed more clearly the dimensions of the financial havoc wreaked on Quebec and Canada from the week of violence.

It was the end, and a bitter one, for Quebec's diminished anglophone minority. The anglos and their businesses had been trickling out of the former province ever since the end of World War I, when the lure of Toronto as the future financial hub of Canada had prompted the first exodus. The Parti Québécois' ascension in 1976 had caused the second exodus; the language wars of the 1990s, the third. The anglophone schools in Quebec had steadily emptied. Educated, bilingual anglo youths were leaving in droves, along with a third or more of the anglophone doctors who had been born and educated in Quebec. Over the past year, anglophones had been selling their homes and properties at fire-sale prices as they fled the language enforcers. Now, in the wake of the riots, the final diaspora turned from an orderly retreat to a wild rush.

Few had imagined that the fate of Canada's 950,000 francophones living outside Quebec would be any more promising. René Levesque had once said they would be welcome in Quebec just as the world's Jews were always welcome in Israel. But, except for some of New Brunswick's 240,000 Acadians departing for the Gaspé across their northern border, few of Canada's francophones chose to cast their lot with Quebec. Even as they recognized the hopelessness of their language and culture surviving, most preferred to face extinction as Canadians. Quebec's separation had rendered them marginal as a society, lumped in with Canada's other ethnic groups; without Quebec, the francophones represented no more than 4 percent of the population. Their language had been dying for generations, the result of francophones intermarrying with other linguistic groups. Half the French-speaking citizens of the three westernmost provinces no longer used their mother tongue at home. The rate of assimilation of francophones into the English-speaking majority virtually doomed their language and culture to eclipse within a generation. The unacceptable alternative was to cling to their ethnicity and become economic and social pariahs like Ontario's half-million francophones, or bullied second-class citizens like the 25 million ethnic Russians living outside Russia in the former Soviet Union.

The sapping heat of August deflated any lingering aggressions and compounded the exhaustion that had settled over Canada and Quebec. Out of the carnage had come recognition that violence was not the answer to unsettled grievances or the need to settle old scores. But out of it, too, had come an awful clarity about what had been lost and what could never be put together again. In the months ahead the temptation to scapegoat would be strong; there was blame to go all around. But a new nation, Quebec, had to recover and find its footing. And an old nation, forever changed, had to heal itself and adjust to its new status in a cold-eyed world.

"We know not whether the French in Canada are to be dreaded as enemies, or to be conciliated as friends."

—JOSEPH SANSOM,
Travels in Lower Canada (1820)

"Strong regional divergencies, the natural North-South pull . . . would probably, inexorably, in time lead to one or more of the provinces or regions breaking away from Ontario / Ottawa domination. Once started, it is questionable whether the process could be stopped."

—*The Quebec Situation: Outlook and Implications,*
document prepared for U.S. State Department,
August 1977

"Canadians' mock horror at the thought of being swallowed by the United States actually masks a deep desire for precisely that. They protest too much. Their lips say, 'No, no,' but their eyes say, 'Yes, yes.' We must embrace them, adopt them, love them and annex them."

—MICHAEL KINSLEY,
Editor, *New Republic,*
in *The Washington Post*

"Every American statesman covets Canada."

—JOHN A. MACDONALD,
Canada's first Prime Minister

6

Canada Without Quebec: The Ultimate Breakup

For all the pain and emotional wreckage the violence surrounding separation had caused, it had also had a purging effect. At a personal level the acrimony between Quebec's francophones and its minorities, between the Québécois and the rest of Canada, would remain for years. Canadians would not easily forgive Quebec's departure and the ugly consequences, the ruin it had visited on Canada's good name and image. But at a higher impersonal level, where policy makers coolly gauge a nation's best interests, the veils had fallen. The illusions of the past had been swept away, the realities of the present and future confronted at last. Grudges were too expensive a luxury for practical statesmen. Canada had no need to foster a permanently hostile foreign nation in its midst. Quebec, in its lonely new status, could ill afford to keep stonewalling and demanding the impossible from its former patron. In the waning months of 2001, accommodations of a sort were finally reached.

Quebec's share of the Canadian debt was settled at 23 percent, the interest-paying period limited to a decade, at which point both nations would reassess the servicing arrangements in light of their economic circumstances. The logjam over the division of assets in Quebec was broken: most of the minor Canadian facilities were turned over to Quebec outright for a lump sum rolled into the larger debt payment; federal facilities of an international security and transport nature would remain in Canada's hands during a protracted phase-out period. Quebec could keep the Canadian dollar as its main currency for the nonce, but would have no say in monetary policy. Once it had gained a surer financial footing, Quebec could decide to print its own currency pegged to the "loonie."

The Natives' issue was resolved in part because wiser and older heads took charge of the negotiations. The fact was, Quebec's leaders had no desire to be categorized as racist or unbending like some white South African regime. As for the elders of Quebec's First Nations, they had been appalled at the suffering instigated by the misdirected young warriors in their midst. Even the precisionlike raid at James Bay had seemed needlessly destructive. In renewed talks between the Natives and the Quebec government, the Mohawks were granted a significant measure of self-government after agreeing to cease all illegal gambling and smuggling activities and to permit periodic inspections by Quebec authorities. The Crees, too, won more autonomy and a pledge from Hydro-Québec to scale down its future expansion plans at James Bay. The Crees agreed to pay substantial reparations for the damage at La Grande-2, to discipline the warriors involved, and to drop all claims to the northern Ungava Territory.

Quebec's other two minorities, the anglophones and French-speaking immigrants, had their day in court, recovering in some cases substantial compensation for injuries suffered or property damaged in the riots. But at best the two groups were diminishing assets and increasingly treated as such. More than 300,000 anglophones were expected to leave Quebec permanently over the next five years. The immigrant populace was already draining away to more amenable cities in Canada and the United States, while potential newcomers bypassed Quebec for more culturally tolerant communities. As their numbers declined, the remaining anglos and immigrants in Montreal received fewer special services, while the ruling francophone establishment stopped making even halfhearted attempts to integrate the police force, the teachers' unions, and other public institutions. Quebec was, for all practical purposes, closing out its accounts with its irksome minorities, becoming at last the thoroughly pure French state it had always dreamed of being.

In purity and independence, Quebec was finally free of the weights imposed by history. It had also ironically diminished its own legend in others' eyes. Once, it had represented a quarter of the population of the seventh richest industrial power in the world. Now it represented itself, a blip on the world's screen, its population smaller than the metropolitan area of Chicago. As a province of Canada, Quebec had successfully portrayed itself as both victim and prince. It had cultivated the image of a society in perpetual bondage, a tribe of wily serfs stubbornly defending their cultural faith. As a province, it had also promoted itself as a lion among sheep, ever eager to roar its singularity, to assert its role as *primus inter pares* within Confederation. Now, in sovereignty, it had forfeited those roles. There was little left to defy or defend against. Quebec was on its own in the great wide world, *primus inter* nothing.

With luck the new nation could survive the economic costs of separation, but they would prove horrific: a drop in productive output of as much as 10 percent in the short run, 5 percent over the long term; unemployment rising to 15 percent as income per capita plummeted to nearly 30 percent below U.S. levels.

The cycle began with the elimination of all federal transfer payments and industrial subsidies, a loss estimated at $25 billion over the next decade. Quebec's formerly propped-up textile and dairy industries, now confined to a much narrower domestic market, withered and died. The cost of natural gas and oil imports, which constituted 60 percent of Quebec's oil requirements, shot up as Canadians refused to further subsidize shipments of western energy to the new nation. In a short while, Quebec faced a serious negative trade balance in energy alone. Its monetary reserves had been hit badly by the flight of foreign capital; now, foreign investors were beginning to bleed Quebec for the privilege of risking their money in the new country. The bond "spreads"—the difference between what a borrower in Quebec paid for needed foreign capital and the benchmark U.S. Treasury bond interest rate—climbed to more than 150 points above the Treasury rate. With mountainous debts compounding Quebec's financial woes, the *péquiste* government had no choice but to kick in the cycle's next phase, an across-the-board tax hike to pay for public services. That, in turn, persuaded many key taxpayers to leave Quebec, saddling those who stayed with a higher taxload. Public services slowly declined, inducing more taxpayers to leave; the cycle spun into its own disabling groove.

Overnight, Quebecers found themselves removed from many of the health care benefits they had enjoyed as mobile Canadian citizens, no longer able to count on free, fully insured medical and hospital treatment whenever they traveled outside their territory. Montreal, one of the most visible casualties of separation, saw its manufacturing base move into advanced stages of decay for lack of new capital investment, its plant capacity become increasingly obsolete. The city struggled to preserve its style, its facade of insouciance, even as the crumbling spread. It suffered the highest unemployment rate of any major city in North America, with no relief in sight. If things kept going this way, some believed, Quebec might eventually end up as a North American Ireland, all slipshod charm and frayed chic, romantic in tongue, pleasantly irrelevant.

That was a premature fear, perhaps, for the Québécois were nothing if not resilient. But the lingering bitterness of Canadians made Quebec's debut as a nation all the rockier. Many Canadian businesses, particularly in the West, had already made good on earlier threats to cease buying from their suppliers in Quebec if the province separated. Quebec-Ontario relations, which had once embraced the largest two-way trade of Canada's provinces, grew chilly. Along the border, where more than $30 billion in goods had once passed freely between the two provinces, a string of customs posts had sprung up, interrupting the normal trade flow. Ontario had always been more important to Quebec in terms of market share than Quebec to Ontario. Now, the Ontarians rubbed their hard feelings into the trade connection, subjecting Quebec goods to unnecessary delays at the customs posts, imposing long lineups for Quebec visitors at immigration control points along the border. The harassment led to short tempers and a rising cost of trade and travel between Quebec and Canada.

By the fall of that year, 2001, Quebec had been officially recognized by most of the world community and had taken its seat in the United Nations. Procedurally, the move from province to nation was hardly a leap in the dark for Quebec. Its Ministry of International Affairs had for years maintained some thirty delegations abroad and an annual $100 million-plus budget; as a province it had signed on its own behalf some three hundred agreements with foreign governments and international agencies. As a nation, however, Quebec faced the reality of having not only to forge important new treaties on its behalf, but having to renegotiate its way into some of the 130 or so bilateral treaties that Canada had concluded over the years with the United States—treaties dealing with international law, environmental and trade issues that could affect Quebec.

As a province, Quebec had profited from Canada-U.S. accords such as the 1965 Auto Pact and the Free Trade Agreement in 1989; under Canada's protective umbrella, Quebec, like the other provinces, had suffered only minimal bruising when U.S. trade actions against Japan or Europe had indirectly struck Canada. Without Canada as a buffer, sovereign Quebec would now have to absorb the full impact of protectionist side-swiping whenever America retaliated against another major trade power. Weakened and alone, Quebec was poorly positioned to compete in the tough international trade arena; in any new trade talks, it lacked the economic weight to exact from its continental competitors the sort of favorable terms it could have won as a province. This was the harsh reality as Quebec prepared to deal itself into the North American Free Trade Agreement (NAFTA) that Canada, the United States, and Mexico had ratified years before. Even if Canada generously decided not to veto Quebec's application to join the NAFTA, Quebec could expect little charity from the other signatories once the negotiating hardball began. "Don't think it's going to be civilized," a high Ottawa official had warned the separatists years before. "Trade wars are wars with the smell of gunpowder in the air. Leave Canada and you'll have the same status as Guatemala. Don't expect special favors."

One area internationally where Quebec could expect a favor or two was the cradle of its culture, France. French Canadians had long nursed a historical grudge against France for having abandoned its colony to the British in the 1700s; on their side, the French tended to be imperturbably snobbish toward their cousins in Canada. But Franco-Quebec relations took a warming turn in the 1960s when Quebec's "quiet revolution" caught the imagination of the French people and, incidentally, coincided with the ambitions of President de Gaulle to extend his country's influence. De Gaulle, on a visit to Montreal in 1960, was appalled by the "Americanization" of the city, the engulfing U.S. commercial and cultural influence. At the same time, he bridled at the Canadian government's tactics to head off efforts by France and Quebec to establish more intimate ties. From then on, de Gaulle was an unabashed sympathizer of the separatist cause, convinced that Quebec would inevitably achieve statehood. He referred to Quebec as "le vrai Canada," and seldom missed an opportunity to annoy the government in Ottawa and its representatives in France. When he prepared to issue his crowning insult in July 1967, as he embarked for Montreal and his celebrated "Vive le Québec libre" speech, de Gaulle explained, "It's the last chance we have to make amends for France's cowardice."

The Québécois cheered that showy bit of noblesse oblige, while Ottawa fumed. Canadian-French relations henceforth were more correct than cordial. Quebec and Paris, however, became entwined in one long, mutually enhancing gavotte. Quebec enjoyed a privileged relationship with the Quai d'Orsay; Quebec's leaders were granted access to France's top officials. La Maison du Québec in Paris had more diplomats than the Embassy of Canada. Student exchanges flourished between the two peoples. France helped the province of Quebec acquire a certain international cachet within the world's Francophonie, the community of forty or so French-speaking nations. Quebec, with its numberless writers and artists, became a protégé that France could eagerly display to affirm its cultural reach into North America. Every so often, to Quebec's secret delight, France would remind Ottawa of its vestigial interests in the Canadian sphere by ordering one of its naval frigates, flaunting the *tricolore,* to evict Newfoundland fishermen from the waters off French-owned St. Pierre and Miquelon.

Small wonder that France was first to officially recognize the new nation and that Quebec's first foreign policy initiative was to seek France's support for Quebec's upgraded role in the Francophonie, its participation in NATO and other European bodies. In Quebec's post-separation era, the French factor in North America would again become a force, and few supposed it would be a benign one.

No country was more concerned with Quebec's courtship of France than the United States, which had recognized the new nation only after lengthy consultations with Ottawa and which did not regard the renewal of France's presence in North America as a particular boon. Ever since the end of World War II the French had challenged or obstructed American leadership of the Western alliance. With the demise of the Cold War, they had been prominent in calling for a marked reduction of American influence in Europe. Thus, the always testy U.S.-French relationship had grown even more barbed throughout the 1990s, a well of mistrust building up on both sides.

Quebec's flirtation with France only reminded the United States that, in the wake of Quebec's unilateral declaration of independence (UDI), America would have to reassess its entire relationship with the new nation that now shared a 487-mile border with four American states. Not only was the Quebec-U.S. trade relationship a $20-billion-a-year enterprise, with Quebec ranked as America's ninth biggest trading partner worldwide; Quebec was a strategic continental security player, straddling the St. Lawrence Seaway and representing an integral part of North American defense arrangements. More than 6 million Americans claimed some form of Quebec heritage, and about one in ten Quebecers regularly spent their winters in America's southern climes, notably Florida, a larger proportion than any other Canadian province. French Canadians had played a contributing role in the history and development of New England, had helped settle parts of Louisiana, and generally felt more at ease with open-hearted and irreverent Americans than with the coolly reserved anglophones of Canada. Quebec's relations with the United States were more extensive and consequential than those between most nations, yet Quebecers had never felt threatened by U.S. political power in the way that English Canadians had.

Quebec and America had shared historical links from the beginning. Frenchmen, from the same explorer class that originally sallied forth from New France with the Black Robes, had discovered the Mississippi and pushed that discovery on to the Gulf of Mexico: Marquette and Joliet and La Salle. Many of America's place names reflected France's role in developing the continent: Detroit, Des Moines, Baton Rouge, New Orleans. Towns of New England—Manchester, New Hampshire; Fall River, Massachusetts; Lewiston, Maine; Burlington, Vermont—became job havens for emigrant Québécois during the nineteenth and early twentieth centuries. Between 1840 and 1930 nearly a million people fled Quebec's overcrowded farms to find work in the factories and textile mills of New England. The emigrant families flowed down Quebec's Chaudière Valley by foot and horse, their leaders dreaming of another Nouvelle France: Quebec grouped with New England under the banner of Catholicism. It was an illusion, like so many of Quebec's, that was dispelled within a generation or two. America's melting-pot experience and the engulfing waves of Eastern European immigrants eroded the Frenchness of the expatriate Québécois. The post–World War II secularism that overtook Quebec, plus the advent of television, finished the job. The parochial schools that had sustained the early Franco-American communities closed down, the anglicization process accelerated. French became the dying language of the old generation.

But the Québécois migration had left its mark: by the late twentieth century there were as many Americans descended from French Canadians as there were Québécois in Quebec. A third of New Hampshire's population claimed descent from Quebecers. The Manchester phone directory was awash in Gagnons and Tremblays, and the town's supermarkets offered specials on *cretons* and *tourtière*. Notable Americans of Quebec ancestry included Jack Kerouac, the Beat writer, singers Rudy Vallee and Robert Goulet, the historian Will Durant, and the famously ill-tempered baseball legend, Leo Durocher.

More significant but less obvious was the psychic imprint of America on Quebec. The American idea had never been embraced with much enthusiasm by Loyalist-descended English Canadians. But French Quebecers, from their earliest days, had taken inspiration from the Declaration of Independence and its statement of rights, even used those principles as a rallying force in the uprisings of the 1830s. Louis Riel, the doomed Métis rebel, had been welcomed in New England in the 1870s when he made several speaking tours to champion his cause, and his execution had especially outraged Franco-Americans. Still, Quebec's later *indépendantiste* stirrings never somehow struck a wholly responsive chord with Americans. Perhaps the two societies' cultures and governing credos were too antithetical: Quebec's willingness to suppress its minorities' language rights, America's insistence that individual liberties outweighed societal obligations. Quebec's reluctance to participate in either of the world wars sat poorly with Americans. Quebecers' insularity, their unwillingness to acculturate easily in either Canada or New England, drove Franklin Roosevelt to write Mackenzie King in 1942, urging that both countries do something to hasten the assimilation of their French Canadian communities "into the whole of our respective bodies politic." Finally, Quebec's sometimes thinly disguised attempts to use its *indépendantiste* cause to drive wedges between the United States and English

Canada, beginning as early as the 1830s with Patriot leader Louis-Joseph Papineau, garnered over time more irritation than sympathy from Washington.

From the 1950s on, Quebec's attitude toward the United States veered between avoidance and courtship. Embracive American culture and business so threatened Quebec's nationalists and intellectuals that the issue became key in the decision by Quebecers in the 1960s to intensify their Frenchness and develop their own economy, distancing themselves from American and English Canadian influence. By the late 1970s it was courtship time, as the reigning Quebec separatists sought to assure U.S. investors and opinion makers that separation would not mean the end of Canada, was very much in the American tradition, and that the Parti Québécois was not a repository of moonbeams and kooks. Still, René Levesque, on a selling mission to the United States, did not captivate New York, and the columnist James Reston wrote that the invitation by Quebec to invest in what amounted to the dismemberment of Canada was the worst proposition put to Americans "since Nikita Khrushchev invited us to accept the emplacement of Soviet nuclear missiles in Cuba."

Americans' fear of subversion and disunion, the legacy of the Civil War, made them suspicious of any talk of secession. They tended to identify the Quebec separatist movement, as one U.S. official observed, "not with Thomas Jefferson, but with Jefferson Davis." Thus, the official U.S. stance on the separation issue remained, right up to the events of December 2000, "neutral in favor of unity." It was not a position entirely pleasing to the Parti Québécois government nor one suggesting a propitious start of U.S. relations with sovereign Quebec.

Although the Parti Québécois had moderated its image since the Levesque era, when Quebec under the *péquistes* was perceived by Washington as a pacifist, left-wing society whose plans as a sovereign state included withdrawing from NATO and NORAD, the new nation remained suspect in defense and economic matters. Sovereign Quebec was sensed to be less supportive than Canada of U.S. security operations abroad; at the time of the Gulf War in 1990, opinion polls had shown widespread opposition in Quebec to the commitment of Canadian forces to the Gulf. Among Canadians, the Québécois had always been more favorably inclined toward "national liberation" movements in the Third World, more pro-Palestinian and less sympathetic to the Israeli cause. There was concern now that Quebec would prove to be an unhelpful neutralist on compelling international issues or, worse, a willing defector to the mischief-making camp of the French. Despite the Parti Québécois' changed views—its professed desire to participate in NATO, NORAD, and UN peacekeeping missions—the newly announced plans for a Quebec army and air force, composed of francophone units from the former Canadian forces in Quebec City and Bagotville, generated uneasiness in Washington. Quebec's modest military would be just enough to enforce its sovereignty in provocative ways, enough perhaps to justify its dubious access to Pentagon plans for North America's defense and U.S. air-defense technology.

What remained troublingly uncertain to the United States was how Quebec, in the aftermath of its violence and the shame of having had to acquiesce in America's armed intervention, would react on such touchy issues as U.S. investments in Quebec, rights of transit on the St. Lawrence Seaway, and uninhibited cross-border trade.

Quebec-U.S. business and trade ties were formidable enough to suggest nothing but a mutually beneficial relationship for years to come. More than 70 percent of Quebec's foreign trade was with the United States; its annual sales to America equaled one fifth of its total gross domestic product. From Quebec, Americans bought billions of dollars worth of cars and trucks, aircraft engines, business machines, electronic parts, newsprint, lumber products, aluminum, food, beer, subway cars, and, of course, hydroelectricity. Quebec did $2 billion worth of trade yearly with California, $8 billion worth with the Midwest states, $5 billion with New England, and $8 billion with New York State. The impact on New York's northern tier was enormous, with nearly forty thousand New Yorkers employed in companies owned by Canada and Quebec. Approximately $5 billion in U.S. direct investment was tied up in Quebec, including the operations of such recognizable companies as Allied Signal, Bristol Myers, IBM, Merck, and General Motors.

Long before it separated, Quebec had curried favor with the United States by stressing its capitalist beliefs and economic practices. It had real entrepreneurial drive, it claimed, with 60 percent of its business generated by small and medium-sized companies. It was an early champion of free trade and had vigorously supported the Canada-U.S. accord when other provinces, notably Ontario, were opposing it. Quebecers were more risk-taking than the cautious anglophones. They were just the sort of trading partner America needed. Still, the more America delved into its hitherto unexamined relationship with Quebec, the more serious differences it perceived. U.S. officials listened to Quebec's pitch with mounting skepticism, privately advising reporters that, without the Canadian fig leaf for protection, Quebec was in for a lot of discomfort if it violated America's notions of fair trade and fair business practices. Quebec was deceiving itself if it thought it could blithely enter into a smiling, untroubled relationship with the United States. It was overreading the friendship factor.

The United States favored an open world economy in which size, the availability of capital, and a skilled, stable labor force were the keys to competitiveness. It frowned on government subsidies (at least, other governments'), discriminatory pricing, and exorbitant taxes. It liked the idea of exporting capital and benefiting from the earnings of its capital investments abroad. Quebec, as a province, had been less wedded to foreign investment as a source of capital supply, preferred to own or control a larger segment of its industry, and relied on far more government intervention than the United States. Quebec as a nation offered a comparatively puny market and limited capital resources. Much of its labor force lacked high-tech training and skills; its track record in labor relations had been spotty, with more days per job lost to labor unrest than in the rest of Canada. It was Quebec's aggressive *étatisme,* however, that most concerned U.S. business interests. Americans saw in the Quebec government a hypertrophied bureaucracy, supported by excessive taxes and dedicated to overseeing every aspect of the new nation's business policy. What Quebec deemed necessary to lend a competitive edge to its undersized market and economy, the United States viewed as inimicable to its trade interests.

In "Quebec Inc." the new nation practiced a version of Japan's *keiretsu,* in which government, business, financial institutions, and labor meshed their interests and clout into a strikingly competitive force. If the United States—which hewed to the tradition of government and business as adversaries—refused to let Japan export *keiretsu* to North America, it could hardly condone "Quebec Inc." Nor could it condone the practices of the Quebec government and its state-owned enterprises like the Caisse de dépôt or Hydro-Québec: they offered hidden subsidies to Quebec companies by way of discounted business favors or encouraged Quebec firms to procure business from them at cut rates below the going market price. Hydro-Québec had reportedly engaged in discriminatory pricing policies, luring multinationals into Quebec by offering them power at rates well below cost or exporting power at rates higher than the domestic price. In addition, Quebec shielded its beer and wine industries through discriminatory listing practices that effectively denied market access to U.S. retailers. Even Quebec's language laws, which regulated the use of French and English in business exchanges, were viewed in some quarters as a non-tariff trade barrier.

Thus America, reassessing its relations with Quebec in late 2001, had to conclude there were doubtful economic rewards in dealing with the new nation to its north, whose citizens favored heavy government intercession in their business affairs, and whose reliance on an intrusive bureaucracy and acceptance of confiscatory taxes ran counter to America's proclaimed faith in unfettered and profitable free enterprise. The test at hand of U.S. convictions was Quebec's application to join the North American Free Trade Agreement. Mexico took no sides, but the United States laid out its differences with Quebec, then carefully weighed Quebec's limited response. Even more carefully, it weighed the feelings of the government of Canada, its closest, most reliable, and now wounded, North American ally. America needed to maintain its comfortably intimate relationship with Canada. And Canada, painfully recovering from Quebec's bloody and acrimonious divorce, was in no mood to accommodate the new nation's trading interests so quickly.

In the end, the United States, with Canada and Mexico acquiescing, rejected Quebec's request to be summarily included in the North American Free Trade Agreement. It was not a total rejection. Quebec would simply have to negotiate its way into the pact by shedding some of its practices and recasting some of its institutions that contravened the spirit or letter of the accord. That was insulting and unacceptable to Quebec, which felt stung by America's action. It had expected more understanding from its southern neighbor, more sensitivity to its pride as a newly sovereign nation. Another illusion shattered.

A frost descended on Quebec-U.S. relations. Over the coming months there was angry talk in Quebec City about rescinding Quebec's participation in some of the NORAD treaties as well as the agreement covering Canada's and America's joint operation of the St. Lawrence Seaway. The government of Quebec assumed a baleful wariness about future tests of its pride and territorial jurisdiction.

No piece of Quebec carried more historic meaning and economic weight than the St. Lawrence River and its manmade Seaway, which stretched 2,300 miles from the Atlantic to the Great Lakes into the heart of North America. And no portion of the Seaway had more potential for a jurisdictional feud than its northernmost section, running some 65 miles northeastward from Cornwall to Montreal, past the shorelines of eastern Ontario, upper New York State, and Quebec.

The river and Seaway served both as national border and as the world's longest inland navigable waterway. The huge "lakers" and "bulkers" that plied it operated under thirty flags and bore every commodity from molasses to pig iron. The St. Lawrence and the Great Lakes affected an area larger than all of Western Europe, their watery trade route bordering on two Canadian provinces and eight states, an industrial kingdom that numbered 100 million people with a purchasing power estimated at $1 trillion. The great river had never been idealized in song and story like the Nile, the Mississippi, or the Danube. Yet its course ran wider than the Danube's, and the traffic through its system was at one time double that of the Rhine. Until the last decade or two, the St. Lawrence had been the lifestream for much of Canada's and middle America's commercial heartland. For Quebec, it had borne on its currents the pain and fortunes of French Canadian history.

Centuries before the economic stakes had become so high, before the French arrived in the late 1500s, the marine wealth of the St. Lawrence's gulf and estuaries had been harvested by the Spanish, Portuguese, and Basques. The river in the 1600s carried the Black Robes and fur traders into the continent's interior to extend the economic and missionary reach of New France. By 1750, France had successfully exploited the St. Lawrence to establish hegemony in North America's midlands. In the century following America's War of Independence, the Loyalists settled in neat villages along the river, while successive treaties split up the natural empire of the St. Lawrence and guaranteed free navigation on the river to Canadians and Americans alike.

Under French rule, economic activity along the river had flourished primarily on the Quebec side, but by the early nineteenth century the population and industrial growth of the Great Lakes states had shifted the economic ferment to the Lakehead and the western source of the St. Lawrence; the building of the Erie Canal had further threatened Canadian shipping interests and the development of Montreal. Canada was thus spurred to begin a construction process in its own interests along the St. Lawrence—deeper canals and locks to accommodate big ships with greater draughts—that would eventually culminate in the vast Seaway project. In the 1950s, the U.S. government was persuaded to join the project along with the Ontario Hydro Corporation, which wanted to harness the power generated by the river's fierce rapids, one of which, the Lachine, just west of Montreal, had forced back Jacques Cartier and denied his dream of finding the Northwest Passage. Before the project was done and the Seaway opened in 1959, planned flooding by dams on the river had swallowed up 22,000 acres of land, including six villages that had been home to six thousand Ontarians. The legend of the "lost villages," many of them French-speaking communities, still resonated along the Seaway four decades later.

So did the resentments of the newly empowered sovereign Quebec government. The St. Lawrence had been good to Quebec, had placed it in an enviably strategic position and made it one of the major maritime regions of the world. But Quebec, the province, had never felt it played enough of a role in organizing and developing the St. Lawrence's sea trade. Not only was it cut out of the joint Canada-U.S. operation of the Seaway, but over the years the Canadian government, which ran the operation on Canada's end of the waterway, had scooped up thousands of acres of choice land along the Quebec side of the river. Ottawa had expropriated this vast stretch of shoreland in order to preserve environmental and historical sites, and had done so in many cases without consulting Quebec.

Quebec had long resented these encroachments. Now, in the wake of separation, the refusal by Ottawa to convert the St. Lawrence Seaway Authority into a joint Canada-Quebec enterprise fueled Quebec's resentment further. Nor did the increase, since the June crisis, of U.S. Air Force surveillance flights over Quebec and submarine patrols near the mouth of the St. Lawrence do anything to assuage the new nation's sense of insecurity. The tensions weren't eased by loose talk in Quebec City of imposing a special levy on Seaway traffic or sinking a couple of ships in the channel to help bring Canada and the United States to terms. By the fall of 2001, the upper reaches of the Seaway near Montreal were dotted with new blue-and-white-hulled Coast Guard cutters and newly acquired patrol craft with missiles (PCMs), aggressively policing the waters, spoiling for an opportunity to assert the new nation's jurisdictional rights.

On a cloudless November afternoon, the U.S.-flagged tanker *Exxon Toledo* was steering for the Beauharnois Locks south of Montreal when it was hailed by the *Georges-Cartier,* a bristling PCM recently donated by France as a contribution to Quebec's embryonic navy. The *Cartier* ordered the tanker to heave to and receive a boarding party of naval inspectors. The 700-foot-long *Toledo,* bound for Sarnia at the foot of Lake Huron with a 250,000-ton cargo of Venezuelan crude and lubricating oils, was already two days behind schedule. The *Toledo*'s skipper, an impulsive Texan, chose to ignore the *Cartier*'s signal. The tanker lumbered on. Outraged, the Québécois captain ordered his PCM toward the *Toledo* at full speed and fired a warning shot across the tanker's bow for good measure. The *Toledo*'s incredulous skipper radioed U.S. authorities at Massena for help, then defiantly ordered his crew on deck, armed to a man with shotguns and pistols. The *Cartier* closed on the *Toledo,* swerved, then raced alongside the tanker and, in a gesture of affronted authority, deliberately sideswiped the *Toledo* amidships, carving a 40-foot gash along its waterline. Shots were fired, several crewmen from both vessels were slightly wounded. The *Toledo* came to a full stop, taking on water while thousands of gallons of its crude began spilling from the gash into the St. Lawrence.

Within days the tides had pushed the gummy ooze into the river's wildlife and fish-spawning habitats, wiping out smelt and salmon, muskrats and mollusks, the marsh birds and vegetation that support the region's fragile ecosystem. Along hundreds of miles of the St. Lawrence littoral, beaches and marinas were soiled. The shorelines of Quebec, eastern Ontario, and northern New York faced a pollution disaster, and Quebec-American relations reached their nadir.

By the dawn of the new year 2002, Canada had finally started to come to grips with the long-term prospect of life without Quebec. The pain had begun to subside. Canada had not lost its heart, as Trudeau had once predicted it would if Quebec left, only its spark. Many Canadians had actually begun to put Quebec out of mind, as they wearily turned to the problems of holding together their truncated, and still divided country.

Canada's dissected anatomy resembled a kind of East and West Pakistan, the Atlantic provinces left dangling by themselves like useless outer limbs. In one cruel slice, the nation's population had dropped by 6 million, to less than 22 million people, half of whom inhabited one province, Ontario. It was as though Texas or New York had taken a walk, leaving California as America's top-heavy giant; Canada's governing institutions had been rocked, their legitimacy weakened: secession had cost the federal Parliament a quarter of its members, the Supreme Court a third of its justices. Montreal was rapidly becoming a memory as the anglophone disapora continued. Vancouver, gateway to the riches of the Pacific Rim, was challenging Toronto to become Canada's top city. The flight of foreign capital had wasted Bay Street, threatening Toronto's primacy as the country's financial center. A new migration had begun, matching that from Quebec in the 1800s: thousands of Canadians from the impoverished Maritimes and Saskatchewan were leaving their seaside villages and worn-out family farms to seek new lives in the more prosperous communities of southern Alberta, British Columbia, and Ontario. The migrants placed new burdens on cities like Calgary and Toronto, where housing shortages spread and welfare costs rose dramatically. The transmigration stirred the chronic resentments between Canada's "haves" and "have nots," the old regional hates. Even with Quebec gone, the divisions remained, fraying the last strands of nationhood.

Beyond Canada's borders, analysts coldly assessed the fallout: Canada would fall permanently behind the United States in trade competition; within a decade, Japan and Mexico would supplant it as America's top trading partners. A diminished Canada would become more dependent on the policies and good offices of Washington. If the Canada-U.S. trade accord had been any indication, with so many of Ontario's plants shut down or crippled, foreign competition in the future could bring even more dislocation to Canada's inefficient economy. Meanwhile, the international community, meeting in emergency sessions in Brussels, Geneva, and at the United Nations, tried to calculate where a humbled Canada would fit in the new world order. The Group of Seven quietly made plans to invite Spain to replace Canada in the world's most coveted club. The Organization of American States and NATO took hard new readings on what further significant contributions Canada could make to their bodies. The United States and Mexico reconsidered their plans for Canada to play a more assertive partnership role in the economic and trade structure of the Western Hemisphere.

Anyone examining the economic prospects of Canada without Quebec would have appreciated the world community's concern. Canada might not have assumed Third World status, a Yemen with polar bears, but it was well on its way to realizing some of the worst-case predictions made by bankers and economists a decade earlier. A year after separation, nationwide unemployment had reached 8 percent and was still climbing; personal income was falling. Canada's standard of living had begun dropping at a rate that would put it within another ten years at 25 percent or more below America's. That was powerful incentive for many Canadians to pack up and move south. Canada had not only lost the cultural vibrancy radiated by Quebec, but was losing the vitality that masses of new and versatile young workers traditionally brought to the labor force. That influx was declining due to the exodus southward and stalled birth rates.

The loss of Quebec's tax base accelerated the decline in federal transfer and equalization payments to the provinces, leading to ever lower incomes, higher taxes, and reduced services in the poorer regions. Ottawa had even less maneuverability now to finance the nation's growth and development, to fund job-creating projects and social needs. The government's ability to cap its spiraling debt had been impaired to the point where the International Monetary Fund had moved in to manage the crisis. At the same time, people's pensions and savings were bound to sink further in value as Canadians and Quebecers anticipated eventually having to deal with two currencies. Quebecers faced the wrench of having to convert everything from their assets and liabilities to salaries and wages into the new currency. Investors faced the risks of having to deal with volatile exchange rates in future transactions in Quebec and Canada.

Canada's economic woes without Quebec had cooled investors everywhere. In the past, foreign investors had always given more credibility to Canada's government bond markets, there being too few world-class corporations in Canada to compete with Ottawa in the borrowing game. Now, even Canada's government paper was suspect. Standard & Poor had long since downgraded the federal government as well as Canada's economically dicier provinces; now, it had put even such heavyweights as Ontario and Alberta on "negative watch," which meant they faced increased borrowing costs. Some provinces were already paying 1 percent higher than the U.S. Treasury rate for thirty-year bonds. Ailing Canadian companies were paying as much as 9 percent to borrow instead of the customary 7 percent, and the moneymen in New York predicted things would only get worse. For Canada, Americans had become the lenders of first and last resort: once Standard & Poor had slapped Ottawa and the provinces with double-B ratings, the bond markets in Europe had shut off the spigot.

The trade picture was cloudy at best. Canada had lost much of the diversity in exports which Quebec had brought to the table via such industries as electronics, mass transit, and aerospace. Political opposition to Canada-U.S. and North American free trade had rebounded with Quebec's departure. Ontario, more powerful than ever and the perennial seedbed of free trade resistance from Big Labor and its New Democratic Party patron, was pressing for abrogation of the NAFTA even as it sought to cut its own intramural trade deal with Quebec. The strains on Canada's wounded federation were compounded by the every-province-for-itself mood which had taken hold since separation. Like turtles retreating within their shells, the provinces dug in behind their trade barriers, further impeding Canada's east-west commerce and accelerating the inexorable flow of trade southward.

Quebec's exit had set in motion fissive tendencies that no planned decentralization could have effected half so swiftly. Overnight, Canada was left holding a checkerboard of provinces dominated by three—Ontario, Alberta, British Columbia—which represented more than two thirds of the population. The provinces in this new era were becoming rival centers of power, their premiers assuming ducal status, several counting themselves as national leaders equal to the Prime Minister. "National" had become interchangeable with "regional." Of the four political parties, only Reform still commanded power over an entire region, the West. Canada's economic woes and decentralizing drift had further weakened the credibility of the socialist New Democrats who controlled only a few scattered seats in the Prairies and Maritimes. Separation had decimated the governing Liberal Party which was discredited for having let Quebec go on its watch. The Progressive Conservatives, destined for eclipse nine years earlier, had struggled back but were still largely confined to minor power sharing in Ontario with the Liberal and Reform parties.

The stunting of the national parties only reinforced the sense of drift at Canada's center, the growing self-absorption of its embittered provinces. The federal government's powers were now confined to national defense, foreign and monetary policies, and international trade. Even the nation's ostensibly national banks danced to the tune of provincial regulation. The

House of Commons in Ottawa, home to a quartet of parties all singing off-key, resembled one of Italy's chaotic "pizza" parliaments. There was talk of eventually winding down the federal Parliament and having Ottawa's remaining powers administered by an executive council of premiers representing the key regions.

Without Quebec's influence, traditional support for redistributing federal funds to the weaker provinces faded. The cost of generosity had always been high, and now it had reached its outer limits. Canadians in the better-off provinces no longer could abide seeing their tax monies flung at empty fishing trawlers in Newfoundland or at an Unemployment Insurance system that encouraged self-enforced idleness. The slow death of federal transfer payments meant that Canada's regions, so diverse in their economies and therefore vulnerable to periodically crushing economic swings—an oil price collapse here, a drought there—could no longer rely on Ottawa's battered fiscal structure to stabilize the impacts. That, in turn, invited the likelihood of sharper and more frequent regional recessions. The provinces would increasingly have to look to their own survival.

They could follow Quebec and form a North American Confederacy of Sovereign States, as a group of anglophone Montrealers had once suggested in 1849, each province a freewheeler within a larger common market. Or they could drastically shift their populations to meet employment realities; the poorer provinces would continue to empty their territories, leaving behind desolate Saharas of the north. Or, the provinces could reconfigure the Canadian map once more, forming regional alliances and economic networks. It was the last idea that began to take shape sometime during 2002.

Cut off from mainland Canada, the vast new country of Quebec having interposed itself between the anglophone cultures of Ontario and Atlantic Canada, the Maritimes and Newfoundland for the first time sought true company in the misery of their isolation. As more of their youth fled westward to the beckoning horizons of Ontario and Alberta, the Atlantic provinces faced the prospect of an aging workforce and increasing irrelevance to the continental economy. Ottawa's largesse was fast drying up, the last economic props slipping away. Provinces which retained cultural and economic ties to Quebec—New Brunswick and its francophone Acadians, Newfoundland with its sales to Quebec of hydroelectricity from its Churchill Falls plant in Labrador—had meager negotiating powers individually. As part of an economic union, however, they could deal in matters of immigration and energy swaps from a stronger base. For too long the Atlantics had competed against themselves, wasting their limited resources ensuring that each province could boast its own public utility board or research center for aquatic technology. For too long Newfoundland's leaders, megadreamers like former premier Joey Smallwood, had convinced themselves that their island, with its offbeat culture and offshore oil, was far too unique to be linked with the Maritimes. Now, all that would change.

In July 2002, the premiers of the four Atlantic provinces signed an agreement of intent to mobilize their economies into a single union, to pool their sizable forestry, mining, and fishing resources, and to henceforth coordinate their various educational, environmental, health care, and business initiatives. The new Atlantic Union would embrace a $40 billion economy, the world's forty-third largest, comparable to Austria's. It would be an economic entity with the leverage to attract possibly one day the acquisitive interests of America's Northeast, in particular New England.

For the rest of Canada, it was Ontario that presented the most visible problem. Its lopsided power now threatened the country with a paralyzing imbalance. Ontario's share of the population, 10.4 million of Canada's 21 million people, had surged overnight from 36 percent to nearly 50 percent; the continuing exodus of anglophones from Quebec would swell that share even further. Ontario's proportion of the gross domestic product had shot up from 40 percent to 55 percent, meaning more than half the nation's economic wealth was now produced in one province. With nearly 100 of the remaining 220 House of Commons seats in its grasp, Ontario not only controlled the federal Parliament, but alone had the potential to veto any further constitutional changes in Canada.

Ontario's distorting empowerment suggested three options. It could submit to its own partition into two new provinces, Ontario East and Ontario West, plus a third province incorporating Metropolitan Toronto (an area of 4 million people, or more than live in all of the Atlantic provinces combined). It could stay put and rely on the regional alliances of Atlantic Canada and the West, plus the creation of new provinces in the North, to correct the imbalance. Or, Ontario could decide, for reasons at least as plausible as Quebec's, to seek independence itself.

The province's staggering budget deficits, the need under free trade to reform its creaky industries, signaled the time had finally arrived for Ontario's withdrawal as chief paymaster for the "have nots," a wearisome role. Ontario had witnessed the slow decline of its prized territorial asset, Ottawa; it had seen the Ontario-Quebec manufacturing axis sundered. It feared for the survival of its prime automobile industry, once secure under the Canada-U.S. Auto Pact, now in doubt because Ontario could no longer deliver the Quebec market. The province faced a shaky new nation on one side, a jealous and resentful region on the other; the West would never accept Ontario's dominance. Ontario was rich and productive enough to make it easily as a sovereign state. Through Toronto's links with cities like Detroit and Cleveland, it might one day even become part of a Great Lakes regional community tied to America. In sum, the context and mood was right for a bid by Ontario for sovereignty.

Canada's West as a regional coalition seemed as unlikely at first glance as an Atlantic Union. Manitoba had more in common with Ontario than with Saskatchewan or Alberta; it had been settled by homesteaders from Ontario, and it shared such commonalities as mining and hydroelectric resources, along with a belief in small-scale manufacturing, activist labor unions, and a strong central government. Saskatchewan resembled Manitoba agriculturally, but had closer resource links to Alberta via oil, natural gas, and uranium. Alberta, in turn, shunned both its Prairie sisters as too poor, too socialist, too anti-free trade, and too dependent on Ottawa. That said, the argument for prairie integration and a three-province western alliance was still persuasive. Plans called for the Prairies to pool their research and educational facilities, form a consortium of their powerful telecommunications companies, harmonize their transportation and farming policies, and establish a Prairie Stock Exchange. The three provinces would underwrite a permanent equity pool for small businesses in the region. It was all a plausible enough dream, lacking only sustained political will and resistance to the growing lures south of the 49th parallel.

As for British Columbia, aloof on the other side of the Rockies, it pondered a private agenda of its own. Its west was the Pacific Rim and the Oregon coast, not Alberta or Manitoba; its future lay in Tokyo and Seattle, not Calgary or Winnipeg.

Behind the maneuverings for regional power blocs lay the unspoken American factor. Canada's provinces would reconsolidate, on the record, in order to preserve some sense of balance against an omnipotent Ontario. But they would also reconsolidate to protect themselves from being swallowed bit by bit by the American Colossus; or, less obvious, to make themselves more alluring economically for an eventual U.S. takeover. That last was the premise behind the Atlantics' union and increasingly it was in the back of the minds of other provincial policy makers. Without Quebec, Canada was more than ever a country in search of its national purpose, some raison d'être that would justify its existing apart on a continent embraced by America. It could pretend to a certain distinctiveness from the United States, keep a formal distance, but without the francophone influence the exercise would appear spurious and self-defeating. The nationalist morality play in Canada was ending its long run, and most of the provinces knew it. The spectacle that dominated the stage now was continental and global economics, and the provinces were shifting the scenery to accommodate it. They would adapt to the new reality, the relentless U.S. hegemonic creep. They would even exploit it. Naturally, the Americans were there helping the process along.

In U.S. border posts like Buffalo, New York, and Bellingham, Washington, the local chambers of commerce outdid themselves to promote their cities as ideal havens for restless Canadian businesses. The cross-border shopping sprees of the early 1990s had declined as the Canadian dollar had dropped in value, but heavy corporate taxes and rigid investment controls were driving more and more Canadian manufacturers into the eager arms of American realtors and economic development sharpies. The Americans offered an array of inducements: lower taxes, cheaper land, below-market rates for borrowing capital to build new plants, special grants to cover the cost of training new employes. The Americans traveled north in droves to make their case; in Vancouver, standing-room-only crowds turned up to hear presentations by officials from Whatcom County below the border. In Toronto, representatives from midwestern states like Ohio, Michigan, and Illinois beefed up their trade offices to spread the message to Canadian executives: locating their operations in the United States could save a pile in labor costs, corporate income taxes, and property-tax liabilities.

Along the Canada-U.S. border, where Manitoba and Saskatchewan bump against Minnesota, Montana, and North Dakota, the first hints of a regional hookup began circulating. Manitobans and Minnesotans shared

Scandinavian roots, a grain-exporting culture, and a history of trading relations along the mighty Red River. At the annual Red River Valley conference, business leaders earnestly discussed the prospects for a new economic sphere to include Minneapolis-St. Paul, Grand Forks, and Winnipeg. Saskatchewan made tentative overtures to Montana, Colorado, and Wyoming for inclusion in a proposed Rocky Mountain corridor where the economic connectors would be cattle, wheat, coal, and hydroelectric power.

Further west, Alberta contemplated a future tied either to a dubious Prairie alliance, an energy cartel linking Calgary to Denver and the Houston–Dallas–Tulsa axis, or a Pacific Northwest economic combine that included British Columbia. Over the years Alberta had been drawn closer to the Pacific Northwest and California, where the markets for its food, forestry, oil, and natural gas products had expanded, and where there was a shared belief in the small business culture. Seattle, as much as Vancouver, had become Alberta's preferred port for its exports to the Pacific Rim. Now, Alberta recast itself from a prairie to a northwest mountain province and elected to take its chances for the long term in a distinctly American-edged coalition.

By mid-2002, Canada's second and third richest provinces had committed themselves irrevocably to the Pacific alliance whose other members included Alaska, Idaho, Montana, Oregon, and Washington. Alberta and British Columbia constituted a little over a third of the region's 15 million inhabitants and annual gross product of $280 billion. The economy of the Pacific Northwest Economic Region was exceeded by only nine nations in the world. The group was a coming force in the export of high technology, aerospace, and finished wood products. It would shortly become the world's major supplier of pollution-cleanup technology, a leading marketer of recycled materials, and a continental trailblazer in the production of fiber optics and computer software. The new territory, with three major ports, formed one of the world's largest shipping centers. It had already created a telecommunications hub linking all of its university libraries. The region was richly served by a transmission belt of hydroelectric power lines, courtesy of B.C. Hydro and the Bonneville Power Administration; the booming industrial corridor of Interstate-5, which stretched from Portland all the way to Vancouver; and a newly inaugurated high-speed bullet train connecting both cities.

In short, Cascadia or Pacifica, as the new region was variously tagged, constituted a perfect vehicle for the gradual assimilation of Canada's drifting provinces into the American matrix.

The portents of America's absorption of Canada had been there right along, certainly since the first stirrings of free trade. British military power and Confederation had blunted the thrust of "manifest destiny," and Sir John Macdonald's high-tariff policies had walled in Canada long enough for it to have developed its own manufacturing base and economy. The place might otherwise have long since been depopulated. But by the late twentieth century Canada's internal strains, the pressures of free trade, and America's enormous gravitational pull had forced the obvious. George Ball had figured it right when he wrote in 1968 that Canada was fighting "a rearguard action against the inevitable," and that sooner or later Canadian-American free trade would impel the integration of the two nations' economies. That, the former U.S. Undersecretary of State had concluded, would gradually require an ever greater degree of "political cohesion," diplomatic puff for the U.S. absorption of Canada.

Others had seen it coming. Charles Ritchie, Canada's Ambassador to Washington in the 1960s, warned that once the British Commonwealth lost influence, Ottawa's balancing act between London and Washington would end and Canada would "inevitably drift further into the American bloc." President Jimmy Carter's national security adviser, Zbigniew Brzezinski, watching the rise of Quebec separatism in the late 1970s, reportedly pegged Canada as "terminal," headed on an irreversible course toward breakup. Quebec's departure had of course accelerated the trend, but so had free trade and the saturation of American culture: cable TV, satellite broadcasting, and round-the-clock CNN. About the time the Free Trade accords with the United States and Mexico had finally turned Canada's north-south trade flows into a torrent, the nation was also surrendering the remains of its cultural independence. Canada, like a great spaceship circling and slipping into the Earth's atmosphere, was revolving at last into America's inevitable orbit.

Canadians—their businesses, their bank accounts, their families and, finally, their flag—followed the economic tidal flow south, with resignation in their hearts. Except for the pain of leaving a country behind, it was reminiscent of the gold rushes of another century. Whole provinces, from Canada's West to its stranded Atlantics, set sail for the big casino across the border. Alberta and British Columbia, wrapped in their protective Pacific alliance, gravitated smoothly into the green and high-tech cornucopia of America's Northwest. Saskatchewan and Manitoba put their granaries and potash mines on the block, and applied for admission to an extended Rocky Mountain–Red River economic community under U.S. aegis. Ontario, protesting to the last, rolled over into the warming hug of the Great Lakes states. The united Atlantics negotiated an interim deal, supported by New England's governors, to become an autonomous commonwealth tied to the United States, another Puerto Rico. Like a massive Arctic cold front, the Canadians swept across the old national border in pursuit of the American dream and trade bonanzas, shoving their investments and new businesses beyond the Buffalos and Bellinghams into the rich U.S. interior, suing by the thousands for American citizenship, statehood, associate status, or whatever, just to belong. At last.

In Washington, American officials watched Canada's slow fade, like the Cheshire Cat, with consternation and regret. They saw nothing joyous or redeeming in the Canadian flight south, little to swell their pride in the provinces' applications en masse for membership in the American republic. Canada's demise had not been in America's best interests. Even as they considered knocking the wheels off the welcome wagon, U.S. policy makers began the painful process of calculating the implications of Canada's ultimate breakup.

"Canada was not here at the beginning of the last century. There is no logic that says it must be here at the beginning of the next."

—JOE CLARK,
Minister of
Constitutional Affairs,
March 1992

"Thucydides wrote that Themistocles' greatness lay in the fact that he realized Athens was not immortal. I think we have to realize that Canada is not immortal; but if it is going to go, let it go with a bang rather than a whimper."

—PIERRE TRUDEAU
before a
Canadian Senate committee,
March 30, 1988

America's attic, an empty room
a something possible, a chance,
a dance
that is not danced.

—PATRICK ANDERSON,
English poet

7

America
and the World
Without Canada

In the real world of today, the notion of Canada breaking up and sliding piecemeal into the American maw might seem a relic of the mind-set that dominated Theodore Roosevelt's era near the turn of the century. But in the Washington of the 1990s real policy makers wrestle seriously with that notion, as Canada continues to walk the thin line between survival and breakup.

The Canada-watchers at the departments of State and Commerce, members of the White House National Security Council, shrewd analysts squirreled away in the alcoves of academe or in the think tanks of Washington and New York, former diplomats and trade negotiators, senior bureaucrats and mandarins, all the expediters and apparatchiks behind the huge, interlacing machinery that propels Canadian-American relations, have puzzled over the consequences of Canada's possible dissolution, but beg anonymity as they discuss the unthinkable.

America and the world would persevere, of course, without Canada or at least the old Canada, but it would be a significantly changed continental environment, a strategically confused and uncertain one. Washington, in the aftermath of a Canadian breakup, would probably find itself dealing with a number of mini-states to the north. It would by protocol still defer to Ottawa, but in fact Ottawa would be just another chair at the negotiating table in binational talks affecting the provinces in a host of areas from trade and investments to energy and transportation. The complex web of agreements and informal arrangements that governs bilateral communications, agriculture, water rights, law enforcement, and intelligence gathering, as well as all the social and professional synergies between the two peoples, would be in danger of unraveling. Washington would face costly and cumbersome adjustments in having to negotiate with not one political entity but as many as nine. It could be easily tarred by getting sucked into sensitive issues between the provinces or between Ottawa and the provinces. The already intricate bargaining that transpires between U.S. consulates in Canada and individual provinces would turn chaotic. Without a strong central Canadian government exerting its authority across the country, the brassier provinces or new coalitions might try to block or renegotiate specific bilateral treaties; and, under the Canadian Constitution, they would have the ability to do so.

A Canada fractured politically would be a Canada fractured economically, with all the inefficiencies and threats of protectionism that implies. Provinces that regularly discriminate against each other within Confederation could readily do the same to outsiders, despite the Free Trade accord, if they felt threatened in a new milieu of fragmentation. Ontario might elect to opt out of the Canada-U.S. Free Trade Agreement, which it never warmed to, and rebuild tariff walls against selective U.S. exports; or it might negotiate a separate Ontario-Quebec customs union that could hamper U.S. exports and investments. Without federal sway in Ottawa, U.S. industries could end up battling with powerful provinces like Ontario over beer prices, British Columbia over lumber subsidies, or Alberta over energy contracts. American businesses would see themselves whipsawed between differing provincial rules and standards, snared within a galaxy of conflicting regulations. Breakup would be horrendous for U.S. firms in, for example, public accounting where practices vary from province to province. For American businesses, the whole commercial intercourse between Canada and the United States would become a nightmare. Only the lawyers might think it a dream.

In the short term, Canada's breakup would unload a mixed harvest on the United States. Much of Canada's investment capital, brains, and talent would pour across the border, fleeing the precariousness of that country's future. U.S. border areas would profit temporarily at least from the inrush of home and land buyers and businesses seeking to relocate. Employment would likely rise in states like Washington, Minnesota, and New York, where some two hundred or more Canadian companies have over the past decade provided fifty thousand jobs to New Yorkers. At the same time, the border cities might suffer severe runs on their banks as Canadians, migrating deeper into the U.S. interior, removed their "hedge" funds and rainy-day accounts to reinvest them on a more permanent basis wherever they finally landed.

Most assuredly, the United States would lose a valued ally in an increasingly turbulent world, would see the North American partnership weakened and future relations with Canada cast in doubt. The United States would also confront to its north a prickly new nation of Quebec with dubious allegiances and an uncertain course.

Canada's dissolution, if it comes, would not present the same dangers it might have twenty years ago when the separatists first came to power in Quebec. Then, the loss of a united Canada would have been a strategic blow to the Western alliance as it sought to maintain a solid front against Soviet expansion. The end of the Cold War has reduced the military dangers of a northern breakup, just as free trade has mitigated the economic perils. But the rupture of Canada would still put at risk many of America's commercial and continental defense arrangements, while entailing substantial costs to its export economy and foreign policy. Canada's reliability as our closest NATO and North American stalwart would be the first big casualty. No superpower like America can give full focus to, and effectively exercise, its worldwide leadership responsibilities with insecurity or turmoil in its backyard. Over the long term, a wounded Canada would act less boldly and swiftly in North America's interests, and would take fewer risks in the international arena. U.S. designs in the hemisphere—for more dependable security structures in Central America and the Caribbean, say, or for more durable democracies in the southern cone—would be that much more difficult to accomplish without Canada's committed support. A fractured Canada would gradually lose its international Boy Scout image, which U.S. diplomats have found immeasurably helpful. When America has wished some other power to take the lead on initiatives where U.S. credibility was weak, it has frequently used Canada as a stalking horse because, as one U.S. diplomat put it, "They can do things that we can't."

Above all, the breakup of Canada would be the death blow of an ideal cherished by America and realized in few if any other parts of the globe: along one of America's two land borders, the enduring presence of a single foreign country that for more than a lifetime has stood for peace, stability, decency, democratic values, and most of those other virtues Americans like to think they have a monopoly on.

Breakup might have a far more prolonged impact, however. American analysts have weighed the possibility of one or more Canadian provinces applying for statehood, considered what the U.S. response might be, and gauged the reaction of Canada's federal government should America decide to accept the provinces. The turning mood of an abridged Canada, riven internally and humbled abroad, could over time result in policies and actions detrimental to Canadian-American relations and dangerous to continental security.

If dissolution occurred and a number of provinces were to court the United States, U.S. authorities would not leap to roll out the red carpet, at least initially. Diplomatically, admitting any provinces would aggravate Ottawa, which has always suspected the United States of annexationist tendencies; in much of the world it would tarnish America's image for seeming overtly expansionist. Politically, Canada's pervasive liberalism and still influential social-democratic left would make its admission as welcome to U.S. Republicans as the idea of crowning statehood on the Democrat-leaning District of Columbia. In economic terms, admitting such welfare cases as the Atlantic provinces or Saskatchewan would simply increase the drag on America's economy.

At bottom, the American leadership might simply conclude that, with rare exception, Canada's provinces were unassimilable. For all the two nations' shared values, history has etched in the Canadian pysche certain assumptions that run square against the American grain: the government dependency syndrome, for one, and the pacifist, flower-in-the-muzzle complex, for another. The Canadian soul is too comforted by authority and order for Americans' tastes, too receptive at times to gauzy chatter about redistributing the wealth. Canadians just might not make very good

Americans. "Being an American is a very serious job," the journalist David Frum has written, "while being a Canadian isn't." Americans, however irrepressible, carry the weight of their responsibility for the world's security, which may explain their hyperactive patriotism. Canadians don't have that sense of responsibility, indeed are repelled by it. Admitting whole chunks of the Canadian populace to the United States would make for a much tougher psychological conversion than admitting the tides of the world's oppressed for whom the American ethos is a coveted grail.

Just as U.S. authorities would prepare to slam the door on the provinces' requests for statehood, however, a second opinion might land on the President's desk. This one, a joint memorandum from the Pentagon, the officials in charge of America's strategic reserves, plus the departments of Agriculture, Energy, and Interior, would offer a reassessment of Canada's natural resources in terms of America's benefit. The memo would start from the premise that Canada—sitting on the world's third richest mineral trove, with the third largest forest area, and 14 percent of the planet's fresh surface water—harbors the greatest resource potential in the Western world.

The memo would note the following: that Saskatchewan's uranium and Manitoba's nickel hoards would be welcome additions to the strategic reserve; that British Columbia's endless forests could prove a boon to the U.S. housing industry; and that even with its depleting oil resources, Canada would still have available by the year 2110 some 16 billion barrels from its remaining reserves of heavy and light oil, a potentially huge windfall if added in part to predicted U.S. reserves of 24 to 30 billion barrels by the same year. The memo would repeat the warning of an earlier President that America's strength is dangerously dependent on a thin line of oil tankers stretching halfway round the globe, originating in the Middle East and the Gulf, one of the most unstable regions anywhere. The memo would add that by the turn of the century, with U.S. energy demands still climbing, America's Prudhoe Bay and Britain's North Sea will have run dry of oil. The authors would end this section with the notation that across Alberta and parts of Saskatchewan lie nearly 50 billion barrels of heavy oil, locked in underground reservoirs, plus an estimated 1 trillion barrels of oil contained in tar sands, all awaiting extraction.

A key section of the memo would address the issue of water, the primary resource question facing North America in the years ahead. At ten times the size of Canada's population and industrial plant, the United States has only half of Canada's water resources, and its thirst increases yearly. The Middle West and Southwest regions cry for more water to irrigate their frequently arid croplands. The experience has too often been an abysmal one of drying rivers, sinking wells, and lower crop yields. Farms in Arizona have shut down for lack of water; in the semi-desert state of Utah, expanding farmland is rapidly using up its water allocations. The massive Ogallala aquifer, which supplies eight Midwest states, will go dry shortly after the year 2000. Tempers are on edge as hard-pressed farm states, whose dams regulate the flows of rivers like the Colorado, rebel at having to pass along torrents of scarce water to generate the hydroelectric power that keeps cities like Los Angeles air-conditioned.

The constant droughts and brownouts have forced ever greater demands on Canada for water exported from its northern regions. There, the vast flows from snow run-offs and glacial ice melts have filled the upper reaches of British Columbia and the Prairies with a lacework of rushing rivers and lakes. Saskatchewan alone boasts an estimated 100,000 lakes; Manitoba's Lake Winnipeg is the world's thirteenth largest repository of fresh water. With such abundance, Canada might seem eager to share its water for a price. But down through the years of Canadian-American relations violence has been known to erupt over the allocation of water rights. As one Canadian politician put it, exporting his nation's water "is the equivalent of selling our blood for money. It's where we draw our line in the sand." Canadians have regularly bridled at U.S. proposals to tap into their river flows and redirect them southward, citing the probability of environmental damage from such diversions. But more than anything, they fear that if they ever signed on to such long-term diversion or water-export projects, America's unslakable thirst would condemn Canadians to a permanent bartering away of their most valuable asset.

The memo to the President would conclude that, although Canadians have traditionally balked at parting with their non-renewable resources, regarding them as valuable bargaining chips, and remain suspicious of U.S. efforts to develop continental resource policies ("our resources, your policies"), the request by entire provinces to enter as new states could change the whole equation and bears serious reconsideration. The admission of several well-endowed Canadian provinces would offer balm to America's parched Southwest, new life to the all-important industry running its exhausted oil patches, and would go far to help replenish its depleting strategic reserves.

It is not inconceivable that, having digested the memorandum, the President would side with his strategic planners and accede to requests by Alberta and British Columbia to be admitted as the fifty-second and fifty-third states after Puerto Rico. Manitoba and Saskatchewan might be placed on associate status, their eventual admission as states dependent on how cooperatively and efficiently their new joint Bureau of Water Exports performs.

Absorption of one or two provinces might stagger an already shrunken Canada, angering it into hostile relations with the United States. In any event, a Canada stripped of its bilcultural peculiarity and fearful of being totally co-opted by U.S. cultural and economic forces might well adopt an anti-American posture as a way of redefining its new identity. Any surge of hardball protectionism from the U.S. Congress would help justify such a stance. At the very least, a beleagured Canadian government, struggling to head off further defections by its provinces, might choose to circle the wagons and hang tough. Canada's leftist New Democrats could very well stage a comeback in this changed atmosphere, rallying anti-U.S. sentiment and influencing government policies that would lead to less cooperation with the United States in NAFTA, NATO, and the United Nations.

America's foremost concern, however, would be the impact of a diminished Canada on continental security, the fact that Washington regards uninhibited access to Canadian territory, airspace, and waters as critical to U.S. defense. An independent, territorially sensitive Quebec could seriously complicate continental security arrangements affecting the use of its airspace, landing, and refueling privileges, the status of NORAD francophone units in Quebec, and the free flow of international shipping through the Quebec end of the St. Lawrence Seaway. The disbanding and relocation to Canada of its Armed Forces based in Quebec, for instance, would cause considerable disarray in Canada's operational effectiveness and its ability to meet its NORAD obligations. A compromised tripartite NORAD command, including Quebec, would hardly appeal to the Pentagon, but remains a distinct possibility. Of graver import would be the will and capability of Canada itself to continue supporting the North American defense structure.

With its ongoing debt crisis, its traditional aversion to U.S. military initiatives, and the fading of the Soviet threat, Canada might reduce even further its NORAD and NATO commitments. It might choose to believe that through its control of territory crucial to the Western alliance, plus its vital natural resources, it could continue to wield disproportionate influence on international and continental security planning. More likely, if Ottawa continued to stint on its defense spending and became increasingly unable to patrol or secure its own borders, the United States would feel compelled to step in and do the job itself. In that event, America would rekindle all the deepest passions about Canadian sovereignty, especially in the Arctic.

For more than a quarter of a century, since a U.S. oil tanker inched its way through the Northwest Passage in 1970 without Canada's permission, Canadians have insisted as a matter of jurisdictional pride that the Arctic waterways belong to them exclusively. They have fretted over the militarization of the area, due to Soviet and U.S. submarine activity, and the environmental degradation that accompanied massive oil and gas exploration by petroleum companies. The Canadians almost went ballistic in 1985 when a U.S. vessel, the icebreaker *Polar Sea,* again navigated the Arctic passage without Ottawa's consent. At one point Ottawa was sufficiently wrought up to have had its Navy install underwater sensors at both entrances of the Northwest Passage to detect American as well as Soviet submarines. Washington's insistence that the Arctic straits remain international has kept the controversy simmering.

Canadian and U.S. differences in the Arctic remind observers of the virtual impossibility that anyone, least of all the Canadians, can properly oversee that multi-million-square-mile domain separating North America from the Russian landmass. A World War II weather station, installed on the Labrador tundra by a Nazi submarine crew, went undetected for four decades. A Polish ship wandered into the Northwest Passage in 1975, and Canadian air patrols still couldn't find it after the ship had announced its presence. There have been rumors for years of reconnaissance and sabotage teams from *Spetsnaz,* the former Soviet Union's elite special force, poking about unnoticed on the Arctic islands. The Canadian authorities have relied mostly on a volunteer force of six hundred Inuit

Rangers to alert them to such suspicious activities. The Rangers, equipped with red baseball caps and World War I rifles, reportedly call an 800 number if they spot trouble.

Comical as they sound, the security arrangements for even such an unlikely prospect as the invasion of the Arctic by an enemy land force suggest the casualness with which Canadians view their defense chores. For more than thirty years the United States has watched the erosion of Canada's military usefulness, and has increasingly questioned Canada's state of readiness, as well as its continuing role as a reliable strategic partner. The Canadian Navy at the end of World War II was the world's third largest; by 1970, it had sold off the nation's only aircraft carrier and was rapidly becoming a minor collection of aging frigates and destroyers. Today's fleet of barely a score of combat ships is incapable of policing Canada's 155,000-mile coastline, the longest in the world. Canada's Armed Forces have dropped from a postwar high of 126,000 personnel in 1962 to below 80,000 today. Some years ago, an internal government study revealed that in a sudden emergency Canada would be able to field only five thousand combat-ready troops, two interceptor jets, and one ship—a situation, according to one Canadian expert, that even the Italians would find disgraceful.

The former Soviet Union's own military decline might alleviate fears for the viability of the North American strategic alliance should Quebec separate and Canada's defenses decline further. In fact, new twists in the nuclear arms game, plus the volatility of the crisis in the old Soviet republics, raise even more questions about Canada-U.S. strategic relations in the years ahead. At the very least, Canada's Arctic could become again a critically important piece of real estate to the United States.

When the great jet bombers of America's Strategic Air Command (SAC) became the world's most formidable nuclear strike force in the late 1950s, the integrated North American Air Defense Command was formed to safeguard the SAC force and assure it adequate warning time to respond to a Soviet bomber attack. The means for this was a soon-completed NORAD system of continental defenses that included, at its peak, 400 radars, 2,600 interceptor jets, 500 missile launchers, and 70 early-warning surveillance aircraft, all manned by up to 248,000 Americans and Canadians. Less than a decade later, when land-based intercontinental and submarine-launched ballistic missiles supplanted the Soviet bomber threat, NORAD was forced to scrap its massive anti-bomber system and became an empire in decline.

Its Defense Early Warning (DEW) line of northern radar posts that stretched from Alaska to Greenland was programmed to track missiles, not bombers, and the Canadian role in this leaner high-tech operation became increasingly limited. Then came the cruise missile, an air-launched, jet-powered nuclear weapon that hugged the terrain as it sped toward its pre-planned target, making it devilishly hard to detect in flight. The advent of the cruise signaled the revival of the bomber as a strategic threat. The best defense against the cruise was to attack the bomber before launch, and that meant the whole air-defense combat arena had to be shifted further north into the High Arctic zone. Thus, the cruise—and the low-flying, radar-eluding bombers that carried it—effectively renewed NORAD's importance and significantly revalued Canada's northern vastness.

By the 1980s, NORAD's geriatric DEW line had become so porous that its operators could no longer guarantee effective early warning of a cruise missile attack. About the same time that noisy "Refuse the Cruise" demonstrations erupted across Canada, opposing U.S. testing of the missile in Canada's North where the terrain matches Russia's, Ottawa and Washington agreed to replace the outmoded DEW line with a modern North Warning System. The new system comprised a necklace of long-range radar sites strung across the Arctic from Alaska to Labrador and bearing code names like Lab-2 or Fox-M. Under plastic white domes resembling giant golf balls, satellite tracking dishes scanned the hyperborean skies to the north, while back-scatter radars peered over the horizons beyond the East and West coasts. A secret satellite communications system linked the new radar sites to Canada's NORAD headquarters at North Bay, Ontario. The whole warning system, supplemented by a handful of forward-area landing strips for NORAD jet fighters, was given the nickname "Paved Paws."

Its development in the late 1980s proved a signal advance in continental security, although some Canadians believed that new radar technology would render the network obsolete by the end of the century. Others feared it would draw Canada further into the Star Wars strategizing of Pentagon planners. Paved Paws did not assuage the larger fear of military analysts that by the early 1990s, after the START Treaty had been signed by the United States and Russia, Canada, as the front line of any nuclear attack on North America, stood to face an expanded armory of Russian cruise missiles which could be launched southward from the Arctic through Canadian airspace. A provision in the treaty to reduce both super-powers' nuclear stockpiles ironically permitted the Russians, as part of a trade-off, to increase their cruise arsenal by nearly half. Thus, instead of land-based ICBMs, easier to track and shoot down with their predictable trajectories, Canada now faces the possibility of some day having to track one or more cigar-shaped cruises streaking at tree level over Canadian territory toward a designated target.

That prospect, however dim at the moment, could take on sharper tones in the context of these possible developments: Quebec's separation and the emergence to America's north of a fragmented Canada, neither event enhancing the continent's security; Canada's military inadequacies and an erosion of Canada-U.S. relations, which might send signals inviting aggression by the Western alliance's adversaries; or a political upheaval in the former Soviet Union, which would precipitate an international crisis. Any prolonged crisis, as security analysts know, involves not only heightened tensions and escalating suspicions but a shift in emphasis to preparing for a very rapid response if hostilities erupt. In such situations the usual safeguards are sometimes apt to be disregarded or even removed.

That is why, with Canada's and Russia's future in doubt today, it is possible to imagine this scenario in the wake of Quebec's secession:

Economic reform has collapsed throughout Russia. Widespread despair over soaring prices, injured pride over Russia's loss of stature, and disgust with Moscow's leadership boil over. A cabal of so-called "Reds" and "Browns"—unreconstructed former Communist officials and neo-Fascist militarists—sweeps the Yeltsin reformers from office. In the name of restoring social order and averting total economic ruin, the leaders of the coup establish an authoritarian provisional government backed by key elements of the disaffected military. The new government resents the Western Alliance for its Cold War triumph and humiliation of the Soviet Union, resents the infatuation with Western culture and consumer products. It especially resents the United States for having won the arms race and reduced Russia to a beggar nation, then acting niggardly in its response to Russian requests for massive economic aid. The Russians,

*who have always regarded Canada as a less vehemently anti-Soviet bal-
ance against the United States in the continental partnership, particularly
resent Canada's fracturing after Quebec's separation and the prospect
of its pieces eventually attaching to the U.S. empire. Russian-North
American relations move from tepid to subfreezing. The new hardliners
running the Kremlin reassess Russia's arsenal of Bear and Blackjack
long-range bombers, its nearly 1,200 air-launchable cruise missiles.
They reanalyze the strategic value of the Arctic, whose jigsawed desert
of ice conceals not only an estimated 500 billion barrels of oil but lurking
nuclear-armed submarines. Then, the Russians order a sequence of air-
borne reconnaissance missions to hard-probe the Arctic and North American defenses.*

*Somewhere on the eastern end of the Beaufort Sea, 30,000 feet above
the approaching Parry Islands, a Russian Bear-H intercontinental
bomber prepares to enter North American airspace clandestinely. The
turboprop bomber, a bright red star on its side, has averaged 400 miles
per hour since it left its base in Siberia and headed over the polar icecap.
It carries inside its bulky frame eight AS-X-15 cruise missiles, each a
little over 20 feet long, each packing a nuclear warhead with more than
five times the power of the Hiroshima bomb. As it wings over Canadian
territory, high enough so that air resistance is minimal, the Bear approxi-
mates the flight mode of a glider, moving silently through the ether except
for short irregular bursts of acceleration from its engines. The bomber is
some 200 miles off Canada's Arctic coast when the ultrasensitive radars
of the North Warning System's CAM-M site at Cambridge Bay pick it up.
CAM-M instantaneously relays the raw data on the unknown aircraft or
"bogie" to NORAD's Region Operations Control Center (ROCC) at
North Bay. In the operations room of the center's subterranean complex,
600 feet deep in a Laurentian mountain, the "ass opers" (Air Surveillance Operators) start a 3¹/₂-minute sequence to establish whether the
bogie is a military or civil aircraft, friend or foe, and the nature of its
flight path and probable destination. The Bear does not respond to ROCC
requests to identify itself. The ass opers within seconds have established
some basic information on the bogie: military, unfriendly, Bear-Hotel
class, and on a flight path pointing generally toward Winnipeg and Min-
neapolis. What the ass opers do not know is whether the Bear is carrying
nuclear weapons, its intentions, and whether it is the vanguard of a possibly larger attack force. At the command post on the floor above the oper-*

*ations room, the commanding major general and two deputies quickly
assess the ass opers' data and order fighter-interceptors to scramble from
an airfield at Paved Paws' nearest Forward Operation Location. They
also notify NORAD's central U.S. command post in Cheyenne Mountain, Colorado.*

*A pair of CF-18 Hornets, attached to the Alouettes, the 425th Tactical
Fighter Squadron based in Bagotville, Quebec, race into the skies and
somewhere above Victoria Island lock their radars onto the approaching
Bear. One of the jets springs a fuel leak and turns back. The other, armed
with six AIM-9 Sidewinder missiles and a 20-millimeter rapid-fire cannon, intercepts the intruder and buzzes it at close range. The young francophone pilot gets no response to his repeated demands that the Russians
confirm whether they are carrying a nuclear payload. He frantically
radios his base command for instructions and zooms in for a closer look
at the bomber, narrowly avoiding the Bear's tail on the pass. The Bear's
pilot takes immediate evasive action, banking his plane steeply at the
same time he finally identifies himself and his payload in angry, almost
threatening tones. For one fearful moment intruder and interceptor seem
transfixed in uncertainty, hovering above the icy barrens of Victoria
Island. The Hornet pilot prepares to respond with a warning burst from
his cannon. The fuming pilot of the Bear considers activating the ejector
cartridges that would thrust a single silvery cruise into the blue, streaking
along its computer-programmed flight path toward a NORAD target.
Then discipline and cold sense reassert themselves. The Bear makes a
shuddering 180-degree turn and heads homeward. The Hornet lingers
several minutes to track the Bear's retreat before it, too, swings back
toward its base.*

In a dangerously unpredictable, post–Cold War world, some arms
experts believe the chances of a fatal miscalculation happening in the
near future are better than 50 percent. The likelier prospect is that a fragmented Canada without Quebec would itself become a lost missile cruising aimlessly through the international sphere, its guidance system
irreparably damaged, doomed to fizzle and fall into some purgatory
reserved for nations that self-destruct.

Canada's demise would be the world's loss. The middle power whose
mediatory diplomacy won it universal plaudits, whose role in the postwar
creation of the United Nations and NATO went far beyond its actual size

and influence, would become a declining power. The Canada of peacekeeping prowess and unstinting generosity to less fortunate nations would fade. The nation whose constructive presence has become a fixture in the world's multilateral architecture—from the Commonwealth to the OECD—would forfeit its active role and its capacity to influence decisions. The world's club of leader nations is relatively small, 30 or so out of a total of more than 170 nations, and within that club less than a half-dozen countries can be regularly counted on to take a world view. Among the latter, Canada—which the economist Barbara Ward once described as the world's "first international nation"—would gradually retreat into a more parochial mind-set, that of a Benelux or Denmark. It would do so, ironically, at a time when new global opportunities and challenges require the dispassionate counsel of just such a nation as Canada; when to withdraw from the world, in former Prime Minister Mulroney's words, "would be an error of historic scale."

The international community would lose not only Canada's valued focus but its special skills and commitments. With Canada unable to act with unilateral authority, the United Nations would find it ever more difficult to rely on Ottawa for prompt military involvement in helping combat aggression or sudden catastrophe in other parts of the world. A unified Canada could continue to play an essential role in helping resolve macro problems like the transfer of human resources from poorer to richer regions or the allocation of food supplies for future Somalias. A Canada fissured would find it increasingly difficult to accept dramatically greater numbers of immigrants or to direct huge quotas of its wheat and grain to the world's starving.

An early casualty of a diminished Canada would be its traditional peacekeeping role, one the Canadians virtually invented. It was their most inspired expression of middlepowership, one that gave Canada a military purpose distinct from the great powers. Ever since a handful of Canadian officers formed part of a small United Nations observer group along the seething India-Pakistan border in 1949, Canadians have made peacekeeping their special identity, serving by the thousands in blue-helmet forces from Angola and Cyprus to the Golan Heights and former Yugoslavia, where they have comprised one of the largest contingents in that decimated country. Few nations in history have deliberately trained their military, as has Canada, for peacekeeping operations thousands of miles from home. No nation has made a greater commitment to the concept. The high financial costs involved, however, have stretched the United Nation's peacekeeping elastic to its breaking point. With a weakened Canada reducing its contribution, the elastic could finally snap.

Another casualty would be the underdeveloped world, which has benefited for decades from a remarkable Canadian generosity disproportionate to the nation's size and wealth. Canada's payments in development aid to poorer countries have ranked it over the years among the top four or five most generous of the developed nations; as a percentage of its gross national product, it spends more than twice what the United States does on foreign aid. Canada, a former U.S. Ambassador to Ottawa acknowledged, "has always had the conviction of America's good intentions." Breakup would harden that soft touch.

Europe would regret Canada's decline, its slow withdrawal from that continent's security deliberations. The withdrawal, however, would hurt Canada far more than Europe. Canada has been reducing its manpower and financial contributions to NATO for decades, and its decision to remove its remaining combat forces from Europe by 1995 has only reinforced the Europeans' perception that, breakup or no, Canada is intentionally marginalizing itself within Western Allied councils. Ottawa may argue that, inasmuch as NATO incorporates North America as well as Europe, withdrawing its troops from Europe to Canada would not be removing them from the common defense. But in doing so, Canada further downgrades its role in the one forum that for nearly half a century has protected Canada from being stranded alone in North America with a domineering United States. NATO has afforded Canada a transatlantic bridge to participation in Europe's military and economic security, a chance to sit at the West's head table and be heard. A Canada broken would see its value to NATO further reduced, ineluctably closing Canada's primary window of international influence.

Latin America would suffer the loss of a potentially useful balance weight against sometimes heavy-handed U.S. policies toward them. Canada historically has preferred to keep a low profile in hemispheric matters, deferring to the preponderant security concerns of the United States. For years it avoided membership in the Organization of American States (OAS), fearing it would be pressured to toe the U.S. line or else appear a spoiler. Since finally joining the OAS in 1989, however, Canada has begun to evince a more than tentative involvement in hemispheric issues, focusing on the democratization of Central and South American countries, and on peacekeeping and the drug trafficking problem in the Caribbean. Canada still keeps a certain distance from the Latin Americans, whom it has regarded in the past as too often undemocratic, more than occasionally temperamental and immature. ("I look on them the way I do my own children," a Canadian bank chairman once told David Rockefeller. "They need to be severely disciplined at times.") But Ottawa has also come to realize that in matters of hemispheric trade and security, Canada, with selected Latin American nations, can effectively counter the United States when it presses too hard for its own way. In the North American Free Trade Agreement, for example, Mexico emphatically wants Canada as an ally, rather than a competitor, when the three NAFTA signatories sit down to iron out specific disputes as they may arise. A devalued Canada is not the ally Mexico has in mind.

A world without Canada, above all, would be a world bereft of the special character and texture that has always defined Canadian international conduct. It may be true, as a comedian joked, that the world needs Canada only because if it wasn't there, the Chinese could sail right across and invade Denmark. It may be truer that the world needs an effective Canada because without it we lose the projection abroad of Canada's largely sensible, compassionate values. On a still dangerous planet burdened by clashing ethnic and nationalist demands, Canada's practiced altruism has been a commodity in short supply, assiduously sought after in the upper strata of international diplomacy.

From his modest office in Ottawa, Mitchell Sharp, a distinguished former Canadian Foreign Minister, can look across the river at the Gatineau Hills turning russet on an early fall day. Sharp recalls that when problems arose, the world's diplomats frequently turned to Canada for help, knowing "we had no ax to grind, no large internal minorities or special-interest groups that would color our ability to act in the interests of world peace." That unusual condition has burnished Canada's credibility in ways that elude America, whose large black population and influential Jewish minority have helped shape, for better or worse, U.S. alliances and policies in Africa, the Middle East, and other volatile regions.

The root and essence of Canada's diplomatic contribution lie in its having carefully bargained, not muscled, its way to its present position of influence in the world. The fact that Canada often sees the world differently from America is one of those intangible benefits that escapes only those who prefer lock-step secondaries as their allies. The nature of Canada, John Holmes pointed out, is that as a nation of limited clout it must tread a more circumspect line, must master nuance rather than bluntness, practice compromise, even occasionally appeasement, as useful means toward productive ends. Holmes grasped that Canadians, "not having the power to contemplate banishing evil from the earth, are less inclined to insist on unconditional surrender."

That has not stopped them from exercising their Scots morality, whether upbraiding deadbeats for withholding their dues to the United Nations or nagging some nuclear powers for not halting their weapons tests. Without Canada, the world would lose a persistent moral voice: the one that helped persuade the Commonwealth in 1986 to impose sanctions against apartheid South Africa; the one that relentlessly champions human rights and made Canada the first nation to officially recognize the newly independent Baltic States; the one that has argued ceaselessly for control of the international arms trade; that has challenged, almost alone within the OAS, human rights crimes and officially sanctioned torture in many areas of Latin America. Without Canada, the world would lose perhaps its most liberal society.

A breakup of Canada would in all likelihood send the world a message of despair. For if Canada, long one of the most successful models of a multi-ethnic society, cannot in the end accommodate the regional and linguistic demands of its constituent parts, the obvious question is, who can? What country and what peoples can hope to succeed if the Canadian experiment in tolerance and cooperation is seen to fail? Canada's disintegration would instruct the world, particularly its less favored peoples, that even the richest, freest, and most developed democracies can die when the will to unify has atrophied. An eclipse of Canada would darken hopes that the democratic ideal is necessarily mankind's salvation.

Nor would the example of Canada's fate sit well with an America that shares in varying degrees many of the same ethnic, linguistic, economic, and fiscal problems afflicting its neighbor. If Canada, with more than a century of democratic governance, cannot hold, so the thinking in Washington goes, it raises questions about America's ability to hold its own sprawling union together. "What then of Alaska, Hawaii, and other remote American territories where there is potential for independence movements?" a senior diplomat asks. Or, what of the prospect of a Spanish-speaking majority emerging at some point in America's Southwest, leading in time to secessionist claims by New Mexico or Texas? Irresponsible ramblings, some may argue. Yet, in the autumn of Canada's 125th year there was near consensus among knowledgeable American diplomats that Quebec would eventually go and that Canada's odds for survival were poor. And responsible Canadians, watching the divisions and rancor spread across their country like some malevolent kudzu, privately warned American visitors that the United States was not immune to the stresses tearing Canada apart.

Stephen Leacock wrote that "The palaces of Nineveh are buried under the Mesopotamian sand, and the Assyrian, who once came down like a wolf on the fold . . . now sells rugs in a palatial hotel in what was once the 'desert of the Saskatchewan.' " It is perhaps too early to consign Ottawa to the fate of Nineveh, Canada to that of Assyria. Some rock-hard stubbornness still lodges in the Canadian spirit, a perseverance to survive the worst. Canada may yet find its compass, the common sense and leadership needed to bridge the divisions that threaten its extinction.

Canadians need to curb their appetite for the perpetual Eden they can no longer afford, and to rein in their sense of being somehow victimized by each other and by the United States. As an American editor wrote more than thirty years ago, they must "put the mirror to themselves and make the harsh decisions that alone can give them the identity they desperately desire." Only then will they regain their footing and purpose as the dependably principled, occasionally ennobling, nation that the world has come to respect.

At sunset in Vancouver, just west of the majestic Lions Gate Bridge, fishermen within a rim of gold-spun sea cast for the coho and Pacific salmon thronging near the entrance to the Capilano River up which they swim to spawn and die. Each season the salmon, born in coastal streams like the Capilano, journey across the Pacific to the Indian Ocean and the Sea of Japan, then return to their haunts in British Columbia—a total distance of almost 7,000 miles. The journey can take as long as seven years. But when the fish return, they miraculously not only zero in on

Vancouver Bay, but with unerring accuracy rediscover the exact river mouth from which they set out on their odyssey years before.

It is an odyssey not unlike the one facing Canadians: an arduous voyage toward self-discovery and renewal, borne along on the currents of hope and redemption.

Acknowledgments

To write of the fate of a country is a presumptuous undertaking. I owe a debt of deep gratitude to the nearly three hundred Canadians and Americans I interviewed, in more than a score of communities in both countries, for this book. I cannot begin to name them all.

I am, however, particularly grateful to a number of Canadian journalists whose guidance was invaluable: Dominique Clift of Montreal, Brian Cole of the *Winnipeg Free Press*, Brenda Dalglish and Bob Lewis of *Maclean's*, Alain Dubuc and Lisa Binsse of *La Presse*, Dale Eisler of the *Regina Leader-Post*, Mary Lou Finlay of the Canadian Broadcasting Corporation, Robert Norman of *Le Soleil*, Jean Paré of *L'Actualité*, Frank Rutter of the *Vancouver Sun*, William Thorsell of Toronto's *Globe and Mail*, David Crane of the *Toronto Star*, Geoff Townsend of the *Charlottetown Guardian*, and Norman Webster of the *Montreal Gazette*. I owe thanks to several American journalists: Laurence Paul of the *Buffalo News*, Trask Tapperson of the *Bellingham Herald*, and my friends and former colleagues in arms, David Greenway of the *Boston Globe* and George Russell of *Time*.

Canadians whose sage advice and support were inestimably helpful include Consul General Allan Sullivan and Curtis Field, director of the Library of the Canadian Consulate in New York City; Rita Dionne-Marsolais of the Parti Québécois in Montreal; James Horsman of the Alberta government; Michael Adams of the Environic Research Group; and such veteran insiders as Dick O'Hagan, Peter Towe, and Jake Warren. Several Canadian and American business executives deserve special thanks for helping me understand the economics of this story: Michael Davies of RBC Dominion Securities, Tom McMillan of Montreal Trust, James Gray of Canadian Hunter Exploration Ltd. in Calgary, Richard Schmeelk and the knowledgeable Joe Taylor of Merrill Lynch's Debt Markets Group in New York. Among the American diplomats I talked with, few have a more informed view of the Quebec situation than Bill McCahill, the former U.S. Consul General in Quebec City.

I am fortunate to have had access to the wise counsel and thoughtful writings of my friends Peter Brimelow, David Crane, William Diebold, Jr., Charles Doran, Richard Gwyn, Peter Newman, Gordon Robertson, Nicholas Stethem, and the late John Holmes.

The following institutions provided me with help in research for which I am indebted: the Canadian Embassy in Washington; the Canadian Consulate in New York; the American Embassy in Ottawa; the Department of State and its excellent consulates in Halifax, Montreal, Calgary, and Vancouver; the Canadian-American Committee and its research arms, the C. D. Howe Institute in Toronto and the National Planning Association in Washington, D.C.; the Canada West Foundation in Calgary; the Fraser Institute in Vancouver; the Canadian National Defence Headquarters and its NORAD personnel; the Hydro-Québec Corporation; the New York Power Authority and the St. Lawrence Seaway Authority; the University of Toronto, the University of Montreal, the University of Saskatchewan, McGill University, and Simon Fraser University.

Not all information comes directly from interviews or publications; much of it comes distilled through informal discourse. I bow in appreciation for the generous hospitality of Brigadier General Romeo Dallaire, Commander of the Canadian Army's 5th Brigade at Valcartier; Professor Robert Dole of the University of Quebec in Chicoutimi; Bob and Louisa Duemling of Washington, D.C.; Peter and Judi Dunn of Quebec City and diplomatic points west; Duncan and Nancy Edmonds of the Old Authors Farm in Morrisburg; the always engaging Mel Hurtig of Edmonton; my old friends Bob and Popsi Johnstone of Toronto and Jim Matkin of Vancouver; the Honorable David Lam, Lieutenant-Governor of British Columbia; the eternally puckish Mavor Moore of Victoria; Leo and Margaret Paré, formerly of Quebec House in New York; Ken and Pat Taylor; Bill and Julia Watson of Montreal; and Tony and Jeannie Westell of Ottawa and Toronto. Thanks all.

For reasons they would understand, I salute the memory of my friend the late Bob Timmins, and thank his widow Pam.

I would not have undertaken this project had not the Americas Society in New York provided me with ten years' worth of accumulated knowledge of Canada and its people. For their support I am especially grateful to George Landau and Stephen Blank, valued colleagues.

Donald Lamm, president of W. W. Norton & Company, my publisher, was an immediate and committed enthusiast of this project; Henning Gutmann, whose thoughtful suggestions and spirited support kept me on keel, was all one could ask for in an editor. I am indebted to them both.

It is ritual to thank spouses for their patience, understanding, etc., but only Ada knows the pains of having had to live for more than a year with a recluse, and how much I cherish her forbearance.

Bibliography

BOOKS, REPORTS, AND ADDRESSES

Adams, Michael. "The Ties That Bound." Notes for address to the Canadian Book Publishers' Council, Toronto, January 22, 1992.

Alberta Select Special Committee on Constitutional Reform. *Alberta in a New Canada: Visions of Unity.* Edmonton, 1992.

Armstrong, Willis. *Canada in Crisis.* Washington, DC: The Atlantic Council of the United States, October 1991.

Aspen Institute for Humanistic Studies. *Canada-U.S. Relations: Perceptions and Misperceptions.* Queenstown, MD, 1987.

Association Canadienne-Française de l'Ontario. *A Canada to Redefine: The French-Speaking Community of Ontario at the Crossroads.* Vanier, Ontario, 1991.

Axworthy, Lloyd. *Prairie Integration: A Blueprint for Economic Renewal.* Winnipeg, February 1992.

Balthazar, Louis. "Quebec: A Distinct Society within a Dynamic Canada." Lecture, Canada House, March 28, 1989.

Barrett, Matthew W. "Renewing Canada: Doing Great Things Together." Address to the Canadian Club of Montreal, May 6, 1991.

Beaudoin, Laurent (Chairman of the Board and CEO, Bombardier Inc.). "Coming to Terms with Canada's Future: A Canadian View from Quebec." Notes for presentation to the Alberta Institute of Chartered Accountants, Calgary, February 18, 1992.

Béland, Claude (President, Mouvement des caisses Desjardins). "Challenging Nineties for Quebec." Notes for presentation to the Americas Society, New York, September 17, 1992.

Belanger, Michel, and Jean Campeau. *Report of the Commission on the Political and Constitutional Future of Quebec*. Montreal, March 1991.

Bercuson, David J., and Barry Cooper. *Deconfederation: Canada without Quebec*. Toronto: Key Porter Books, 1991.

Berton, Pierre. *Why We Act Like Canadians*. Toronto: McClelland & Stewart, 1982.

Blank, Stephen. *The Crisis in Canada and the Emerging Architecture of North America*. New York: Americas Society / Pace University, September 1992; Global Business Policy Council Brief.

Blank, Stephen, and Guy Stanley. *Is Canadian Federalism a Model for Europe and the Soviet Union?* International Economy, November 1990.

Breton, Albert, and Raymond Breton. *Why Disunity? An Analysis of Linguistic and Regional Cleavages in Canada*. Ottawa: Institute for Research on Public Policy, 1980.

Brimelow, Peter. *The Patriot Game: National Dreams and Political Realities*. Toronto: Key Porter Books, 1986.

Business Council on National Issues. *Canada and the 21st Century*. Ottawa, April 26, 1991.

Canada West Foundation. *1991 Annual Report*.

Canada Year Book 1992. Publications Division, Statistics Canada, Ottawa.

Canadian-American Committee, 1957–92, A Thirty-Fifth Anniversary Retrospective Toronto; Washington, DC: C. D. Howe Institute and National Planning Association, 1992.

The Canadian Provincial Story. Merrill Lynch, Pierce, Fenner & Smith, Inc. Budget briefing paper; June 21, 1991.

Canadian Upstream Oil & Gas Industry Profitability. September 1991; executive summary prepared for the Canadian Petroleum Association and the Independent Petroleum Association of Canada.

Carver, George A., Jr. *The View from the South: A. U.S. Perspective on Key Bilateral Issues Affecting U.S.-Canadian Relations*. Washington, DC: Center for Strategic and International Studies, Georgetown University, 1985.

Charlottetown Agreement, Consensus Report on the Constitution. August 28, 1992.

Chartier, Armand B. *Franco-Americans and Quebec: Linkages and Potential*. Paper presented at the World Peace Foundation Colloquium, Harvard University, September 1982.

Clarkson, Stephen. *Canada and the Reagan Challenge*. Toronto: James Lorimer & Co., in association with the Canadian Institute for Economic Policy, 1982.

Clift, Dominique. *The Secret Kingdom: Interpretations of the Canadian Character*. Toronto: McClelland & Stewart, 1989.

Confederation for the Twenty-First Century. Discussion Papers on British Columbia in Confederation. Victoria, B.C.: Canadian Cataloguing in Publication Data, 1991.

Conference Board of Canada. *Provincial Outlook*. Winter 1992; economic forecast.

Cook, Ramsay. *Canada and the French-Canadian Question*. Toronto: Copp Clark Pitman, 1986.

———, with John Saywell and John Ricker. *Canada: A Modern Study*. Rev. ed. Toronto: Irwin Publishing, 1971.

Courchene, Thomas J. *In Praise of Renewed Federalism*. Toronto: C. D. Howe Institute, 1991.

———. *Global Competitiveness and the Canadian Federation*. Toronto: C. D. Howe Institute, 1992.

Courtney, John C. "Spectators on the Playing Field: The Changing Dynamics of Canadian Politics." Address to the Americas Society, New York, March 14, 1991.

Crane, David. *The Next Canadian Century*. Toronto: Stoddart Publishing Company, 1992.

Curtis, Kenneth M., and John E. Carroll (with a foreword by Cyrus R. Vance). *Canadian-American Relations: The Promise and the Challenge*. Toronto: Lexington Books, 1983.

Davis, Robert H. *Canada Cavalcade: The Maple Leaf Dominion from Atlantic to Pacific*. New York: D. Appleton-Century, 1937.

DeMille, Dianne. *Accidental Nuclear War: Reducing the Risks*. Ottawa: Canadian Institute for International Peace and Security, January 1988.

Department of National Defence. *Challenge and Commitment: A Defence Policy for Canada*. Ottawa, 1987.

––––––. *Defence Update 1988–89*. Paper presented to the House of Commons Standing Committee on National Defence, Ottawa, March 1988.

Desbarats, Peter. *Canada Lost / Canada Found: The Search for a New Nation*. Toronto: McClelland & Stewart, 1981.

Diebold, William, Jr., ed. *Bilateralism, Multilateralism and Canada in U.S. Trade Policy*. A Council on Foreign Relations Book. Cambridge, MA: Ballinger Publishing Co., 1988.

Doran, Charles F. *Forgotten Partnership: U.S.-Canada Relations Today*. Baltimore; Johns Hopkins University Press, 1984.

––––––, and John H. Sigler, eds. *Canada and the United States: Enduring Friendship, Persistent Stress*. Englewood Cliffs, NJ: Prentice-Hall, 1985; sponsored by the American Assembly and the Council on Foreign Relations.

Doran, Charles F., with Puay Tang. *Canada: Unity in Diversity*. Headline Series. Foreign Policy Association, Winter 1989–90.

Economic Council of Canada. *A Joint Venture: The Economics of Constitutional Options*. 28th Annual Review, 1991.

Energy Resources Conservation Board. *Energy Alberta 1991*. Review of Alberta Energy Resources in 1991, Calgary, 1992.

Feldman, Eliot J., and Neil Nevitte, eds. *The Future of North America: Canada, the United States, and Quebec Nationalism*. Lanham, MD: University Press of America, 1979; sponsored by the Center for International Affairs, Harvard University, and the Institute for Research on Public Policy.

Fox, William T. P. *A Continent Apart: The United States and Canada in World Politics*. Toronto: University of Toronto Press, 1985.

Fry, Earl H. "A Chronology of Canada's Constitutional Crisis: Background Information for the U.S. Community." Briefing Paper. Department of Canadian Studies, Brigham Young University, October 1991.

––––––. *Canada's Unity Crisis: Implications for U.S.-Canadian Economic Relations*. New York: The Twentieth Century Fund Press, 1992.

Gandhi, Prem P. *The Free Trade Agreement and Canadian Investment in Northern New York*. Plattsburgh, NY: State University of New York Press, 1991.

Garreau, Joel. *The Nine Nations of North America*. Boston: Houghton Mifflin, 1981.

Gill, Robert M. *Language Policy and the Status of French in Quebec*. Radford, VA: Radford University Press, 1991.

Gogo, Jean L., ed. *Lights on the St. Lawrence*. Toronto: Ryerson Press, 1958.

Government of Alberta. *Rebalancing Federal-Provincial Spending Responsibilities*. May 1992.

Government of Canada. *The Indian Act of 1876* (extracts).

––––––. *Prosperity Through Competitiveness*. Consultation paper; 1991.

––––––. (Minister of Supply and Services). *Our Future Together: An Agreement for Constitutional Renewal*. Ottawa, 1992.

Government of Newfoundland and Labrador. *Change & Challenge: A Strategic Economic Plan for Newfoundland and Labrador*. Policy paper; June 1992.

Government of Quebec. *The St. Lawrence: A Vital National Resource*. Report of the Projet Saint-Laurent; June 1985.
———. *The Basis of the Quebec Government's Policy on Aboriginal Peoples*. 1988.
———. *The Quebec Manufacturing and Trade Sectors in 1991*.
———. *Quebec's Traditional Constitutional Positions 1936–1990*. Working paper; 1991.
Grady, Patrick. *The National Debt and New Constitutional Arrangements*. Working paper prepared for the Economic Council of Canada, Ottawa; 1992.
———. *Quebec Through Darkly Tinted Lenses: Economic Consequences of Quebec Sovereignty*. Comments prepared for the Manhattan Institute, New York, January 1992.
Granatstein, J. L., and Norman Hillmer. *For Better or For Worse: Canada and the United States to the 1990s*. Toronto: Copp Clark Pitman, 1991.
Grant, George. *Lament for a Nation: The Defeat of Canadian Nationalism*. Ottawa: Carleton University Press, 1986.
Gray, James K. *Who's in Charge?* Paper presented to Alternatives '91 Constitutional Conference, Canada West Foundation, Banff, Alberta, September 28, 1991.
The Group of 22. *Some Practical Suggestions for Canada*. June 1991.
Gwyn, Richard. *The Northern Magus: Pierre Trudeau and Canadians*. Toronto: McClelland & Stewart, 1980.
———. *The 49th Paradox: Canada in North America*. Toronto: McClelland & Stewart, 1985.
Hampson, Fen Osler, and Christopher J. Maule, eds. *A New World Order?* Ottawa: Carleton University Press, 1992.
Hart, Michael. *A North American Free Trade Agreement: The Strategic Implications for Canada*. Ottawa: Institute for Research on Public Policy, 1990.
Henrikson, Alan K. "The North American Perspective: A Continent Apart or a Continent Joined?" Chapter from *NATO After Forty Years*, Lawrence Kaplan, ed. Wilmington, DE: Scholarly Resources Inc., 1990.
Hero, Alfred O., Jr., and Marcel Daneau, eds. *Problems and Opportunities in U.S.-Quebec Relations*. Boulder, CO: Westview Press, 1984.
Holmes, John W. *The World According to Ottawa*. Lecture paper delivered to Americas Society, New York, 1981.
Hydro-Québec Corp. *James Bay: Development, Environment and the Native Peoples of Quebec*. September 1989.
———. *Future Hydro Development in Northern Quebec*. May 1991.
Jackson, Robert J. "The Challenge of Canadian Federalism." Study paper; Department of Political Science, Carleton University, Ottawa, 1979.
Lamont, Lansing, and J. Duncan Edmonds, eds. *Friends So Different: Essays on Canada and the United States in the 1980s*. Ottawa: University of Ottawa Press, 1989.
Latouche, Daniel. *The New Continentalism: Prospects for Regional Integration in North America*. January 1992.
Leacock, Stephen. *Canada: The Foundations of Its Future*. Montreal: Gazette Printing Company, 1941.
Lemco, Jonathan M. *Canada-U.S. Outlook: Turmoil in the Peaceable Kingdom: The Quebec Sovereignty Movement and Its Implications for Canada and the United States*. Washington, DC: National Planning Association, March 1992.
Lindsey, G. R. "Strategic Aspects of the Polar Regions." In *Behind the Headlines*. Toronto: Canadian Institute of International Affairs, 1977.
Lipset, Seymour Martin. *Continental Divide: The Values and Institutions of the U.S. and Canada*. New York / London: Routledge, Chapman & Hall, 1990; sponsored by the C. D. Howe Institute and the National Planning Association / Canadian-American Committee.

Lisée, Jean-François. *In the Eye of the Eagle*. Toronto: HarperCollins, 1990.

Macfarlane, David. *Come From Away: Memory, War, and the Search for a Family's Past*. New York: Poseidon Press, 1991.

MacLennan, High. *Two Solitudes*. Toronto: Macmillan of Canada, 1945.

———. *Rivers of Canada*. Toronto: Macmillan of Canada, 1974.

Mackness, William. *Big Government and the Constitution Crisis*. Toronto: Mackenzie Institute, 1992.

Malcolm, Andrew H. *The Canadians*. New York: Times Books / random House, 1985.

Maly, Stephen. *True North. Part 1*. Hanover, NH: Institute of Current World Affairs, October 1990.

———. *Fields of Vision*. Report on Manitoba and Saskatchewan prepared for the Institute of Current World Affairs, Hanover, NH, May 1991.

Manitoba Constitutional Task Force Report. October 28, 1991.

Martin, Lawrence. *The Presidents and the Prime Ministers: Washington and Ottawa Face to Face: The Myth of Bilateral Bliss 1867–1982*. Garden City, NY: Doubleday & Co., 1982.

McCall-Newman, Christina. *Grits: An Intimate Portrait of the Liberal Party*. Toronto: Macmillan of Canada, 1982.

McDougall, Barbara (Secretary of State for External Affairs, Canadian Government). Statement to the UN General Assembly, New York, September 24, 1992.

McNaught, Kenneth. *The Pelican History of Canada*. New York: Penguin Books, 1976.

Meech Lake 1987 Constitutional Accord. Text of accord and constitutional amendment, approved June 3, 1987.

Morris, Jan. *O Canada: Travels in an Unknown Country*. New York: HarperCollins, 1990.

Morrison, Alex. "Canadian Resources for Peacekeeping." Briefing notes for presentation to the Senate of Canada, Subcommittee on Security and National Defence, June 16, 1992.

———, ed. *Divided We Fall: The National Security Implications of Canadian Constitutional Issues*. Toronto: Highnell Printing, 1991.

Mulroney, Brian. Notes for addresses at Quebec City, February 13, 1991; Calgary, April 22, 1991; and Toronto, December 11, 1991.

National Planning Association. *The Future of North American Defense*. Canada-U.S. Outlook Series. Washington, DC: National Planning Association, February 1991.

Organisation for Economic Co-operation and Development. *OECD Economic Surveys*. August 1991.

Parkman, Francis. *France and England in North America*. 2d eds. 2 vols. New York: The Library of America, 1983.

Parti Québécois Task Force. *The English-Speaking Community: An Integral Part of a Sovereign Quebec*. Montreal, 1993.

Porter, Michael E. *Canada at the Crossroads: The Reality of a New Competitive Environment*. Ottawa: Harvard Business School and Monitor Company, October 1991; study prepared for the Business Council on National Issues and the Government of Canada.

Powe, Bruce Allen. *Killing Ground: The Canadian Civil War*. Toronto: Peter Martin Associates, 1968.

———. *The Aberhart Summer*. Toronto: Lester & Orpen Bennys, 1983; New York: Penguin Books, 1984.

Prospects and Opportunities in Quebec-U.S. Economic Relations. Proceedings from a conference sponsored by Ecole des Hautes Etudes Commerciales, Montreal, and World Peace Foundation, Boston, at Seven Springs Center, Mount Kisco, NY, December 1981.

Report of the Special Committee of the Senate on National Defence: Canada's Territorial Air Defence. Ottawa, October 1, 1992.

Richards, John, François Vaillancourt, and William G. Watson. *Survival: Official Language Rights in Canada.* Toronto: C. D. Howe Institute, 1992.

Richler, Mordecai. *Oh Canada! Oh Quebec! Requiem for a Divided Country.* New York: Alfred A. Knopf, 1992.

Riggs, A. R., and Tom Velk, eds. *Federalism in Power.* Vancouver: The Fraser Institute, 1992.

Robertson, Gordon. "To Nobly Save." Address to the Federation of Canadian Municipalities, St. Johns, Newfoundland, June 8, 1991.

Royal Bank of Canada. *Unity or Disunity: An Economic Analysis of the Benefits and the Costs.* Montreal: Royal Bank of Canada, September 1992.

Schlesinger, Arthur M., Jr. *The Disuniting of America: Reflections on a Multicultural Society.* New York: W. W. Norton, 1992.

Scott, Graham W. S. "Canadian Cultural Issues." Notes for an address to the American Bar Association, Washington, DC, January 28, 1988.

Scott, Stephen A. "Issues Relating to Quebec Independence." Notes for presentation at Pointe Claire, Quebec, February 19, 1992.

Scowen, Reed. "New Relationships: Quebec, the U.S. and Canadian Constitution." Address to the America Society, New York, October 13, 1992.

Shaping Canada's Future Together, September 1991; initial proposal of federal government leading toward Charlottetown Agreement.

Simeon, Richard, and Mary Janigan, eds. *Toolkits and Building Blocks: Constructing a New Canada.* Toronto: C. D. Howe Institute, 1991.

Stethem, Nicholas. *National Security in a Changing World Order.* Study paper; Vancouver, November 24, 1990.

Stewart, Walter. *Shrug: Trudeau in Power.* Toronto: New Press, 1971.

Tangled Web: Legal Aspects of Deconfederation. Series on the Economics of the Breakup of Confederation. John McCallum, series editor. Toronto: C. D. Howe Institute, 1992.

Tonra, Ben. *Canada's Identity Crisis.* Washington, DC: Center for Strategic and International Studies, February 5, 1991.

U.S.-Canada Working Group. *Canada's Crisis and American Interests.* Washington, DC: The Atlantic Council of the United States, April 1992.

U.S. Department of Commerce. *U.S. Industrial Outlook '92: Business Forecasts of 350 Industries.* Washington, DC: U.S. Department of Commerce, 1991.

U.S. Department of Defense. *Soviet Military Power.* Washington, DC: U.S. Department of Defense, 1986.

U.S. International Trade Commission. *The Year in Trade: Operation of the Trade Agreements Program 1991.* 43d report. Washington, DC: U.S. International Trade Commission, 1992.

Varty, David L. *Who Gets Ungava?* Vancouver: Varty & Co., 1991.

Wade, Mason. *The French Canadians 1760–1967.* 2 vols. Toronto: Macmillan of Canada, 1968.

Watson, William G. *The Stay Option: The Economic Feasibility of Self-Determination for Quebecers Opposed to Secession.* Study paper; McGill University, Montreal, 1992.

———. "Separatism and the English of Quebec." In *Survival: Official Language Rights in Canada.* Toronto: C. D. Howe Institute, 1992.

Watts, Ronald L., and Douglas M. Brown, eds. *Options for a New Canada.* Ottawa: University of Toronto Press in association with the Institute of Intergovernmental Relations, Queen's University, and the Business Council on National Issues, 1991.

Weaver, R. Kent, ed. *The Collapse of Canada?* Washington, DC: The Brookings Institution, 1992.

Wilson, Edmund. *O Canada: An American's Notes on Canadian Culture.* New York: Farrar, Straus & Giroux, 1965.

Woehrel, Steven J., and Arlene E. Wilson. *Canada's Constitutional Crisis.* Washington, DC: Congressional Research Service, The Library of Congress, December 19, 1990.

ARTICLES

The American Review of Canadian Studies, Twentieth Anniversary Double Issue (Summer–Autumn 1991).

Bergquist, Laura. "French Canada's Strange Revolt," *Look* magazine (April 1963).

Bissonnette, Lise. "Quebec 1990: Towards a Renewed Internal Consensus," *American Review of Canadian Studies* (Summer 1990).

Blank, Stephen. "The Emerging Architecture of North America," *The G-7 Report* (October–November 1992).

Blank, Stephen, and Guy Stanley. "Is Canadian Federalism a Model for Europe and the Soviet Union?" *International Economy,* November 1990.

Bromke, Adam, and Kim Richard Nossal. "A Turning Point in U.S.-Canadian Relations," *Foreign Affairs* (Fall 1987).

———. "Tensions in Canada's Foreign Policy," *Foreign Affairs* (Winter 1983–84).

Conference Board of Canada. "Canadian Outlook," *Economic Forecast* (Spring 1992).

Courchene, Thomas J. "Death of a Political Era," *Toronto Globe and Mail,* October 27, 1992.

Galt, George. "Can't Live with Them, Can't Live without Them," *Saturday Night* (June 1991).

Hodgin, Deanna. "Canadian Crack-up," Insight on the News, *Washington Times,* June 18, 1990.

Hutchison, Bruce. "Canada's Time of Troubles," *Foreign Affairs* (October 1977).

Jockel, Joseph T. "If Canada Cracks Up: Implications for U.S. Policy," *Canadian-American Public Policy* (September 1991), University of Maine, Orono, ME.

Kierans, Eric. "How Ottawa's Hunger for Power Created Our Constitutional Mess" and "The Source of All Our Troubles," both in *Canadian Forum* (May 1992).

Latouche, Daniel. "Quebec and Canada: Scenarios for the Future," *Business in the Contemporary World* (Autumn 1990).

Lemco, Jonathan, and Peter Regenstreif. "The Fusion of Powers and the Crisis of Canadian Federalism," *Publius: The Journal of Federalism* (Winter 1984).

Linden, Eugene. "Bury My Heart at James Bay," *Time* magazine, July 15, 1991.

"Maclean's CTV Poll," *Maclean's* magazine, January 4, 1993.

Mothner, Ira. "The Unknown Canadians," *Look* magazine, April 9, 1963.

Nuechterlain, Donald E. "The Demise of Canada's Confederation," *Political Science Quarterly* (Summer 1981).

Pelletier, Francine. "Mon Pays," *Saturday Night* (June 1991).

Pinard, Maurice. "The Dramatic Re-Emergence of the Quebec Independence Movement," *Journal of International Affairs* (Winter 1992).

Richler, Mordecai. "Inside / Outside: A Reporter at Large," *The New Yorker* September 23, 1991.

Ritchie, Charles. "My Washington Years," excerpt from *Storm Signals: More Undiplomatic Diaries 1962–1971* (Toronto: Macmillan of Canada, 1983). In *Saturday Night* (August 1983).

Robertson, Gordon. "The Amending Formula," *Policy Options* (January–February 1982).

————. "Homespun Mending of Canada," *Policy Options* (March–April 1982).
Rotstein, Abraham. "Canada: The New Nationalism," *Foreign Affairs Review* (October 1976).
Scully, Robert. "What It Means to Be French in Canada," *Washington Post,* April 17, 1977.
Sharp, Mitchell. "Canada-U.S. Relations: Options for the Future," *International Perspectives* (Autumn 1972).
Smith, Alan. "National Images and National Maintenance: The Ascendancy of the Ethnic Idea in North America," *Canadian Journal of Political Science* (June 1981).
Sokolsky, Joel J. "The Future of North American Defence Cooperation," *International Journal* (Winter 1990–91).
Stethem, Nicholas. "Canada's Crisis: The Dangers," *Foreign Policy* (Winter 1977–78).
Stothart, Paul B. "Seven Costs of Quebec Sovereignty," *Policy Options* (March 1991).
Verhoevek, Sam Howe. "Power Struggle," *The New York Times Magazine,* January 12, 1992.
Vesilind, Priit J. "Common Ground," *National Geographic* magazine (February 1990).

Miscellaneous:

"Canada 2000: Reflections on What's Ahead," *Time* magazine, December 14, 1992.
"Getting Their Pact Together," *Time* magazine, June 18, 1990.
"For Want of Glue: A Survey of Canada," *The Economist,* June 29, 1991.
"One Nation Divisible," *Forbes* magazine, July 20, 1981.
"Report of the Nation: Forecast for Canada in the '90s," *The Financial Post* (Winter 1988–89).

Index